KU-606-861

Love of My Life

WITHDRAWN FROM STOCK
DUBLIN CITY PUBLIC LIBRARIES

Also by Lesley-Ann Jones

Bohemian Rhapsody: The Definitive Biography
of Freddie Mercury
Ride a White Swan: The Lives & Death of Marc Bolan
Naomi: The Rise and Rise of the Girl from Nowhere
Imagine
Tumbling Dice
Who Killed John Lennon?: The Lives, Loves and
Deaths of the Greatest Rock Star
Hero: David Bowie
The Stone Age: Sixty Years of the Rolling Stones

131523

Love of My Life

The Life and Loves of Freddie Mercury

Lesley-Ann Jones

Leabharlanna Poiblí Chathair Baile Átha Cliath
Dublin City Public Libraries

Leabharlann na Cabraí
Cabra Library
01-2228317

CORONET

First published in Great Britain in 2021 by Coronet
An imprint of Hodder & Stoughton
An Hachette UK company

This paperback edition published in 2022

2

Copyright © Lesley-Ann Jones 2021

The right of Lesley-Ann Jones to be identified as the
Author of the Work has been asserted by her in accordance
with the Copyright, Designs and Patents Act 1988.

All rights reserved. No part of this publication may be reproduced,
stored in a retrieval system, or transmitted, in any form or by
any means without the prior written permission of the publisher,
nor be otherwise circulated in any form of binding or cover
other than that in which it is published and without a similar
condition being imposed on the subsequent purchaser.

A CIP catalogue record for this title is available from the British Library

Paperback ISBN 9781529362367
eBook ISBN 9781529362343

Typeset in Plantin Light by Hewer Text UK Ltd, Edinburgh
Printed and bound in Great Britain by Clays Ltd, Elcograf S.p.A.

Hodder & Stoughton policy is to use papers that are natural, renewable
and recyclable products and made from wood grown in sustainable
forests. The logging and manufacturing processes are expected to
conform to the environmental regulations of the country of origin.

Hodder & Stoughton Ltd
Carmelite House
50 Victoria Embankment
London EC4Y 0DZ

www.hodder.co.uk

Note to the reader: The astrological symbol for the planet Mercury – ☿ – which also represents the Greek/Roman messenger god's winged helmet and caduceus (serpent-entwined wand) has been used throughout the text in place of asterisks.

To Kathleen Mary Jones
my mother

IN MEMORIAM

Farrokh Bulsara: Freddie Mercury
5 September 1946–24 November 1991

Ursula Ledersteger: Barbara Valentin
15 December 1940–22 February 2002

James Hutton: Jim Hutton
4 January 1949–1 January 2010

Maria de Montserrat Viviana Concepción Caballé i Folch :
Montserrat Caballé
12 April 1933–6 October 2018

Show me a hero, and I'll write you a tragedy.
F. Scott Fitzgerald

Contents

1 Souvenirs ... 1
2 Reflections ... 15
3 Roots ... 29
4 Ritual ... 41
5 Stone Free ... 59
6 Hendrix ... 73
7 Leader ... 91
8 Queen ... 107
9 Secrets ... 119
10 Mary ... 135
11 Jim ... 151
12 Barbara ... 171
13 Redemption ... 185
14 Montserrat ... 201
15 Love of My Life ... 221
16 Finale ... 239

Chapter Notes ... 249
Tributes ... 267
Select Bibliography ... 273
Acknowledgements ... 279
Index ... 285

CHAPTER ONE

SOUVENIRS

The Freddie Mercury who haunts me wears no costume. He commands no madding crowd. He is not the classic yellow-and-white-clad poser leading a thousands-strong throng through improvised call-and-response, nor a velvet-cloaked and crowned finale king. It is not his unitarded prancer, his leather biker, his vested rocker nor any other stage or video incarnation of him who lurks in my mind. The version of Freddie I like to remember is a low-key, clean-cut forty-something in denim and plaid, with nothing at all about him that gives away 'rock star'. That Freddie could have been anyone. We came across him when and where we least expected to: at dusk, alone, unfettered by minders, in the back-bar dinge of a local pub.

I say 'local'. While I have been floored by a few places in my time, a more magical setting is hard to imagine or describe. Queen's home-from-home on Switzerland's Vaud Riviera during the band's eighties heyday, when they owned their own recording studios there, could have been the archetypal chocolate-box image. The town of Montreux's retro charm complements the immense natural beauty of the landscape. I remain captivated to this day by that lake and those mountains. I still think of the place as more of a *Ballets Russes*-style backdrop for *Swan Lake* or *Giselle* than as a location indelibly linked with rock'n'roll. I have been back a couple of times in recent years, not least to pay my respects at the late Irena Sedlecká's striking bronze statue of Freddie, three metres high, on the promenade at the Place du Marché. It was unveiled on 25 November 1996, five years after his death, in the presence of his parents, sister, bandmates and Spanish soprano Montserrat Caballé, one of Freddie's most cherished friends.[1]

Suspended against the blur of Lac Leman, as Lake Geneva is called there, the Chablais Alps loom as darkly today as they did that memorable night in May 1986, when Roger Tavener and I, showbiz reporters deployed by rival English newspapers, came stumbling past the Château de Chillon in search of a drink.[2] The wind was up, and the trees were swaying. We lurched away from the lake and into the White Horse. Freddie was within, holding court. At this, the only tavern in town, he was a regular. He was hanging towards the rear in the company of strangers: half his age, male, trim and tightly belted. They jousted in French, jostled for position and dangled on his every word.

It was one of those moments that can be neither contrived nor repeated. While by no means the first time I had been in his company, I believe this was the only occasion when I met the real Freddie.

In the absence of personal assistants, publicists, roadies and gofers, that irritant from their management office, the taciturn blonde to whom they referred as his 'common-law wife', we were neither ignored nor banished. Despite which, we kept our distance. Because of this, he came to us. 'Ciggie,' he pronounced pointedly, as if it were someone's name. I glanced around for 'Phoebe', the affable Peter Freestone, who was Freddie's constant companion and acknowledged best friend. Unusually, he was nowhere to be seen. Nor were any other members of the entourage present, specifically Brian, Roger and John – aka the band. How was Freddie going to pay for his drinks, I wondered. Though it wasn't my business, the thought preoccupied me. Peter himself once confided that his boss never carried cash. Nor cheque book, nor credit cards, nor even his own passport, as though in homage to the monarch herself.

My companion, meanwhile, pulled out a packet of Marlboro Red. 'I prefer Silk Cut,' frowned Freddie, tutting and snatching one anyway. We smiled and bought a round – a large vodka tonic for Freddie, a bottle of Pinot Noir and some beers – and withdrew, to flirt with friends who had made it there ahead of us. Freddie, we realised, would not be leaving us alone. He'd soon come sniffing again.

Queen were riding high at the time. They were the toast of the world, having stolen Live Aid from under the noses of Bono, Bowie, Elton, Macca and all those other music legends at Wembley Stadium the previous July. Rethinking retirement, they'd hit the road again, for what no one could have known at the time would be their final outing with Freddie. Widely criticised for 'cashing in' on the plight of Ethiopia's starving millions, the band advanced from Stockholm to Slane to Stevenage on a last hurrah with their fearless frontman.[3] Contrary to what the 2018 film *Bohemian Rhapsody* depicts, Freddie had not yet been diagnosed with HIV. The twenty-six-date *Magic* tour was attended by more than a million fans. The fat lady warbled at Knebworth that August. Five years later, Freddie was dead.

☿

Bohemian Rhapsody the movie had been in development for a decade when it saw the light of day towards the end of 2018. Many of those dismayed by Queen's jukebox spectacle *We Will Rock You*, an outstanding success at London's Dominion Theatre between 2002 and 2014 before cleaning up across the globe, feared that a big-screen version of the musical and its futuristic plot must be imminent. Never knowingly predictable, the band and their management went one better, summoning an autobiographical motion picture out of Queen's real life. I should I say, from Freddie's. Because no significant aspect of the existence of guitarist Brian May, bassist John Deacon or drummer Roger Taylor could ever trouble Mercury's unbelievable back story.

What a binge of control-freakery and dissent the film production was. So far, so Queen – who, as Freddie said, argued 'about every little thing, even the air that we breathe.' They played down much of what had really gone on. There were plenty of baffling distractions, including a record label executive by the name of Ray Foster, played by *Wayne's World* star Mike Myers, who was invented for the piece. Why? When it came to real musicbiz monsters, they would have surely been the first to admit that they were spoilt for choice.

Despite the years of ranting that led to the side-lining of celebrated screenwriters and the dropping of directors and leading men, the film was made. Born-to-be-Mercury *Borat* star Sacha Baron Cohen demanded to play Freddie warts, tantrums, orgasms and all, but was sent packing in 2013. We lamented that development at the time, only to capitulate down the line, agreeing that he would not after all have been suitable. The result would have been a film about Baron Cohen playing Mercury. Instead of Ben Whishaw (Q in Bond) or Dominic Cooper (*Mamma Mia*), both of whom had been in the frame, we got to feast our eyes on Egyptian-American actor Rami Malek (*Mr Robot* and *Twilight*), whose vocal performance was enhanced here and there by Canadian Freddie impersonator Marc Martell. Not that the producers advertised this. Could Malek really capture Freddie's nimble stage skip, his fist-clench, his pout, the beckoning digit, the flickering, finger-licking tongue? By Jove, he nailed it. The BAFTAs, the Screen Actors Guild, the Golden Globes and the 91st Academy Awards all Best-Actor-ed Malek for his masterclass in impersonation. Steering the production towards its conclusion in place of alleged sex offender Bryan Singer (allegations he has always denied), Dexter Fletcher (*Sunshine on Leith, Eddie the Eagle, Rocketman*) directed anonymously, but did receive an executive producer credit. The script was crafted by *The Queen, Frost Nixon* and *The Crown* writer/creator Peter Morgan CBE, with input from Anthony McCarten,

Justin Haythe and Christopher Wilkinson. Morgan's name remains, writ large and deserved.

I had dealings with Morgan. After reading my first biography of Freddie, published in 1997, he flew to London from Vienna to entice me to schnitzel among the blondes at Daphne's.[4] He wanted to know the truth about Freddie. 'Read it again,' I said. He'd devoured every Freddie and Queen book, but had found in mine, he wooed, 'the meat, the bones, the broth of his wrath. His oscillator, his battery, his mainspring.' Charmed? Cat got an ass? So I helped him a little.

Music biopics are in the danger zone. Get it right and the world karaokes. Fall short and you're torching alone. We all have our favourites. I'll take *The Rose*, which is sort of about Janis Joplin, and for which Bette Midler bagged a Golden Globe; *The Runaways*, presenting Kristen Stewart as Joan Jett; Ken Russell's *Lisztomania*, featuring Roger Daltrey as the world's first rock star and Rick Wakeman as Thor; *The Doors*, bringing sublime, ridiculous, poetically constipated Val Kilmer as Jim Morrison; and *Ray*, serving up Jamie Foxx as Ray Charles. The Academy caved. Could Queen live up to any of them? Because, get this: the Queen story was never about the band. It was about a misfit boy born Farrokh Bulsara in Zanzibar.

Perhaps the most perplexing thing about *Bohemian Rhapsody* is that Freddie's early years are barely referenced. Books and documentaries have also tended to sail myopically through that period, preferring to kick-start the story from the moment he washed up in London. What was it that made them ignore his mysterious colonial past? It's not as if they would have had to dwell on it. Even hazy glimpses of those distant islands off the east coast of Africa would have sufficed. We needed something of the circumstances of Freddie's birth. We could have done with a little detail about his father Bomi's employment as a cashier in the High Court of the British Colonial Government, and the advantages to his family that that work might have generated. We would have benefited from a little analysis of the Zoroastrian Parsis, the community and religion of which Freddie's family were part. Why? Because that creed and culture had such an impact on the way he was raised; and because it cast such long shadows over the life he would ultimately choose to live. Above all, the warning signs should have been flagged: Freddie's volatile relationship with his father, his abandonment at boarding school in India three thousand miles away when he was only eight years old, and his awakening to the fact that he was, give or take, homosexual. These and other elephants were studiously ignored throughout the picture. Nor did we get the full eighties Munich experience, a crucial and dangerous last hurrah for Freddie before he relinquished hedonism and began the process, reluctantly or deliberately, of winding down his life.

When the band and the film's producers were called out for factual inaccuracies – not only by the press and wider media but by a string of websites that listed errors in detail – they were forced to defend themselves. Brian May and Roger Taylor engaged in public damage limitation. 'We weren't making a documentary,' Brian told *Guitar World* magazine. 'It wasn't supposed to be, "This happened, and then this happened." This was an attempt to get inside Freddie Mercury and portray his inner life – his drive, his passion, his fears and weaknesses. Also, we wanted to portray his relationship with us as a family, which was pretty much a part of what made him tick. And I think Freddie would love it, because it's a good, honest representation of him as a person.'

It's not, though, is it? For reasons which we will come to.

I was prompted to reconsider the fall-out from *Bohemian Rhapsody* when I read Bel Mooney's comments about Peter Morgan's magnum opus *The Crown*: the historical drama multiseries about the reign of Her Majesty Queen Elizabeth II, broadcast to great acclaim by Netflix. *Daily Mail* columnist and Fleet Street veteran Mooney had never watched it.

'I heard the early, historic episodes (with Claire Foy as the Queen) were excellent, but Olivia Colman as Elizabeth II? What a piece of sad – even insulting – miscasting,' she said. 'As for watching the tragic (Princess) Diana story unfold in fiction . . . no thank you. You might think I sound holier-than-thou (I'm not!) but I've no time for cheap gossip aimed at hurting living people.'

Bel proceeded to discuss the 2012 film *The Iron Lady*, which earned Meryl Streep a Best Actress Academy Award for her portrayal of the later former British Conservative Prime Minister Margaret Thatcher. It was, concluded the journalist, 'a good performance, if you relished a cruel impersonation of one of the most effective Prime Ministers of the twentieth century reduced to a friendless wreck with dementia. Lady Thatcher was still alive. Yet she had no redress, no voice – and was shown no mercy. Nor were those who loved her. I felt soiled by it. It was full of lies, as well as a gross invasion of somebody's privacy. Oh, but when "creatives" make TV or films, they can get away with murdering the truth. That's why I won't be watching the Royal Family I love mimicked into monsters in *The Crown*.'

Is misrepresentation more acceptable when the subject is deceased? I must argue that it is less so. There is a duty of care to reflect Freddie as he was, and not as those who shared his orbit might have preferred him to be, precisely because he is not here to give his side of the story. The sad fact is that Freddie's X-rated lifestyle was diluted, simplified and sanitised by this production in order to render him acceptable and appealing to the widest possible audience: one with a PG-13 certificate in the UK, meaning that it is not recommended for children under the age of thirteen. This rating was crucial to the film's blanket success. It meant that 'moderate' sex and drug references got past the censors: lines of white powder, the popping of pills, buttock-slapping, crotch-grabbing, and a cosy gay-club scene in which males parade about in bondage gear. So, too, did 'offensive language'. There are references to orgies, a guy telling a gal she's 'an epic shag', insulting euphemisms for Pakistani people and members of the LGBTQ community, and a smattering of 'wanker', 'screw', 'twat', 'shit', 'bloody', 'arse' and 'bollocks'.

Bohemian Rhapsody raked in an estimated $1 billion at the global box office. It also became the fastest-selling digital download film of all time, shifting two hundred and sixty-five thousand downloads in a week, and selling a record number of DVD and Blu-Ray copies, some four hundred and sixty-five thousand units during the same period. And counting ever since. Its success also had a knock-on effect on sales of Queen's musical back catalogue, which rose fantastically from the picture's release onwards. The remains of the band – Brian, Roger, Adam Lambert as Freddie, plus sidemen – then embarked on a sell-out world *Rhapsody* tour in 2019. It was unfortunately curtailed by Covid-19, but they'll be back.

☿

I have lost count of the number of rock stars I've interviewed, the number of tours I've been on, the number of hours I must have squandered in the company of artists. Spend enough time around these people and you are soon au fait with the signs. Although they may differ dramatically from one other in terms of personality type, musical genre, songwriting and instrumental ability, presentation style and so on, they are often alike in fundamental ways. They can be control freaks, attention-seekers and shot-callers. They can, like Freddie, be conflict-conjurers and tantrum-throwers: not 'because they can', lest we forget who's in charge/picking up the tab/is the point of all this, or when the boredom and tedium of the road set in, or because they are essentially insecure; but because they depend on conflict to fire their generators, enabling them to go out there and muster the magic that fuels their performance. They are often impractical, inefficient, disorganised and immature. They can be monstrously selfish, cruel, petulant and paranoid. Out on stage before the baying mob, they rise to the occasion, shakin' that ass, wielding that axe, thrashing hell out of a drum-kit; producing bloodcurdling, other-worldly sounds from apparently superhuman throats, and rejuvenating themselves on the nectar of adoration the way vampires feast on blood. Out there, doing what they do, we forgive them anything. Backstage, before they go on and after they come off, they behave like (and are treated like) babies. When they threaten to boycott the gig, they have to be sweet-talked, pampered and cajoled into going on. Someone pours or mixes their poison, cuts the crusts off, dishes their meals. Someone else does up buttons, zips flies, laces boots, tousles hair. Every last thing is done for them short of wiping their bottoms, and sometimes even that, I am reliably informed: because, in the words of one personal assistant who should be awarded a knighthood for lifelong dedication, it 'frees up their mind to focus on the job in hand, which is to go out there and sock 'em the most sensational show they've ever seen in their entire lives.' To the point that they shit themselves? If it's that stressful, why do it? Because it sells their recorded music and (not to be ignored) their merchandise. Now that the biggest bands on earth can earn insane percentages of their revenue from merch sales, the old adage that goes 'been there, seen it, got the T-shirt' has never been more apt.

Quiz them about their childhood and they are reluctant to be drawn. Manage to extract a few details and you're onto something: the same thing in too many cases for it to be coincidental. Many lost themselves in music at a young age as an antidote to adversity. They got creative in order to exorcise demons; wrote songs to expunge torment and to dilute despair. It soon got the better of them, to the point that they could no longer *not* do it. They joined bands in order to immerse themselves in the company of like-minded, equally damaged lost boys. They sought fame as an escape from their insecure past, mistaking the adulation of millions of strangers for love. They excused their sex-drugs-and-booze debauchery as coping mechanisms. They ached to fill the void but just made it bigger, missing the point.

Freddie filled his own void with Western pop. He channelled every spark of spare energy into his schoolboy band, the Hectics. He returned home to Zanzibar, for good or so he thought, in

1963. After the revolution the following year, which barely scraped into the history books, the Bulsaras boarded a flight for England with their children. Did they run for their lives with a couple of suitcases between them, or make a controlled departure within six months? No one can remember. Whatever, they settled in west London.

Peter Freestone once remarked that Freddie would have cancelled his entire childhood if he'd had the choice, and would have begun his life at the age of twenty-one in Feltham. In other words, he would have preferred to have been born 'ordinary' and 'English' over 'exotic' and . . . what? In geographical terms, he was Zanzibari, and therefore African. By virtue of racial ancestry and ethnicity, he was Indian. Or was he? Although he was proclaimed posthumously to have been 'Britain's first Asian pop star', he wasn't really that. Not only was he not born in an Asian country, but Freddie's lineage was Persian. Although the Zoroastrian Parsis had migrated centuries earlier from the Western Asian land now known as the Islamic Republic of Iran, to escape Muslim persecution and settle in India, their tightly knit, devoted community never integrated completely. Culturally, Parsis did not consider themselves to be Indian. Despite the fact that Freddie's parents had been born in pre-independence colonial India and that their legal nationality was 'British Indian', they would identify for life as 'Parsee'.[5]

Freddie never talked about his Zanzibar roots. Those who had no inkling that he'd been born in such a place didn't need to know about it. It was history, it didn't matter, he was a Brit now. He downplayed his ethnicity. He kept his memories to himself, and never looked back. History drew a veil over Zanzibar's darkest chapter. I admit I'd never known a thing about it until I began researching Freddie's life five years after his death. Were he alive today during the age of #BlackLivesMatter (BLM), would he have managed to avoid discussing it?[6]

Plenty of rock and pop stars have thrown their weight behind political causes and humanitarian crises down the years. Freddie himself did so when he performed at Live Aid in 1985 in support of Ethiopian famine relief. He referred, that day, to the 'guilt' he had felt as a boarding school pupil in India, when he became aware that most other children in the world were by no means as fed or as fortunate as he was. Did his mind rewind at that point to Zanzibar, and to the early childhood and late teen years he had spent there? Freddie was eighteen when revolution erupted. His sister Kashmira, six years his junior, was twelve. Yet their mother Jer spoke in a documentary about the moment when she and her husband took the decision to leave their adopted country because they 'had young children', and moved to England to start a new life. Was she, too, obfuscating the horror and shame of Zanzibar's past? To revisit significant periods of his life of which Freddie was so dismissive is to begin to understand the secretive, unsentimental, progressive, forward-facing determination of his character.

Most of Zanzibar's Parsis made their way to India, the UK, USA or Canada in 1964. The Bulsaras, who had family in England, swapped canopy skies and coral-reef sunsets for cold, grey, self-contained Feltham, settling at 22 Gladstone Avenue. If the lifestyle change was drastic, there were modest compensations. English suburbia might be drab, but at least it was safe. In place of a home overlooking palm-fringed shores and talcum beaches, there were identical, viewless streets of brick and pebbledash. There were no glistening, crystal waters to swim in, but there were Hounslow's pungently chlorinated municipal baths. No merchant ship to sail between Malindi and Mumbai, but you could rent a rowing boat on the lake at Inwood Park. If the local market lacked the spicy street food that Freddie relished, there were at least coconut buns and banana milkshakes to share with new friends.

There was also music. That summer saw the opening of the Attic Club on Hounslow's High Street, which would welcome an extraordinary wealth of talent. The Swinging Blue Jeans, Geno Washington and his Ram Jam band, Georgie Fame and the Blue

Flames, P.P. Arnold, Manfred Mann, the Graham Bond Organization, Long John Baldry and the Hoochie Coochie Men and more were there to ramp up Freddie's appetite for Western rock and pop. When he discovered Jimi Hendrix, he said, his life was turned upside down. As an art student he would work part-time in Heathrow airport's catering department (not as a baggage handler, as depicted in the film), on a trading estate and as a nude life model while sketching a new identity at art school. He immersed himself in the Swinging Sixties, but couldn't decide which way he swung. He squatted, dossed, tossed, fucked, ducked in and out of groups, flogged threadbare garb, Hendrix sketches, even his college thesis on Jimi in Kensington Market; met some egghead academics posing as rockers; inveigled his way into the band, insisting on the name 'Queen' despite his bandmates' overwheening machismo; created their defining song *Bohemian Rhapsody* only a beat into their existence, and never again returned to the land of his birth.

The Bulsara family's escape from political and social revolution and their relocation to London was, then, the cause and catalyst of Freddie's personal revolution. What might have become of him, had he and his family opted to remain in Africa? Might he have moved to the mainland to find work, or have returned to India to study Law, Accountancy or Medicine at the University of Bombay and have followed a respectable profession, as his parents were desperate for him to do? With leaving school grades as inferior as his, it seems unlikely.

As for his sexuality, while a couple of close former school friends insist that Freddie was 'obviously heterosexual' during the Panchgani years, one in particular claims to have been aware that his friend was experimenting. How could he be sure?

'Because he tried it on with me,' the married father and grand-father confided during our encounter, on written assurance of anonymity. 'I wasn't interested, and he wasn't embarrassed about it. He just said, "It was worth a shot!", laughed it off and moved on to the next chap. Whenever he caught my eye, which was infrequently after that as I decided to keep my distance, it was always with a certain flourish and a toss of the head as if to say, "You don't know what you're missing!"

'I knew of several boys he had "experiences" with,' his former classmate went on. 'I also knew about some of the girls from the girls' school, as well as one or two who seemed unsure. You know, in terms of whether they batted or bowled as it were. People are inclined to believe that homosexuality, lesbianism and bisexuality hadn't been invented in those days, because it was considered indelicate to discuss such matters. Did Freddie take advantage of their indecision? He wasn't predatory, if that's what you mean. I'm sure it was mutual. At least one of our teachers fell for his charms, though who knows whether or not they took things further. I wouldn't wish to speculate.

'Bucky, as we called him, much to his irritation and annoyance, was a most unusual and mysterious-looking boy. There was a proud sadness about him that brought out the fixer and carer in some of those around him, if you read me. Something about the eyes. They seemed to arouse a maternal instinct in the girls, while lots of the boys found themselves drawn to him and wanting to be chums with him. Yes, he was popular in a curious and unexpected way, I would say. I wouldn't have been at all surprised to hear that there may have been others. Teachers interested in him, I mean. There was gossip about all that. Nothing more. It was the 1950s, you know? Hush hush, stiff upper lip. Things were swept under the carpet in those days, especially when it came to matters personal.'[7]

Back in Zanzibar under a Muslim regime, Freddie could never have experimented sexually without risking imprisonment. To this day, gay males there face up to life behind bars if caught. Orthodox Zoroastrians, too, support the suppression of homosexuality. Their sacred text, the Vendidad, denounces gay people as 'demons', their behaviour as 'devil-worship'.

Sexual activity between two adult males was de-criminalised in the UK in 1967: three years after Freddie and his family arrived. If he was already embracing alternative sexuality, he was at last free to try on different identities for size and to become who he really was. So why was so much of the life he went on to lead at best furtive, and at worst a lie?

CHAPTER TWO
REFLECTIONS

Freddie Mercury was one of the greatest pretenders of all time: a posing, posturing English eccentric with a faux plummy accent and a fake aristocratic air. He was also plagued by contradictions. Vivid, arrogant and fearless in public, he could be raw, vulnerable and uncertain behind closed doors. According to some of those who shared his life – his PA Peter Freestone, former barber turned live-in lover Jim Hutton, German actress Barbara Valentin and others – he wasn't hard to read. He wore his heart on his bicep. At times, more than one. Emotionally addicted to the soft affection of women, he came to prefer hard sex with men. Irrefutably though the global homosexual community has claimed him, he clearly kept his options open. Would we not therefore, by contemporary definition, consider him to have been 'bisexual'?

Peter Freestone warns against it. Freddie's factotum for the final twelve years of his life believes that his friend was unequivocally gay. At a fabulous dinner in Peter's honour hosted by our Italian friend Federica Dini in June 2019 at Shezan in Knightsbridge – a superior Indian restaurant and once a favourite haunt of Freddie's – we discussed it at length.

'Even though Freddie never came out,' he said, 'we should be wary of categorising him as bisexual. As far as I'm concerned, and I was there – in the next room, or quite often in the same one – he lived the life of a gay man. It was the lifestyle he wanted. Why didn't he share that with the world? He had his reasons.'

Peter should know. I have known and loved 'Phoebe' for thirty-five years. I also saw and heard enough to wonder. True, Freddie never came out officially during his lifetime. He dropped hints and made cryptic comments, such as his famous line 'I'm as gay as a daffodil, my dear!' Peter flagged up that Freddie did in fact speak quite openly about his sexuality in a couple of interviews: 'It's there if you look!' It wasn't obvious to all, clearly. Freddie did indeed have his reasons, which we will explore. Because he has been outed posthumously, he is denied the right to reply. Nor did he confirm that he had AIDS until the night before he died, when he issued the following statement to the media through Queen's manager Jim Beach:

'Following enormous conjecture in the press, I wish to confirm that I have been tested HIV-positive and have AIDS. I felt it correct to keep this information private in order to protect the privacy of those around me. However, the time has now come for my friends and fans around the world to know the truth, and I hope everyone will join with me, my doctors and all those worldwide in the fight against this terrible disease.'

'It was a load off Freddie's mind,' said Jim Hutton, his presumed partner for the final few years. 'He did seem calmer after that. Though I have often wondered, did he know that was it, and that he would die the next day? Or was that just coincidence?'

It was uncanny, inexplicable and very Freddie.

☿

Freddie's former girlfriend and primary beneficiary Mary Austin has long been paraded as the Grieving Mother Mary. Why did he leave her his palatial Kensington home and most of his chattels and fortune when the pair had not been an item for fifteen years – and were 'just good friends' for infinitely longer than they were romantically and sexually entwined? Could it have been part of the construct – the elaborate mythology fashioned to hoodwink the world into believing that Freddie was a gay man whose tragedy was that he had fallen in love with a woman? That his orientation would otherwise have been 'straight', but for a single inconvenient bio-blip? The implication being that we might have forgiven Gaia her thoughtless aberration, which Freddie could 'not have helped', whereas we might not so readily have accepted him as bisexual . . . because there was, at least in the 1970s and '80s, a popular tendency to interpret the latter as 'greedy'. The 'biphobic' suggestion that Freddie could not possibly have been that way inclined would today be regarded as an example of 'bisexual erasure'.

'Traditionally, our understanding has been that if you're male and have even a slight attraction to the same sex, then you must be gay,' explained Ritch C. Savin-Williams, professor emeritus of development psychology at New York's Cornell University.

'Even if this isn't immediately apparent, we tell men it will become so once you come to terms with your true self and exit your 'phase' of bi-curiosity or questioning. Women, by contrast, we give more space to be sexually fluid, as the sizeable literature on the subject attests.'[1]

British psychotherapist Richard Hughes is on the same page as Peter Freestone.

'I'm pleased you mentioned it,' he said. 'I know from what you have written in the past that you hang quite a lot on Freddie's Barbara Valentin episode. But tread carefully. I really do think that Freddie was a gay man. Homosexual males can easily have sex with women, especially when loads of drugs and partying are involved.

'I do believe that Barbara had a sexual relationship with Freddie. Having said that, this kind of relationship doesn't necessarily make a man bisexual. He can still be gay. Who is a hundred per cent gay? Can anyone define themselves as completely anything? And of course all of this, in turn, is defined by the language and theory of our times. There is more nuance and difference now than there has ever been.

'While Freddie is generally regarded as a gay man,' Hughes adds, 'there was also something queer about him.' A pejorative term for a homosexual person in the past, 'queer' has been revived of late and is used by people who do not identify as normative. Homosexuals, bisexuals, non-binary and transgender people might all define themselves as 'queer' – as might heterosexuals who identify beyond the norm. The language, particularly to older generations, can be confusing. 'Non-binary', for example, refers to those who do not identify exclusively with traditional gender or sexuality definitions and labels. 'Bigender', 'agender' and 'gender-fluid' are not the same thing as 'both genders'. Many bisexuals define 'bisexual' as being attracted to two or more genders. But some bisexual people are attracted to women and men only, and not to non-binary people. Curiouser and curiouser? What about pansexual people – who can be attracted to people of all genders, and who describe their propensity for attraction as relating to an individual's personality rather than biology or orientation? To such folk, gender and sexuality can be irrelevant. In an age in which the majority understand that all orientations and identities are acceptable and valid, how might Freddie have fared?

'Who knows how he would have reacted to a non-binary approach?' says Richard Hughes. 'He was fascinated by all facets of sexuality, identity and gender, and he would have continued to explore and play with that, challenging boundaries creatively and personally.'

I have long believed that Freddie enjoyed taunting the world with the mystery of what he might or might not be. He had the devil in him, to use an old phrase. He didn't want to be defined. He wanted people to wonder.

'Exactly,' agrees the psychotherapist. 'Alienating the whole of America with "I Want to Break Free", for example. Which was *so* bold. What was he saying? "I'm actually gay"? Or, "I wear women's underwear in private, you know, aren't I risqué!" Or both! Yes, it was John Deacon's composition, but look what Freddie made of it. He took it all the way. The whole thing was a provocation. As for the video, it was outrageous for its time. Rockers in drag, sending up *Corrie* was always going to puzzle them in the US. They had no idea what *Coronation Street* even was, so the joke fell on deaf ears.[2] America was all chinos and baseball hats. They didn't get it. Many of them still don't get it. They were also offended by what they saw as cross-dressing. We knew it as 'drag' and thought nothing of it here, we'd grown up on Dick Emery, Stanley Baxter and Danny la Rue.[3] But the drag-queen scene in the States was still years away. Hard to imagine, isn't it, now that RuPaul and his glam queens are part of mainstream culture and almost universally admired? But back then, Queen were widely criticised for having made a career-damaging mistake. Did they? I have to say, I love that level of arrogance. "Break Free" was extraordinary. That video, that music. It packed such a punch, and hasn't dated at all. It was all so ahead of its time. It's why Freddie is a superstar, because of creations and daring like that.'

Had Freddie lived, he would have been at the forefront of LGBTQIA+ identity today, believes Hughes.

'I imagine him as an amazing protagonist too,' he says. 'Giving him labels such as "gay" or "bisexual" is too limiting. I sort of feel that while his general flavour was a gay man, he was much more complex than that.

'It's ironic that he never came out, but that he has been taken up as a major gay icon. The nineties were dominated by gay politics because of the AIDS crisis. It was all about "equality" and the Pink Pound.[4] Freddie set the scene for that narrative. He became the gay martyr of HIV and AIDS. But when we evaluate him today, his relevance has increased, particularly from an intersectional perspective of race and class. What is fascinating about Freddie is that he spans different eras. Language and attitudes have changed dramatically. He also lived through several eras during his own lifetime. To the point that we have to stop and think: which era Freddie are we talking about?'

Most people today are more aware of, and more comfortable with, the infinite variety and multiple sub-categories of sexuality, gender and identity. Freddie's tragedy was never that he fell in love with a woman. It was that, due to the prejudice of the times, he was never able to be honest and open about the flexible nature of his identity.

☿

Mary Austin was by no means the only woman in Freddie Mercury's life.

Freddie worshipped another woman so intensely that he seemed almost enslaved to her for a while. She not only awakened him to the three-sixty heterosexual experience, but also indulged and encouraged his obsession, as she put it, with 'cock'. She was a woman with a sexual appetite as insatiable as his; who got him to a T; who brought out his sweetest and his ugliest; who purchased an apartment with him in Munich during the death-or-glory days; and who was at his side when he discovered that he was incurably ill. She was the late Austrian-born 'German Jayne Mansfield', actress Barbara Valentin. That's her in Queen's video for their July 1984 single 'It's a Hard Life'. Shot in Munich, it is perhaps the most preposterous they ever made. The video is loaded with symbolism, much of which is obscure. Its setting is Venetian masked ball meets lavish operatic production, featuring King Freddie in his court of misfits and freaks representing the Elizabethan and Renaissance eras, the Decadent movement and the Age of Enlightenment. Freddie sports a skin-tight, red, feathered, fish-eyed costume that makes him look like a giant prawn. Barbara is lush in a black off-the-shoulder number complete with bejewelled skullcap. Leaning over a balcony to gaze adoringly at the star of the show below, her exuberant bosoms are practically spilling all over him. In one sequence he passes her on the grand staircase, and the camera zooms in on their bare feet. Barbara is seen grinding her naked foot on top of Freddie's. This lends the piece an unequivocal sexual vibe, the foot being an obvious phallic symbol. We can safely assume from this, as well as from the ecstatic expression on her face, that there is more than a handshake going on between them in real life.

But her existence was not so much as hinted at in the *Bohemian Rhapsody* film. I was both bewildered and angered by their neglect of her . . . until I remembered when, where and why I had felt that way before.

When I attended the 'David Bowie Is' exhibition at the V&A in 2013, I found not a trace of his first wife Angela. Not a syllable of recognition was she granted for her considerable contribution to the creation of David's defining alter ego, Ziggy Stardust. Angie Bowie, she who used to hand me signed black-and-whites of her local-hero husband when I was a schoolgirl, on the doorstep of Haddon Hall, their home in Beckenham, Kent, had been comprehensively airbrushed from his life. But she had been such an indelible part of it. Who sanctioned that? It could only have been David himself. What he hadn't bargained for was that to exclude his indomitable ex was to draw mass attention to her absence. People were bound to notice and to comment. She had been such an assertive creative influence on David throughout their relationship that she ought to have been acknowledged. Just as Barbara ought to have been for her importance to Freddie.

On the first of several days I spent in Munich with Barbara in 1996, we talked from teatime until dawn about the secret Freddie she knew. I heard first-hand about what they saw in each other. He was flawed and frail and flamboyant. A cursed exotic, a damaged diva. So was she. They mirrored each other perfectly. They were equals. Mary Austin didn't get a look-in on that level. She was not blessed with Barbara's huge personality, and wouldn't have dreamed of behaving like her. She never flaunted an upholstered embonpoint, never snogged Freddie in public, never drank herself stupid, never swore, sang, wept all over him, picked fights with flirts who tried to muscle between them, nor made everyone aware that she was there. Mary was demure, dignified and reticent, both publicly and in private. She knew her place, and never drew attention to herself. She never put a foot wrong. She was thrifty and fastidious. She was kind and polite towards but wary of and cautious around

Barbara. Apart from the fact that both were blonde, they could not have been more different. Mary must have fretted that she might be usurped by this explosive femme fatale. Perhaps she even feared that Freddie might marry her, which of course Barbara desperately craved. At which point, Mary's hold over her former lover turned friend and employer would have disintegrated. She would not be living where she lives today, nor have Freddie's fortune at her disposal.

Barbara and I remained close until she died in 2002, aged sixty-one. I sometimes stayed with her in Germany. I made a point of doing so after Freddie's funeral, from which, distressingly and unfathomably, she was banned. She returned the favour by flying to London to attend my book launch. Her recollections of Freddie and of their time together were too detailed, too nuanced, too finely tuned and emotionally forensic to be fraudulent. Dishonesty and exaggeration have been widely implied, not only by those who resist inconvenient truth as an impediment to a good story, but by one of Barbara's own adult children. While I sympathise – there must be a certain level of embarrassment attached to the thought of the whole world knowing that your late mother used to have sex with a gay rock star – I beg to differ. Barbara was frank about the fact that her relationship with her kids was not close. The Freddie whom Barbara shared with me rang true. He harboured a death wish, she told me. He strode defiantly into the eye of the global HIV/AIDS storm, doing 'everything with everybody' – just as he had insisted he would to broadcaster Paul Gambaccini during a visit to London's Heaven club after HIV had emerged, and was tightening its grip on the world. The movie failed to capture all that. Freddie, a figure of unassailable legend, was not portrayed as accurately as he deserved to be. Would he have wanted to be? I think so.

I rewrote my original biography of him after meeting screenwriter Peter Morgan. The new book was published in 2011. Of the forthcoming movie, barely a whiff. The memories, meanwhile, began to gather like clouds. Much of the gossip and rumour about Freddie was apocryphal, I knew that much. I trusted what his close friends had told me, and what I had witnessed first-hand. Not usually, it should be said, in professional settings: Freddie could be clipped and monosyllabic in interviews, primarily because he couldn't be arsed. He was also shy. He grew bored easily, which made him irritable. He had the attention span of a seven-year-old. But there were sometimes opportunities for peripheral people like me to join in surreptitiously. To blend with his entourage and fold into his schedule for a couple of days or nights. On such occasions, the crop could be gold.

There were wondrous Swiss dawns down by the lake, where from 1979 until 1996 Queen owned Mountain Studios, the multi-track recording facility housed in the Casino Barrière de Montreux where they recorded seven albums. Freddie would acquire his own luxurious home nearby. Too late: his illness prevented him from spending much time there. But a few years before his demise, peering out into the black, we had him to ourselves and he did let his guard down. The waspish Freddie who was inclined to tell pushy female interrogators where they could park their pudenda had receded by then. He no longer reached for the narcotics that had fuelled debauched capers in the company not only of rent boys but female models, actresses, whatever. In those somewhere-towards-the-end days, when he seemed more middle-aged and resigned if not exactly regretful, I struggled to reconcile him with his earlier incarnations. The Freddie who had orchestrated a £200,000 'Excess All Areas' launch for Queen's *Jazz* album at the New Orleans Fairmont Hotel in 1978, during which strippers writhed starkers in baths of chopped liver, bare buttocks were caned, prostitutes were positioned at the disposal of four hundred guests, serpents were charmed, queens were dragged, and oysters, lobster, caviar and cocaine were circulated on silver platters strapped to the heads, chests or backs of naked dwarves (depending on whom you believe). Who storyboarded video shoots depicting gaggles of naked female cyclists. The supplying store refused to accept the borrowed bikes back, post-shoot, because the leather saddles had been 'contaminated'. 'I sniffed them, darling,' Freddie snorted, 'they were right!' Who commissioned hookers to mud-wrestle and perform live lesbian sex acts backstage, for the amusement of band members, liggers and crew. Who threw a party for his own thirty-fifth birthday in New York to which guests arrived on Concorde for a three-day break and wound up staying three weeks. He put them up at the Berkshire Place Hotel on East 52nd Street and plied them with £30,000-worth of champagne. Another, his thirty-ninth, at Mrs Henderson's transvestite club in Munich, generated the video for his 1985 solo single 'Living on My Own'. Three hundred guests including Steve Strange, Mary Austin and former manager John Reid took part. Yet another, his forty-first, at Pike's Hotel on Ibiza, involved seven hundred revellers, Boy George, Bon Jovi and Kylie Minogue among them; three hundred and fifty bottles of Moët & Chandon, and pyrotechnics that could be seen a hundred miles away in Majorca. Who unnerved a young Michael Jackson by chopping coke in front of him and snorting lines through hundred-dollar bills at the Jackson family's Encino abode, the pair having convened there to co-write songs.

I don't imagine that Freddie ever set out deliberately to shock or amaze. Excess and exaggeration came naturally to him. He is supposed to have composed Queen's 1979 single 'Crazy Little Thing Called Love' in a Munich hotel bath, demanding of his concierge that a piano be dragged to his tub. Well, good story. He dedicated his 1985 solo album *Mr Bad Guy* to some of his beloved cats, with the postscript 'screw everybody else'. He sent Spanish soprano Montserrat Caballé recordings of the complete works of Queen when the pair were toying with the idea of recording an operatic duet. When she travelled to London for an engagement at the Royal Opera House, he invited her to dinner at his home, Garden Lodge, then kept her up until dawn with *Barcelona* producer

Mike Moran at the piano, jamming the band's greatest hits – to which stately, fragrant 'Montsy' had memorised the lyrics.

He had calmed considerably by the eighties when I came in. He no longer insisted on separate hotels from the rest of the band and their entourage, to facilitate his sanity-threatening nightlife. When he took up with Irish former barber Jim Hutton and paraded him within inner circles as his partner, the latter rose credibly to the occasion. Freddie swapped one-night stands for board games, and memorably played reverse Scrabble: starting with a full board and taking letters away to leave complete words. He took to acquiring art at auction, resumed painting and worked on his stamp collection.

I once found him in his Budapest suite in a velvet smoking jacket and silk cravat. He was hosting a cocktail party for the journalists and photographers on the *Magic* tour. It wasn't really his thing. A global superstar with a legendary reputation for living it up, he could be hopeless at one-to-one small talk. Only once the throng were in place and were getting stuck in did he emerge. He seized two bottles of champagne and went round topping up the guests' flutes, thus avoiding the obligation to linger and converse.

Although I could never profess to have known him intimately, he had a profound effect on me. I was in thrall to him for years, and in many ways still am. I cried the day he died: 24 November 1991. He did not, as he had promised, make old bones.

☿

'It's an arduous thing to tell someone's life in just two hours,' observed Rami Malek of the film in which he excelled, and which went on to become a major international box office success. It grossed close to £700 million on a production budget of less than £39 million. It was the sixth highest-grossing film worldwide of 2018 and is said to be the most successful music biopic of all time. In addition to Malek's achievements were three further Oscars at the 91st Academy Awards for Best Film Editing, Best Sound Editing and Best Sound Mixing. It was nominated for Best Picture but lost to *Green Book* starring Viggo Mortensen. It took the Golden Globe for Best Motion Picture: Drama and received nominations for the Producers Guild of America Award for Best theatrical Motion Picture and the BAFTA Award for Best British Film.

'What's the nature of celebrating a life?' Malek went on. 'Definitely not avoiding his death in any way, or what caused his death, which is the AIDS virus. But I think if you don't celebrate his life, and his struggles, and how complicated he was, and how transformative he was – and wallow instead in the sadness of what he endured and his ultimate death – then that could be a disservice to the profound, vibrant, radiant nature of such an indelible human being.'

Dreams, above all else, were the essence of Freddie's being. Even towards the end, virtually blind and bedridden, he was still insisting to all who came near that he was one of the 'lucky ones'. Most people's hopes and aspirations are extinguished by disappointments and relentless grind. He could have been forgiven for growing bitter at the way things panned out. Beyond his death, his flame flares on, unthwarted. Films come and go, but his music's not going anywhere. On 9 October 2020, the band celebrated the success of *Queen + Adam Lambert Live Around the World*, their tenth UK number one album, and their first in the UK for twenty-five years. It is a compilation of highlights from the band's ten years on the road with replacement frontman Adam Lambert, a former *American Idol* contestant. The band's previous chart-topper had been 1995's *Made in Heaven*, their final offering of new songs featuring Freddie's vocals. Though Lambert never set out to eclipse Freddie, well aware that no one could, he has done his bit to keep the great legacy alive.[5]

What kind of party, meanwhile, would Freddie have hosted for his fiftieth, sixtieth and seventieth birthdays, all of which he missed? What about the big one, his seventy-fifth, which would have fallen in September 2021? How might he have liked us to mark the thirtieth anniversary of his death? Would he have wanted us to?

☿

My first biography of Freddie was published in 1997. What with that and the *Definitive Biography* of 2011 and the *Bohemian Rhapsody* edition of 2018, you might think that I have said all that I want to say. But no story is ever finished. There are always aspects of a life to reconsider. Interest in Freddie, his music and legacy has never waned. Hence, the success of both the stage musical and the biopic; the immense popularity of all the post-Freddie Queen world tours; and their chart-topping 2020 offering that drove legions of new young fans back to the original albums, of which Queen have sold more than three hundred million, buying themselves more time on the UK charts than anybody else, including the Beatles. In a 2002 BBC poll of the Hundred Greatest Britons, topped by Sir Winston Churchill, Isambard Kingdom Brunel and Diana, Princess of Wales, Freddie was voted fifty-eighth. He was chosen as the second greatest lead singer of all time by readers of *Rolling Stone* magazine in April 2011, behind Led Zeppelin's Robert Plant but ahead of U2's Bono (third) and Mick Jagger (fourth). He was also named eighteenth best rock singer ever by that publication's editors in the same poll. Because he was the first rock star to die from AIDS, his name became synonymous with the disease. The Freddie Mercury Tribute Concert for AIDS Awareness at Wembley Stadium in 1992 sold out seventy-two thousand tickets in five hours and was watched around the world by a billion people. The Mercury Phoenix Trust launched that day has poured millions in funding into aid and research in Freddie's name. All of which makes him one of the most important individuals in HIV and AIDS history.

But Freddie was more than AIDS. He was more than hits. He was more than a singer with a song, wielding a broken mic stand provocatively on a stage in front of a band who never seemed to know what he might do next. He was infinitely more than sex and shopping. He represents something that appeals to people of every generation, nationality, ethnicity, occupation and persuasion. What *is* that? Perhaps the answer lies in revelations shared with me by some of his nearest and dearest which for various reasons I chose not to disclose, but which now seem too relevant to keep concealed. Especially now, during more enlightened days, and at a time when truth and transparency are more vital than ever.

'Life is about alternatives and compensations,' a three-parts-pissed and unexpectedly contemplative Freddie mused, that long-ago evening in Montreux. 'I don't think about it too deeply. Whatever I have to say about it, or about anything else for that matter, won't mean a stuff when I'm gone. But when I do think about it, I realise it's about only one thing. You just have to find it.'

Was he telling us that he'd fathomed the secret of life?

'Fuck off!' he screamed, 'There *isn't* one!'

The questions never vary. They ask pretty much the same things in every interview and television documentary. Who was the real Freddie? Why does he seem in this, the thirtieth-anniversary year of his death when he would have turned seventy-five years old, more alive and more relevant than ever? What was it about him that still fascinates and enthrals us? Why has the music endured and never dated, to the point that Queen's catalogue is more valuable today than it was during his lifetime? What is 'Bohemian Rhapsody' about? Who or what were the people or things most precious to him? And who *was* the love of his life?

CHAPTER THREE

ROOTS

We are still in the dark as to why Freddie took the name of the moon-less planet closest to the sun which was rising at the moment of his birth. Nor do we know whether his assumed surname was inspired, as has been suggested, by the winged messenger of the Roman gods (Hermes to the ancient Greeks), the clever god of translators and interpreters who ruled over wealth, good fortune, commerce, fertility and thievery. The liquid metal common in Hindu and Chinese culture and found in the tombs of the ancient Egyptians might also have had something to do with it. Speculation raged during Freddie's lifetime. To some extent, it still does. He never confirmed or denied a single theory. Brian May has long been convinced that the source is Freddie's song 'My Fairy King' about the fantasy world of Rhye (as in 'Seven Seas of . . .'), which Queen recorded for their eponymous debut studio album of 1973. The somewhat twee, frantic song demands indulgence: you need to be a die-hard Queen fan to want to play it again. But it may be significant for its line, 2.55 minutes in, in which Freddie sings mournfully, 'Mother Mercury look what they've done to me/I cannot run, I cannot hide.'

'And it was after that he said, "I am going to become Mercury, as the mother in this song is *my* mother," remembered Brian. 'And we were like, "Are you mad?" Changing his name was part of him assuming this different skin. The young Bulsara was still there, but for the public he was going to be this god.'

No one really knows why Freddie restyled himself 'Mercury'. One possibility that had previously escaped me was outlined in 2019, in an unsolicited email from Larry André: since November 2017 the United States Ambassador to the Republic of Djibouti.[1] With his kind permission, I reproduce an extract here:

'I spent a lot of time on Zanzibar's main island between 2008 and 2010. My circle of Zanzibari and long-time expat friends there attributed the choice of "Mercury" as a stage name to the existence of a Mercury Space Program tracking station just outside Stone Town during the period after Freddie returned to Zanzibar from India and prior to the family's departure following the Zanzibar uprising/revolution. I researched to confirm, and found that there was indeed a Mercury space program tracking station on Zanzibar at that time. My friends tell me that Zanzibari families frequented the site to enjoy its extensive, well-kept lawns. In the end, who really knows for sure? But this seems a worthy theory.'

I had twice travelled to Zanzibar, in 1996 and 2010. On neither occasion did I come across the remnants of Project Mercury: the five-year, US$400-million-dollar operation launched by NASA in October 1958 to test the viability of manned and unmanned space travel in preparation for expeditions to the moon.[2] I subsequently learned that the satellite-tracking station on Zanzibar had been built in 1960. It was part of a network of tracking stations across the world, overseen from the Mercury Control Center at Cape Canaveral, and taking in, among others, sites on Gran Canaria, Kano in Nigeria, the Kanton Island atoll in the South Pacific, and the US Navy ships *Rose Knot Victor* and *Coastal Sentry*. The Zanzibar installation straddled two sites: a US$3-million-dollar manned receiver location inland at Tunguu, and an unmanned transmitter site close to the east-coast town of Chwaka. The team of astronauts selected to mount the missions became known as the

'Mercury 7'. Twenty-eight orbital flights were charted during the early 1960s, twenty of them unmanned, two with chimpanzees aboard, and six piloted by humans. During the earliest test launches, astronauts were projected into space in a parabolic arc from Florida to East Africa. Zanzibari kids got into the habit of memorising the schedules of satellite launches. It became a thing among teenagers there to gather on the beach at night, lie on the sand gazing up at the stars, and await the overhead passing of the American space-ship. Sixteen-year-old Freddie was back from his boarding school in India by then. Although he shared next to nothing about his life in either location, he did sometimes allude to the enjoyment he had derived from hanging with his friends at the beach. It does not seem far-fetched to imagine him as one of those fanciful stargazers, nor to guess that the name and obscure connotation of 'Mercury' might have enthralled him to the point that he would one day adopt its name.

Zanzibar was a favoured assignment for America's space techni-cians, being one of the few foreign territories to which they could bring their families. Their community numbered around sixty. They lived close to Zanzibar City and commuted to work by car along what were, during the sixties, excellent roads. But everything changed after the revolution of 1964. The new Zanzibari govern-ment felt vulnerable to attack. They feared that their country could become a target in the event of nuclear war between the Soviet Union and the United States. Claiming that the station's telemetry towers could be used to guide missiles towards the island, they ordered the Project Mercury station to be dismantled. Its American and allied-national personnel and their families were repatriated. Most were lifted in a swiftly organised exodus, involving a secret convoy of vehicles to transfer them from their homes to the Africa House Hotel near the city harbour. Small dinghies conveyed them to the American destroyer USS *Manley*, which took them home.

Fifty-six years later, parts of that disused station still stand. Locals refer to the ruins as 'the Americani buildings'. Somewhere within lies what may well have been the inspiration for Freddie's rock-god name. That he went on to form a band with a guitar-playing astrophysicist takes on new meaning. Was Freddie not proud of his homeland for having played a significant part in the exploratory missions preceding the July 1969 Apollo 11 moon landings?

☿

Zanzibar's most valuable export today is neither the cloves nor coir for which it became renowned, but a Disneyfied fantasy of its perceived *One Thousand and One Nights* past.[3] The more remote island of Pemba has become a popular honeymoon haven. Sister island Tumbatu is of great archaeological significance, some of the earliest Swahili settlements having been uncovered there. Its Shirazi inhabitants can claim descent from the Persian royalty who migrated there during the ninth century. The largest, main island of Unguja, also known as 'Zanzibar Island', is promoted as a 'spectacular' holiday destination with 'something for everyone': snorkelling the coral reefs of the Indian Ocean, whale-shark-watching, wild swimming with dolphins, paragliding and exclusive spa resorts. The 'jewel in the crown of empires' boasts unspoilt sands, colonial inns and the 'haunting remains of a once eminent slave trade' – a typically insensitive travel site entry. Visitors head for both the capital, Zanzibar City, known as 'the Paris of Africa' by the time of the Great War, and for Stone Town, which in 2000 was declared a UNESCO World Heritage site.[4] They come in search of crumbling architectural wonders, the remnants of ancient cultures and for the endless array of exotic street food. They take the world-famous Spice Tour, learn to cook with African seasonings, and pick pineapples, custard apples and passionfruit from the trees. They marvel at the ruined Mtoni Palace and at the Beit-el Ajaib, House of Wonders, once the tallest building in East Africa, and where Freddie's father Bomi Bulsara once worked. They linger atop the Africa House and watch the sun set over the ocean. The better-heeled head under the silken mosquito nets of luxurious thousand-pound-a-night hotels, domed pavilions and veranda'd villas converted from merchants' mansions, and sun themselves on the remote private white beaches of Paradise Found.

Some come to find Freddie Mercury. The roots of him, at least. Though his popularity in the land of his birth has risen since the success of Queen's film, there are little more than traces of him. I was surprised, during my first visit, to discover that his connection to the country was barely acknowledged. He had never enjoyed star status there. Although I was introduced to proud owners of residences in which 'Freddie and his family had once lived', none of them could verify it. I was enticed to six different dwellings said to have been their home. A couple of tour operators running 'Discover Freddie Mercury' holidays to his homeland sold little more than accommodation with tenuous connections to his clan, excursions to restaurants with gorgeous views over the ocean, and detours to gift shops. Nor could I find any mention of him at the local museum. I couldn't even locate his birth certificate at the official records office. It had been stolen years earlier, I was informed, and was now believed to be in a private collection in Oman. This was indeed the case: a copy made its way to me eventually from the capital Muscat.

In 2004, Zanzibar officially outlawed gay relations. When, two years later, plans were announced to commemorate what would have been Freddie's sixtieth birthday with a 'gay-tourist beach party', there was vehement objection from UAMSHO, the Association for Islamic Mobilisation and Propagation. Their grievance centred on the belief that Freddie had violated the morals and mores of Islam with his defiantly gay lifestyle, even though Freddie had never lived openly as a homosexual in his life. The many thousands of fans from all over the world set to land there for the festivities were warned to stay away or face dire consequences.

While acceptance of the LGBT community continues to expand around the globe, homosexuality remains illegal in dozens of countries. Still a capital offence in a handful of territories, many others still impose fines, lashings, custodial sentences and even life imprisonment. According to ILGA, the international association which campaigns for lesbian, gay, bisexual, trans and intersex rights and against discrimination, some seventy United Nations member states still criminalise consensual same-sex sexual activity. Many of these are repressive regimes. Others, such as Singapore, Malaysia and Zanzibar, are popular tourist destinations.

Given Zanzibar's stance, I was surprised to find that the world's first museum dedicated to Freddie's life and music had been opened there in November 2019. Housed in a plain old building believed to have been Freddie's final family home before their sudden escape to England, it can be found off the beaten track down a narrow back alley in Stone Town. There is little to alert the passer-by, save for a handful of curling, sun-bleached photographs displayed in wall-mounted cases on either side of a spruced-up main entrance. Inside, a crammed gallery of framed images and faded newsprint cuttings illuminate the way to the exhibition's central attraction: a black piano that Freddie is supposed to have played. There is nothing about his personal life, still a controversial subject there.

The 'museum' – something of an overstatement – was the creation of Javed Jafferji, a Zanzibari businessman who converted to Queenism while studying in London during the 1980s, and who had long cherished the idea of establishing a permanent tribute to Freddie back home. In 2002, he opened a modest souvenir shop there on Kenyatta Road, which he named The Mercury House. When Queen guitarist Brian May and his wife Anita Dobson visited Zanzibar, posed for photographs outside Jafferji's shop and posted them on Instagram, Javed saw them and a light went on. He talked a friend into business, enlisted the support of the band's management company Queen Productions, and converted his tiny emporium into his dream. It opened to the public on the twenty-eighth anniversary of Freddie's death. But when the coronavirus pandemic struck in February 2020, they like everyone else were forced to close. The imminent launch of their guided walks, the Mercury Tour of Stone Town, had to be postponed.

We cannot help but recall having seen more substantial exhibits elsewhere. In 2009, on the eighteenth anniversary of Freddie's passing, two thousand Queen fans from around the world converged on Feltham town centre to witness his eighty-seven-year-old mother Jer and Brian May unveil a granite commemorative plaque: the first British monument to Freddie if you don't count the temporary statue of him that stood outside London's Dominion Theatre for the run of their musical *We Will Rock You*. But the Feltham memorial did not last. It was neglected, suffered acute weather damage, and fell into such disrepair that it became almost unrecognisable. It was later removed by the council, who promised a suitable replacement. They were as good as their word, but let Freddie and Queen fans down with a plain engraved stone that in no way mirrors the glamour of the original. It is not even in the original location, but sits outside number 21 High Street, Feltham.

To commemorate the band's fortieth anniversary in 2011, Queen launched 'Stormtroopers in Stilettos', a touring exhibition revisiting their earliest days. Two years later, they opened 'Queen – the Studio Experience' in Switzerland. Housed in their original Mountain Studios in Montreux, it told of their association with the studios and the town, and went behind the music they made there. It also showcased an evocative range of memorabilia including instruments, recording equipment, records, costumes and handwritten lyrics – most notably the last-ever lines written by Freddie in 1991. The control room had been preserved virtually as it was during their tenure.

In 2016, English Heritage installed a commemorative Blue Plaque on the front wall of the Bulsaras' Gladstone Avenue, Feltham home, which was unveiled by Brian and Kashmira, Freddie's sister. And in February 2020, a street nearby was renamed in Freddie's honour. Family, friends, fans, residents, local MP Seema Malhotra and Baron Bilimoria of Chelsea, the first Zoroastrian Parsi to sit in the House of Lords, gathered to watch Kashmira unveil the street sign. It is situated, appropriately, in front of the headquarters of the WZO, the World Zoroastrian Organisation – the address of which is now Number 1, Freddie Mercury Close.

But at the time of writing, Freddie does not have his Graceland. I've lost count of the number of times that Peter Freestone and I have lamented this fact over lunches and dinners down the years. Freddie left Mary Austin his eight-bedroom neo-Georgian home Garden Lodge on Kensington's Logan Place, its contents and the lion's share of his multimillion-pound fortune. She chose not to live there most of the time, taking advantage of a mews cottage behind Freddie's house from which she could keep watch over the main abode. With no other shrine to visit, fans continue to make pilgrimages from across the world on the anniversary of his death to what *Time Out* magazine called 'London's biggest rock'n'roll shrine'. They congregate in the road outside. They light candles, leave notes and poems, chalk tributes on the pavement, and sing Queen and Freddie songs into the night. It's only once a year: how vexatious to Mary and her neighbours can it be? In the good old days, Ms. Austin would emerge from the green door in the wall to accept flowers, thank the fans, and read out a poem or a prayer. But the novelty must have worn off. Large Perspex sheets affixed to the brick walls to cover the scrawlings, notes and messages were later torn down. Warning signs appeared, threatening anyone leaving tributes that they were at risk of being reported to the police. Anti-graffiti paint was applied to the fencing above the brickwork. While it was claimed that the paraphernalia deposited there antagonised other residents, home-owners in the vicinity who were interviewed by the *Mail on Sunday* in 2017 contradicted the statement and insisted that they had no problem with it at all. They found it 'charming' and 'special', they said, that Garden Lodge still attracted so many visitors, some of whom travelled thousands of miles at considerable expense to honour their hero in the cold and the dark.

I went down there year after year on the anniversary. My cousins Trev and Debbie came down from Birmingham to accompany me once. The last time I went, three years ago, it was to find that the pavement had just been hosed down. The candles and blooms had been swept away. I was perplexed. Why would Mary deny fans the right to commemorate the passing of their idol at the only place they have?

On 24 November 2020, one dejected fan from overseas wrote on the Official International Queen Fan Club Facebook page about her experience at Freddie's old house:

'It was very sad today at Logan Place . . . when I came there after 7 p.m. there were five people, plus security guards. They were there last year and this. They spoiled the atmosphere and everything. They take flowers, cards. They told us to go away. Other fans told me that police came and asked them to go away. A police car drove through. The atmosphere is over. Something has finished. We went behind a corner with other Queen fans to chat. We came back to take a goodbye picture and security blocked the entrance to Garden Lodge, to ruin the picture. I have no words.'

Other fans pointed out that London was in lockdown at the time, and that no one should have ventured there at all. We get her point, however.

Meanwhile, on the twenty-ninth anniversary of Freddie's death, Man Friday Peter Freestone took technological baby steps and appeared on YouTube for the first time, to address the fans he had missed at a string of annual gatherings cancelled by Covid.

'I know, I understand, that so many people are sad today. But Freddie is around,' he reassured them, 'for anybody who really needs him. You just have to talk to him. For me, it's the time that Freddie was finally without pain. We should celebrate his life, and think of what he has given us: the legacy, the music and the legend. He will always be around.'

One of the places Peter missed especially during lockdown year, he revealed, was Montreux: whence Freddie returned to London on 10 November 1991, all too aware that he would never see his beloved haven again.

There is no obvious grave to visit. No public London statue. Despite fervent efforts by Queen's fan club to have an effigy of Freddie erected at Imperial College Kensington or opposite in Hyde Park, every application has been rejected. Such an installation would, they were told, invite defacement and desecration. Why? Because of his sexuality? In the end, they 'just gave up'. The only official statue in existence, as far as anyone knows, is almost six hundred miles away in Montreux. What became of the twenty-feet-high bronze-coloured copy of the Montreux statue that once towered above the entrance of the Dominion Theatre on London's Tottenham Court Road, during the twelve-year run of Queen's musical *We Will Rock You*? Ah, that one's in drummer Roger Taylor's back garden, at the exquisite Grade II listed Puttenham Priory, Surrey, that he calls home. He was told by Guildford Borough Council in February 2015 that the installation had breached planning rules, and was forced to apply for retrospective permission. This was granted, provided that Roger and his South African-born wife (and stepmother to his five children) Sarina Potgieter Taylor lug the giant figure with them if and when they move house.

☿

We can but ponder Mary's long career as the official love of Freddie's life. She has lived as a cosseted 'widow' on the back of her place in his heart. If she was truly the closest person to him, why would she not bend over backwards to please his fans, just as he did? If I had a quid for the number of times I have wished this: that she had converted Garden Lodge into a tourist destination, creating a lasting monument to the greatest showman for the enjoyment of all.

'Many of you have asked if Garden Lodge will become a museum,' said Peter Freestone on his 'Ask Phoebe' blog. 'I really don't know. I remember many times walking around the house with him and he constantly complained how it felt like a museum, and how he hated the fact. I could only tell him that he should stop buying antiques, at which point he just laughed. Freddie had a very eclectic taste, but it was firmly set in the past, whether from the 1920s and '30s, back to Louis XV furniture. If you buy and utilise antiques, your house will look like a museum. So will that happen to Garden Lodge? Who knows?'

Mary should perhaps have a heart-to-heart with Lisa Marie Presley, who inherited her father's mansion in Memphis when he died in August 1977. It quickly became one of America's most popular tourist attractions, and is today the second most visited home in the United States after the White House. Along with its Meditation Garden, where Elvis, his parents and grandmother are buried, it opened to the public in 1982, five years after the King's death. Thirty-four years later, in May 2016, it welcomed its twenty millionth visitor. By my reckoning, that's an average of five hundred and eighty-eight thousand ticket-buyers a year, equating to almost fifty thousand visitors per month. The great and the good have graced it with their presence, from Bob Dylan, Sir Paul McCartney – who left a guitar pick on his grave so that Elvis could 'play his guitar in heaven'– to Paul Simon, who wrote the title track of his 1986 Grammy-winning album *Graceland* following his visit; from President George W. Bush and Albert Grimaldi, Prince of Monaco to British royals William, Harry, Beatrice and Eugenie. Its exhibit complex features Elvis's costumes and clothes, his cars and awards, his furniture and many other personal effects. Interest in the compound subsequently generated Elvis Week, a spectacular annual parade, and even a dedicated church mass. The celebrations are covered by international media.

Don't give me all that about vulgarity. Don't tell me that Freddie was far too dignified for such frivolity, or that he had infinitely better taste. He did and he didn't. In any case, what else have the remaining members of Queen (bar bassist John) been doing all these years other than keeping the dream alive by any means imaginable? I'm thinking specifically of the 'Freddie for a Day' campaign, launched in 2010 and held on Freddie's birthday every year, when fans are encouraged to dress up as their idol or just wear a moustache to get sponsored, go to work and about their business, raising money and awareness for the Mercury Phoenix Trust. About that: imagine the millions that Mary could raise for the Trust by creating a museum and shrine in Freddie's own home, where she could oversee proceedings and retain complete control. Mary, Mary, you're missing a trick. Fans the world over would adore you for it.

CHAPTER FOUR

RITUAL

Jer Bulsara was delivered of her firstborn at the Government Hospital on 5 September 1946, the Parsi New Year's Day. Her husband's niece, Perviz Darunkhanawala, told me when I visited her in Zanzibar that Freddie's mother was only eighteen years old when she had him. According to official records and press reports, Jer was ninety-four when she died in 2016, which would have made her twenty-four when Freddie was born. There is no obvious explanation for the discrepancy. What is more interesting, if records were accurately kept (there is every chance that they were not), is that Bomi Bulsara was thirty-eight years old when he became a father for the first time. A fourteen-year age gap between him and his bride, coupled with the fact that he began fatherhood in what would, in those days, have been considered middle-age, is surprising. This must have been challenging for the diligent and dignified but also authoritarian, antagonistic, confrontational and inflexible man whom Freddie knew as 'Dad'. How do I know this about Bomi, given that he never gave interviews and that Freddie did not discuss his parents publicly? Because Freddie confided in his lover Jim Hutton in the years preceding his death, and Jim shared those memories with me. It was to Jim that Freddie lamented the lack of affection in his young life, and his bewilderment at being sent away to school. He did not want to go, but his pleas to remain at home fell on deaf ears. Jim also revealed that Freddie had never understood

41

his father. How could he have done? How could Bomi have understood him in return? There was no intimate, emotional communication between them. Indeed, there would be hostility, objection and disapproval in years to come, when Mr Bulsara came to believe that his son and heir had forsaken his heritage, offended their religion, and heaped shame upon his family via his excessive lifestyle. Old for his years and set in his ways, he was never going to be the dominant role model or macho hero to his impressionable young son. Having always felt more at ease among the females of the family, Freddie was not destined to follow in his father's footsteps. To be clear, he did not say that Bomi was a bad father; merely that he was an emotionally distant one. The love he would yearn for in later years was his mother's.

Freddie's father did not witness his birth. He had not been expected to. Despite which, it fell to the patriarch to decide on the infant's name. He chose carefully, with hope and optimism, praying for a blessed life for his child. 'Farrokh' is an ancient Persian name meaning 'fortunate and happy'. How hurt Bomi and Jer must have felt when their painstaking choice of the 'popular name' was abandoned in favour of 'Freddie'. It is unlikely that Freddie gave thought to his new name's significance. He opted for the contraction, probably unaware that the full version 'Frederick' is derived from the Germanic words 'frid', meaning 'peace', and 'ric', for 'ruler' or 'power'. There was an uncanny pre-echo of fate in 'peaceful ruler'.

It is often attested that Freddie 'spent most of his childhood in Zanzibar'. He did not. He spent only the first eight years of his life there. When he was five, his mother enrolled him at the local missionary school, where he was taught by Anglican nuns. At seven, having started to sing in the local temple, he became a fully-fledged Zoroastrian. He was subjected to the Navjote ceremony which initiates a Parsi child into the ancient religion, and which corresponds to the Christian confirmation or the Jewish bar mitzvah. At the time, 1954, there were around three hundred Parsis living in

Zanzibar. But their temple was long ago abandoned, and only a handful still live there today.

The ritual, which was lengthy and involved, is worth pausing over for its beauty and humility. After taking the prescribed sacred bath, the Nahan, Freddie was presented to assembled priests, relatives and friends in a ceremonial chamber. There, he found four trays: one bearing his sacred white cambric shirt, the 'sudreh', symbolising a blessed path through life. The shirt features a 'giriban', a small pocket below the throat area representing the initiate's obligation to be virtuous as well as industrious, and to fill his purse with righteousness as well as money. The multi-stranded 'kusti', a sacred thread or belt, stands for the seventy-two chapters of the Yasna, the book of liturgical prayers. Woven from lamb's wool to evoke innocence and purity, with tassels at both ends, it is wound around the waist three times as a symbol of the *Humata, Hukhta, Huvareshta*, the 'good thoughts, good words, good deeds' expected of the recipient. It is then knotted at both front and back to signify a lasting commitment to the faith. This tray also bears a few 'good luck' charms: a handful of Rupees, some betel nuts and leaves, grains of rice, some sweets, and a metal cup filled with kanku: the red vegetable-based powder made from turmeric or saffron and slaked lime that we would call vermilion powder, and which is used to make the tili (red mark) on the forehead; a tray of rice to be presented afterwards to the priest as a symbolic 'payment'; another of flowers to be distributed among the guests at the ceremony's end, and one of pomegranate grains, rice, raisins, almonds and coconut slices, to be sprinkled on the child to summon future prosperity. There was also a lighted lamp, probably burning with clarified butter, and incense, of sandalwood and frankincense.[1]

It is likely that Freddie went through these ritualistic motions without protest. He would have been expected to submit and obey. What else do we do, as young children? Only as adults do we think and reflect. Having bowed for years to parental demand, there comes a time to look inwards, to ask questions and to think for ourselves. Because he discussed neither his faith nor his withdrawal from it, we have no way of knowing at what point Freddie disconnected from it. We know only that his parents remained devoted all their lives. Mindful of their standing within their close-knit community, he went to great lengths to protect them and to preserve their dignity. It was the reason why he kept his thoughts and his lifestyle to himself.

Opportunities to further his education in Zanzibar were limited. Influenced by friends who had already despatched their children to well-regarded and expensive public schools in India, the Bulsaras took a reluctant decision. In order to give their son the most privileged start in life that they could afford, they followed suit. How hard must it have been for his mother to part with him? What made her agree to send her son so far away from home at such a young age for so many years? The suggestion is that both parents were keen for him to experience the culture of their own homeland. In which case, why send him to an English-style boarding school in the 'Western Ghats' among the misty Sahyadri Mountains, a range older than the Himalayas? Yet it is what they did, enrolling him at St Peter's Church of England School in Panchgani: a lush, idyllic hill station which had been a popular summer resort for rich Bombay residents during the era of the British Raj. St Peter's had first operated as The European Boys School for Anglo-Indian students, housed in the boys' section of Kimmins Girls School until its own building was completed in 1904. The school motto was, and remains, 'Ut Prosim': 'That I May Serve'. The establishment had its own Christian church on campus. While a range of religions and backgrounds were welcomed and tolerated, all boys were required to attend the Eucharist on Sundays. Whether or not his exposure to the liturgy of the Church of England influenced him, or whether he kept up his Zoroastrian rituals while away at school, is not known. Close friends have confirmed that, while he did not practice as an adult, he never turned his back completely on the mother faith. Years later, when asked whether Freddie Mercury would go to heaven or hell after his death, presumably because of his sexuality and hedonistic behaviour, a priest of his acquaintance is said to have responded diplomatically, 'From what I gather, he had the Zoroastrian traits of generosity and kindness.'

Once Freddie began at St Peter's, he would return home only once a year. Fellow pupil Subhash Gudka, who attended St Peter's from 1958 to 1962, sometimes made the journey with Freddie. 'There were about sixty of us East Africa students travelling to India to study then,' he remembered. 'For the school year, we'd take the same ship to India, Freddie boarding at Zanzibar and me at Mombasa. I'd join him in First Class.'[2] Given that each journey exceeded three thousand nautical miles, the boys spent their weeks at sea intensely bored, poorly fed, and herded in endless lifeboat drills and strictly controlled racial mingling. Once the ship docked at Bombay, they scrambled through the madness to lofty, stained-glass-windowed Victoria Station, twenty minutes or so away by taxi or rickshaw, to locate the train for Poona. What a culture shock Bombay must have been to small schoolboys from the back of beyond. How frantic and frightening it must have been. If only Freddie had ever felt like sharing his reminiscences of arriving in that city for the first time, sailing towards a majestic view of the great Gateway of India and its architectural neighbour the Taj Mahal Palace, the finest hotel in the East.[3]

Subhash recalled a timid, uncommunicative, rather homesick Freddie. He also remembered a very musical one. Every class at St Peter's had between three and five boys who would sign up for music lessons, of which Freddie was one. Although books talk of him having 'excelled' at piano, he pounded rather than played the school's solid teak Moutrie upright and made it only to Grade IV in both Theory and Practical & Performance out of a possible eight grades in each category.[4] Freddie, his friend Peter Freestone reminds us, never actually claimed to be a great pianist. He would defer to the expertise of professionals Spike Edney and Mike Moran in years to come.

He spent most of his school holiday breaks with his aunts, Jer and Sheroo, in Bombay. Even that was a considerable journey from the green paradise they referred to affectionately as 'Panchi': a sixty-mile bus or taxi ride to the railway station at Pune, then a hundred-mile, three- or four-hour journey by train into Victoria railway terminus. It would have taken five hours by road, not that there was anybody to drive him. Little Freddie did all his coming and going alone, or with fellow boarders heading is the same direction. His parents never visited him at school. Distance determined that exeats – temporary leave of absence to go home – were out of the question.

Gita Choksi, who as Gita Bharucha was part of Freddie's inner circle while she was a pupil at Kimmins Girls', recalls that she never once met Mr and Mrs Bulsara. 'They never came. Which I always thought was strange,' she admitted. 'Freddie didn't seem bothered by it, but you never knew, with him. I felt for him when so many mothers and fathers would arrive for the sports days, the plays and concerts, the parents' evenings and the open days, but Bucky never had anybody to watch him or go around with him. Most likely there were financial constraints. I didn't have the impression that his family was wealthy. How could they have afforded to travel thousands of miles each time to attend such events? It was understandable, but sad for him.'

Even though we are talking about the distant past, some sixty-six years ago, Gita's memories are sharp. 'I would have been six or seven years old when Farrokh and I first met,' she told me. 'And it was always "Farrokh", never Freddie. He chose to change his name only much later. We were all friends, the boys and the girls together. Pesky little fellows, those boys were, too. I remember that feeling quite distinctly. There was nothing so special about Bucky, as we started calling him, in those days. Nothing that stands out. It has been written that we were "joined at the hip" or "in love" or whatever you want to call it. It's nonsense. There would never be anything like that between us. I was never more than a close friend.

I was neither "Freddie Mercury's first girlfriend" nor the "love of his life".

Gita spoke to me from her home in South Mumbai (she still refers to it as 'Bombay') more than twenty years after we had first met. The daughter of the personal pilot to the Maharaja of Jaipur, her mother was a widow by the time Gita was six months old. Mother and daughter relocated to Bombay. By 1997 Gita was living in Frankfurt, where she worked for an Indian travel company. I tracked her down, and she came to meet me in London. She lent me original photographs from her personal albums for my first book about Freddie, which were later destroyed accidentally by the publisher. I got to know her son Aarish, who attended my book launch that summer. I was heavily pregnant with my second child at the time, and had a third baby nineteen months after that. Because I was up to my eyes in children, Gita and I lost touch. Twenty-three years later, I was about to go looking for her again for this book when an email from her landed in my inbox. She had found me via my website. Her tragic news was that her son had died, unaware that his young wife was expecting their first child. Gita seemed to be taking stock of her life and getting her house in order. We talked again about the Freddie she knew. Grief had exposed a deeper layer of this thoughtful lady. This time round, her opinions were more blunt.

'Do you know,' she said, 'I make no bones. I acknowledge that he achieved greatness, touched the world with his music, was loved by millions and is adored to this day. I understand that he is even more popular today than he was during his lifetime. But in truth, I was not a fan of Freddie Mercury. Why? Because he totally disowned his antecedents in India, and that does not sit well with me at all. I have racked my brains as to why he might have done that. The only thing that I can think of is this: during the sixties and seventies, Indians were not very well treated in the UK, I am afraid to say. Probably he didn't want to display any links with India because of that. As if he feared that he too might be persecuted. But it came across that he was ashamed of his roots. Anyway, as close as we were as children and as teenagers, he left school before I did, and that was the end of it. After that, I never heard from him again.'

Gita prefers, she says, to cherish fonder memories. She recalls occasions when they would all meet up and hang out together at both schools, at fetes and sports days and at inter-school and inter-house dramatic competitions.

'There were boys from Nepal, Nairobi, other parts of East Africa. Diplomats' children. During the May summer holidays, Bucky and several others stayed back. They didn't go home. This was great for those of us who lived there. We would meet at the Panchgani library in the evenings, which was lovely. Panchi was delightful in those days: a very pretty hill station with old bungalows built on either side of just three roads. The name meant "Five Plateaus". Panch as in "five", gani as in "plateaux". There was a V-shaped part known as Tigers' Leap. Whether tigers leapt there, God knows. All the bungalows were named after where the original owners had come from. Our family bungalow was called "Maidstone", and it was very charming. Our road was on the lower side, facing the Krishna River valley. The climate was so good, despite the monsoon. It was because it was in the rain shadow that they founded the boarding schools there. You could live there twelve months of the year and not be driven out by the rain. There were "points" – Sydney Point, Parsi Point – and Tableland and the Lingmala waterfall, all with beautiful scenic views, for recreation. Where people could relax. There were many beautiful birds. There were also plenty of spiders and snakes, which Bucky hated, he absolutely couldn't stand them. A lot of the dogs got bitten by snakes. But there was also the mongoose. There were panthers, wild boar and deer. There was the occasional leopard. Imagine all of this. It seems wondrous, looking back on it. Panchi was a kind of paradise. We had an idyllic child-hood there.'

Apart, that is, from the food: 'Oh, my goodness, the food at my school was God-awful. At St Peter's it was even worse! The *world's* worst, Bucky used to say. We had no choice but to eat it, we would have starved otherwise. There was nothing else.'

Freddie displayed an incredibly modest appetite in later life. It seems likely that dreadful school dinners were at least in part to blame.

'Our schools were very strict, but not suffocating,' said Gita. 'Our main teachers were missionaries from the UK. I thank them still for our missionary values. There were many opportunities for much creativity. For sport, we played hockey, basketball, throwball, badminton, the works. We followed the Church of England holidays. During Parsi New Year in September, we spent two weeks in Bombay. The same at Christmas. Bucky would go to aunts in Bombay, I know. He never complained to me about his homesickness. You had to be rough and tough and not display weakness. You couldn't go wetting the bed and be cowering away like babies. He had to present a façade, and to cover up any signs of insecurity. I know, however, that he did share his feelings with one or two of the boys.'

Had she any inkling of homosexuality brewing in Freddie?

'None at all, I swear. In those days, for us to be *gay* was to be happy and exuberant. We didn't know what "gay" as in homosexual was. Not a clue. People would use words such as "pansy" and so on, but it went over our heads. Only when I was at university did I become aware of certain men being different. Much later, about women being different. There was an art teacher at St Peter's called Mrs Blossom Smith. I knew her daughter, Janice Smith. Years later, she said to me, "Mum always felt there was something different with Bucky." "What do you mean by different?" I asked her. But we didn't take it further, and I didn't know what she meant.'

The schoolboy Freddie whom Gita recalls today was 'not exactly shy, just not as forthcoming as most of the other boys. A few of them had girlfriends, but we were all a group together. We were the privileged Hectics gang, hanging around with Freddie's band' – in which Freddie played the ancient school upright piano while his classmate Faran Irani manhandled a skiffle-style tea-chest-and-string bass.

'We were into Elvis Presley, Cliff Richard and Little Richard,' remembered Bruce Murray, the Hectics' founder and frontman, lead singer and guitarist who later migrated to England, played in a string of bands and ran the Music Centre store in Bedford. When his son became a member of the Quireboys, he helped to run the band. 'Also, other popular musicians of the fifties, like Fats Domino, Ricky Nelson and Fabian. We did numbers like "Yakkety Yak", "Ramona", "Girl of My Best Friend", "Rock Around the Clock" and "Tutti Frutti". We wore tight trousers, thin string ties, pointy shoes and Brylcreemed hair with big "puffs", like our idols, Elvis and Cliff Richard. We really thought we were hot stuff.'

Hectics drummer Victory Rana dismisses rumours about Freddie's inspiration.

'I've heard stories that Freddie was inspired by Bollywood music, and Lata Mangeshkar,' he said, 'but that is a lot of rubbish. The only music he listened to, and played, was Western pop music.'[5]

Victory remembers Freddie as 'hugely talented': 'He was a natural musician. He had an amazing voice. He could sing anything – from rock'n'roll to classical music. For example, apart from the Hectics, he was also part of a Western classical music group at school, where three boys would sing in three different keys. And that is probably one of the reasons for the eclectic sound he created for Queen in later years. By the way, his voice never changed over the years. If you listen to a Freddie Mercury CD, it sounds just like the young Freddie did back then, singing for the Hectics in Panchgani.'

'He was a prodigy,' enthused Bruce Murray. 'He could play anything! He had the unique ability to listen to a song on the radio, just once, and be able to play it perfectly. Our favourite programme was the "Binaca Hit Parade" (presented by Greg Roskowski on the hugely popular commercial service Radio Ceylon), which was broadcast every Wednesday, if I remember correctly. If we heard a new song and liked it, Freddie would quickly learn the chords, and

I would scribble down the words. And it would be the Hectics' next hit number. Simple!'

Fellow Hectics Derrick Branche, Bruce Murray, Farang Irani and Victory Rana would follow careers in film and television, music, hospitality and the military. The two who wound up distinguishing themselves most, Victory and Freddie, had been The Boys Least Likely To. Their classmates would have found hilarious the thought of the former drummer becoming the very model of a modern Major-General – Victory went on to train at Sandhurst, was made a Major General in the Nepalese Army and concluded his career as his country's Ambassador to Myanmar.[6] As for the shy, goofy ivory-tickler growing up to be not only one of the greatest singers in rock history but also the creator of one of the most popular songs of all time, it was all too much.

But Freddie's obsession had its downside. 'I did notice that when he was at the piano, whether on or off the stage, he was totally different,' said Gita. 'Music changed everything for him. He was so obsessed with it that everything else fell off the side. He won the Junior All-Rounder trophy, which was for studies, elocution, dramatics, sports and extra-curricular pursuits. You got a double promotion from fifth standard to seventh for that. His parents must have been extremely proud of him. But in standards eight and nine, things changed dramatically for him. He threw it all away. The only thing he cared about was his music. It must have come as both a shock and a dreadful disappointment to them. They had invested so much money, which can't have been easy for them, and now it seemed to be all for nothing. He was sixteen when he left. He should have stayed longer.'

Years later, when she was flicking through her mother's *Woman's Weekly* and *Woman's Own* magazines, Gita recognised an image in one of the articles.

'I started screaming, "Oh my God! This is Bucky! It's Bucky!" We had no idea until that moment that he had become the rock star Freddie Mercury.

'Much later on, I did go to see the *Bohemian Rhapsody* film. I enjoyed it, but I ask you: not even *three minutes* spent on his child-hood in Panchi? It was a travesty! I was so angry, I was grumbling and mumbling. They are disowning his past, but they shouldn't do that. His childhood was where it all began.'

☿

Freddie's eight-year tenure at an English-style public school instilled in him, whether consciously or not, a fervent desire to shake off Persian, Indian and African roots and influences. He needed to anglicise himself fully in preparation for a more liberated and less confined future. During the St Peter's years, discipline, manners and etiquette were prioritised. He couldn't speak to his parents on the phone, as lines of communication were not yet established. He wrote formal letters home heaving with pain between the handwrit-ing, to 'Dear Mum and Dad'. The shy introvert was obliged to grow up quickly. He learned to stand on his own two feet; to fight his own battles; and to maintain the requisite stiff upper lip which in his case protruded in a pronounced overbite possibly caused by hyperdon-tia, the clinical term for supernumerary or 'extra' teeth. Whether he did have four extra teeth in the back of his mouth or whether he had four enlarged 'third molars' or wisdom teeth which shoved the inci-sors forwards, has been debated for years. Photographs show that his teeth looked much larger in his face when he was small than they did during adulthood, even though he had never had anything done to them. He grew into and learned to live with them, it seems, though they always provoked conversation. They earned him the aforemen-tioned nickname 'Bucky'. Which he naturally disliked almost as much as he had loathed his given name.

Many years after they had all left school, Gita ran by chance into Derrick Branche, the Hectics guitarist who had moved to Australia and had become an actor. He appeared in the 1980s British televi-sion series *The Jewel in the Crown*, about the last days of the Raj, and in feature film *My Beautiful Laundrette*. 'Derrick told me that he had been terribly excited to get tickets for a Queen concert in London, at Earls Court,' she said. 'He couldn't wait to see our old school friend afterwards. He went backstage with his companions after the concert, explained to the security people who he was, and they allowed them into the dressing room area to wait for Freddie. When eventually Freddie came in, he spotted Derrick, looked down his nose, didn't say a word, then turned around and walked back out. '"Only five minutes earlier," Derrick said to me, "I was telling my friends how Freddie and I were not only at school together but in a band together, and how thrilled I was that I was about to see him again. He recognised me, I know he did. But he ignored me. And in that moment, he made me out to be a liar." It makes me so sad to recount this to you. I have never forgotten it. Freddie never looked back in his life. It's a shame but it's true, that in the end there was no long-term loyalty in Freddie.'

☿

The love of Freddie's life was not his homeland. Although he had been none the wiser when he left for India, he was fully aware of Zanzibar's dark and shameful past when he returned home under a cloud at the age of sixteen. From history lessons, he knew all about Dr David Livingstone (I presume), the late nineteenth-century explorer and Christian missionary who had once lived in Stone Town.

'The stench arising from a mile and a half or two square miles of exposed sea beach, which is the general depository of the filth of the town is quite horrible ... It might be called Stinkabar rather than Zanzibar,' wrote the doctor in his diary of the city which brimmed with starving slaves infected with VD, cholera and malaria. For hundreds of years at that point, the island's clove plantations had been worked by enslaved Africans from the mainland, twenty-two miles west across the Zanzibar Channel by dhow, the traditional wooden sailing vessels still in use. At that point, this fabled land of spices that had once been the domain of Portuguese settlers but had been conquered in 1650 and was later controlled by an Omani Arab ruling elite, was one of the richest and most God-forsaken places on earth. It has been estimated that forty to fifty thousand Africans from as far away as central Africa's Great Lakes were shipped to Zanzibar each year. Many died en route to the Stone Town slave markets, from overcrowding, starvation and disease. Countless more expired in the terrible shelters into which they were crammed like animals before being paraded naked in the marketplace to be sold. Those who survived were prized for their hardiness, and fetched premium rates. But even the most robust would go on to die on the plantations they were enslaved to, throughout Zanzibar, North and South America, the West Indies, the Ottoman Empire, Egypt and the Middle East, from neglect, abuse and overwork ... thus creating the need to mount further expeditions, and to take even more slaves.

During the mid-nineteenth century, when the British began to colonise the Dark Continent, Indian labourers were transported to East Africa to work on the railways and in construction. There, they established their own communities. Between 1840 and 1950, many thousands more Indians migrated there in search of opportunity and a better life. Under British colonial rule from 1896 until 1963, a constitutional government and political party system were imposed in nearby Zanzibar. When independence from Britain was granted on 10 December 1963, the islands' population consisted of fifty thousand Arabs, twenty thousand Asians and some two hundred and thirty thousand Africans. Advantages had long been weighted in favour of the ruling Arabs. Economic inequality, adverse working and living conditions, an education system unaffordable to the majority, unfair taxation, and a trade crisis that saw the price of cloves drop dramatically on the world market, leading to hardship for many: all of this contributed to mounting unrest. The problem was compounded by religious intolerance, mainly of Christianity and traditional African beliefs and practices, as the Arabs strove to Islamise the islands. Tensions erupted. A short, sharp, racial rebellion was launched on Sunday 12 January 1964, timed to coincide with the Ramadan celebrations. It caught the police, the military and the government unawares. Armed rebels entered Zanzibar city, assembled in the African quarters, and carried out their surprise attack with machetes, spears and a handful of stolen guns. The predominantly Arab government was overthrown, and a republic was proclaimed. The eleventh Sultan, Jamshid bin Abdullah al-Said – who had only been in power since his father died the previous July – was deposed. His palace was seized by revolutionaries. He escaped with his entourage on the royal yacht, intending to settle in the motherland, Oman. Thousands of Zanzibari refugees had fled there, including the Sultan's seven children and two of his siblings. But his pleas to be admitted were rejected on grounds of security. He flew instead to England, where he remained for nearly sixty years.[7]

The Indian and Arab minorities were mostly massacred or expelled. No peaceful coup d'état, this. Castrations, beheadings, gang-rape and infanticide were rife. Entire villages were decimated, and thousands of corpses thrown into mass graves. Some people surrendered to the new regime. Those who managed to escape left with what they stood up in, fleeing to neighbouring countries such as Kenya and Tanganyika. Others headed for Saudi Arabia and Europe. Those who came West crossed the water to Dar es Salaam, negotiated passages on ships of various nationalities to London via the Suez Canal, reached Dover several weeks later and proceeded to Victoria by train. Others, like the Bulsaras, purchased plane tickets. In the words of an online documentary featuring rare footage from the period, 'the sins of the Arab fathers who had owned African slaves and caused the most appalling wastage of human life in capturing them throughout Eastern and Central Africa had been visited terribly on the third and fourth generations.'

Kiswahili, an Arabicized form of Swahili, was now declared Zanzibar's official language. The country was annexed to Tanganyika. This new union became known as the United Republic

of Tanzania. One of the twentieth century's most horrific geno-
cides was thereafter swept under the carpet. We speak freely today
of the Holocaust, the slaughter of Rwanda's Tutsi, the extermina-
tion of Muslims in Bosnia, the long-running persecution and
murder of Yazidis in Iraq. It is hoped that the act or remembering
will prevent reoccurrence. But of the Zanzibar Revolution, most
people know nothing beyond the fact that Freddie Mercury was its
most famous refugee. As for Freddie, he told Jim Hutton that his
connection to it 'appalled' him. He had wanted nothing to do with
it, he said, and couldn't wait to get away.

'Freddie told me that he didn't know anything at all about what
had gone on in Zanzibar over the centuries when he went away to
India as a little boy,' Jim told me, during the first of several interviews at his home in Bennekerry near Carlow town, south-east
Ireland.

'But he'd learned about it at school, and it nagged him. He talked
to me about the servants who worked for his family. There had
been some kind of nanny, not a trained one or anything, just a poor
local girl who helped his mother. He couldn't really remember her.
How could he have done, he was only a baby! He couldn't tell me
her name (she was called Sabine). He had a bee in his bonnet about
"the Africans". Almost as if it had just dawned on him, the whole
slavery thing. He talked about Zanzibar being "a cauldron". He got
very angry about it. I didn't really know what he meant at the time.
No, I didn't want to ask. I was used to Freddie pontificating, I just
let him bang on. He liked a drink, and he would get more and more
irate. I tried not to get into those kinds of conversations. I wasn't
educated compared to him. I always felt self-conscious about looking ignorant in front of him.'

'But now,' Jim said, 'I think he meant that all the slavery in the
world must be the fault of Zanzibar in some way. It wasn't, of
course, it was only part of the greater horror, which you don't want
to think about really. "All those poor people, hundreds, thousands,
must have been millions of them," he would say. "Wrenched from

their families. Dragged out of their tribal villages. Marched until they couldn't stand. Thrown on top of each other on ships and traded like goats in a marketplace." It played on his mind when he'd had a few. It felt to Freddie as though the evils of the world all started there, in the place where he himself had been born. It tormented him, he couldn't stand it. He thought a good deal about the fact that his own family had once had poor Africans working for them for little reward. He felt terrible about it.'

Jim cast his mind back to Live Aid day, 13 July 1985, which we both attended. He accompanied Freddie and witnessed Queen's triumph.

'I remember Freddie was talking to his favourite journalist David Wigg, they were doing an interview that day, about the cause and all. He told David that when he'd watched the report about Africa's starving millions, he'd had to switch the television off, it upset him so much. He said the word "Africans" and he glanced at me. I wasn't right next to him, I was further away, but I could literally feel him flinch. You could see he was uncomfortable. That old guilt again, I thought to myself. He didn't say it. We didn't talk about it afterwards. I always knew not to quiz him. I knew my place. But I understood what was going through his mind. "I'm an African, Jim," Freddie said, "and this whole fucking thing is all a sham. I am *one of them*. I am a hypocrite. So what do you think of that?"'

CHAPTER FIVE

STONE FREE

The genie had delivered. Auspiciously, symbolically, during a Leap Year. A clean slate, a fresh start and a new beginning: what a priceless opportunity for Freddie to leave his old self and previous life behind. He was burdened by neither baggage nor unfinished business. Consigning mistakes and failures to a past he would never revisit, he was now set to create a whole new persona and future ... in London! Far from frozen by fear of change, Freddie was ready. Not only had he been rescued from a backwater he abhorred, he was whisked from one extreme to another and landed as if by magic in the capital of cool. Old memories were discarded en route. Ghosts were banished with a toss of his head, don't come around here no more. Yes, the Bulsaras entered England as impoverished refugees, and their vastly different new environment would take some adjusting to. But as far as Freddie was concerned, this was the best thing that could ever have happened to him. His new address, if somewhat threadbare, was right up his street. His younger sister, who was twelve at the time and perhaps less aware at first of the extent to which the move would improve their lives, recalled being struck by how 'conspicuous' she and her family felt on the streets of West London's Feltham. Changes would have to be made if they were to integrate successfully. Freddie's sixties Indian schoolboy quiff, he decided, was the first thing that had to go.

'He was a bit embarrassed and he quickly grew his hair and would never stop grooming it!' Kashmira said.

The family held their breath for a while, anxious that they would not be accepted. They soon settled. Although immigrants were unwelcome minority 'misfits' in 1960s Feltham, seventeen per cent of people now living in the London Borough of Hounslow, of which that town is part, identify themselves as ethnic Indians. Lord Karan Bilimoria, founder of the Cobra beer brand and a fellow Zoroastrian Parsi, spoke of the 'glass ceiling' that existed in this country when Freddie's family arrived here. He credited them and others like them for their courage and perseverance, which enabled them to overcome racial differences in order to survive and thrive. 'It's people like Freddie Mercury who smashed through it,' he said. 'Hounslow is a shining example of multiculturalism and the opportunity that Britain offers.'

He makes it sound easy. It wasn't. Freddie's old school friend Gita was frank about the difficulties he and others like him would have faced, and pointed out how grudgingly the Bulsaras would have been received in their new country and community. This was the deplorable era of 'No Blacks, No Irish, No Dogs', when seventy-five thousand ethnically diverse immigrants were arriving in Britain each year, and when racial tension was tearing communities apart.[1]

Bomi and Jer struggled to secure jobs. In the face of lost status, they held their heads high. Freddie's father accepted employment inferior to the level he had enjoyed in Zanzibar, as a low-ranking accountant for the Forte catering group. His mother settled for shop assistant at a local branch of Marks & Spencer, selling jumpers, knickers and hot cross buns. Even after Freddie had made it a few years hence, and could afford to keep his family in style, she was reluctant to relinquish her position and independent income. Throughout those early years, money was tight, treats were rare, and domestic servants were a distant, embarrassing memory. 'We got real when we got here,' Freddie would later tell his last lover Jim Hutton, 'but I always felt that my mother deserved better. It made me wince to watch her go out to work, and then have to come home and do all the housework. I had to make it, you see, so that she no longer had to.'[2]

Just turning eighteen and with no clear idea as to 'what he wanted to be when he grew up' – at least, not anything he could admit to – Freddie enrolled at Isleworth Polytechnic and Hounslow Borough College in September 1964, to embark on a two-year art foundation course.[3] He would later explain that this was all part of his cunning master plan. Aware that London's art colleges were breeding grounds for bands, he had plotted a route to pitch himself into the favoured milieu of young musicians. The big drawback was having to live by strict parental rules, forced as he was to remain under their roof for the duration. There were insufficient funds to rent student accommodation, or to pay his way on a flat with friends. Frustrated by the threats of his draconian father, the restrictions imposed and the all-round domestic disharmony and disapproval – of everything from his hair and his clothes to the hours he kept to the perceived degenerates he was wasting his time with – Freddie champed at the bit to spread his wings in 'swinging London'. The throbbing capital lay just forty minutes away by train, from Feltham to Waterloo. From there, the hub of Soho was merely a sprint over the bridge and a dash up through Covent Garden. The bright lights, sights and sounds of the big city were close enough to taunt and distract him.

There may have been no better year than 1964 for a fervent music fan to land in Blighty.[4] Already sold on the music of rock'n'roll's first Golden Age – Elvis and the hillbilly cats out of Memphis, Fats Domino and Little Richard via New Orleans, Bo Diddley and Chuck Berry from Chicago and other fifties musicians sucked into their orbit whose songs Freddie and the Hectics had covered at school, here he was now in the eye of the sixties rock and pop storm. Thanks to the Beatles, this sceptred isle became the epicentre of a quake that would never be calmed.[5] Having turned their homeland on its head, the Fabs' sensational appearance on

The Ed Sullivan Show on 9 February, watched by a record seventy-four million Americans, catapulted the band to international stardom. Their single 'Can't Buy Me Love', issued four days ahead of the UK release date in March, shot soundly to number one. The next four songs down on the US chart were also Beatles songs, while another nine dominated the Top 100. In the UK, this was their third offering to shift more than a million copies. It was wall-to-wall Ringo, George, John and Paul, everywhere you looked. Unless, that is, you happened to be more inclined towards the edgier and ruder Rolling Stones, who released their eponymous debut album that year; or the foppish, camp-ish R&B ravers the Kinks, who did the same. Meanwhile, nineteen minutes away via the Chertsey Road, the Who's bellicose Pete Townshend destroyed his first guitar at Richmond's Railway Hotel and set the tone for a nearly sixty-year rebellion ... without a pause.[6]

Seminal pop show *Top of the Pops* had made its debut on BBC television that January, serving up the hits, the glitz and a must-watch chart rundown every Thursday night that was the talk of every classroom on Friday morning. It would become the world's longest-running weekly music show. The UK's third channel, BBC2, was launched in April, and soon evolved into the nation's cultural go-to. The *Sun* newspaper arrived in September, originally as an addition to the Mirror Group's titles and far-removed from the soar-away red-top we love and loathe today. And Radio Caroline, the UK's first pirate station, set sail, broadcasting from a boat anchored somewhere off the east coast of England.

Freddie had a happy-go-lucky time of it at the Poly. Pleasantly surprised by the way he was accepted into this new group, he got stuck into the college choir and won a part in the Christmas drama production, *The Kitchen*, which was the late 1950s debut of playwright Arnold Wesker. Freddie played Dimitri, one of the kitchen staff with a sideline in radio construction.

'Fred was charmingly shy, but also very engaging, and he desperately wanted to fit in,' recalled fellow student Adrian Morrish. 'He dressed weirdly in drainpipe trousers that weren't quite long enough, and middle-aged jackets that were slightly too small."[7]

Through a friend, Freddie started doing freelance layouts for the National Boys' Club magazine, to earn pocket money, and found he wasn't as good an artist as he wanted or needed to be. Still, he now had the wherewithal to venture out to clubs with his friends at weekends. The gang frequented local haunts and London blues clubs, where bands like the Bluesbreakers, Steampacket and the prototype of Peter Green's Fleetwood Mac would play. At the Eel Pie Island Hotel on Sunday nights, the gang would enjoy the Yardbirds, Howlin' Wolf, the Rolling Stones and the Tridents, Rod Stewart and Long John Baldry. Freddie would often raise eyebrows by departing alone before the end, explaining that he had to get back to do his piano practice. He rushed off, more likely, because his father had reminded him of his curfew. He clearly found time for his piano, however. Classmates would later recall him being able to summon songs from the keys that he had only just heard on the radio that morning, ahead of lessons. Even at that stage, Freddie was striving to go one better.

'He'd say, "But we can do this or we can do that . . ." and start improvising to try and make (the song) sound better,' remembered his friend Patrick Connolly. Freddie, Patrick and their guitarist pal Paul Martin started writing original songs together. 'I wasn't very interested in pop music and I didn't think I could sing,' confessed Patrick. 'But the three of us would sit around the piano (in Freddie's front room on Gladstone Avenue). Fred's enthusiasm brought us together. He'd actually encourage me: "Look, Patrick! You're singing, you can *do* it!"'

At one point, he started auditioning musicians with the intention of putting his own polytechnic band together. Nothing came of it. Freddie worked on both his music and his look, swapping the musty tweeds and trews for garments with 'Levi's' on the labels, and pulling girls at parties and gigs alongside everybody else.

Freddie graduated from the polytechnic in 1966 with his art A level, then vanished into thin Ealing Art College. The establishment was part of Ealing Technical College and School of Art, and was based on the same St Mary's Road site as the University of West London is today. The graphic design course to which he transferred after a year is today under the umbrella of the University's London School of Film, Media and Design. During the 1960s, the college ran courses in fashion design, graphics, industrial design, photography and fine art. Pete Townshend of the Who had studied there from 1961 until 1964, while the Rolling Stones' Ronnie Wood had enrolled in 1963. Freddie signed up as a dedicated follower of fashion. Which must have been the nail in the coffin as far as Bomi Bulsara was concerned.

Now that his son was twenty years old, Freddie's father realised with dismay that he was fighting a losing battle. Freddie would soon be staying out all night, dossing on friends' floors and skulking home to cacophony. While his tender, supportive mother Jer, of whom Freddie was almost a mirror image and to whom he was exceptionally close, would sigh, 'Boys will be boys' and hand him a hot meal and a pile of freshly ironed shirts, his short-fused father was enraged by the feisty wannabe rocker. According to Jim Hutton, Bomi denounced Freddie as having 'brought shame on the family' and for being 'impossible to control':

'The memory of that particular argument bothered Freddie a lot,' recalled Hutton. 'Not so much the "shame" bit, it was that word "control". It horrified him that his dad still needed to dominate him and try and run his life, even though Freddie was now an adult. Twenty is twenty, right? Lots of people are married parents themselves by then, at least they seemed to be in those days. What was lacking in Bomi's own life, Freddie wondered, that his father needed to be so regimental about his? He spent a lot of time thinking back over this and trying to work out his dad's thinking. "He was so *mercurial*," he used to say to me, to the point that I started wondering whether *that* mightn't have been the reason behind the name Freddie took for himself. Or he could have done it subconsciously, who knows.'

'We'd sit up talking about it all,' said Jim, 'really late at night. Sometimes it could be morning by the time we stopped. "I can say things to you that I can't say to anyone else," he'd tell me. The problems he'd had with his dad couldn't just be about their family's religion, Freddie thought. There had to be more to it. He didn't know all that much about his father's early life, nor his mother's, come to that. I did suggest for him to try and see someone at one point, you know, a counsellor or a doctor or something, because he was so cut-up about it all. So tormented. Even with all his success, he'd never managed to shake off his worries. He was such a famous rock star, loved all over the world, but he was still upset by the way his father had treated him when he was young. He had never come to terms with it. I think it must have been because his life ran away with him and everything else just got put on hold. I told him I thought he should read one of those self-help books, you know, to try to get to the bottom of their strained relationship. Just to help him to come to terms with things and be happier. But he wasn't interested in going deeper. He didn't have the patience, you know? He wasn't much of a reader, either. I don't think I ever saw Freddie read a whole book, in all the time we were together.'

Was Freddie's twenty-first birthday, his coming of age, significant? There is nothing on record. It seems likely that it passed without fanfare. Perhaps he felt hard-done-by as a result, having attended, as he would have done, the parties of friends, because 'Twenty-One' was such a big deal in those days. Being handed the 'Key of the Door' was a major rite of passage. It seems significant because as soon as he'd made it, Freddie marked every birthday thereafter with an extravagant no-holds celebration, and out-did himself year by year. It is worth noting here that the age of majority in the UK, including the legal voting age, was twenty-one until 1970, at which point it was reduced to eighteen. Freddie was therefore not yet eligible to vote in the 1964 General Election, when the Labour Party's Harold Wilson ended a thirteen-year Tory reign; nor in 1966, a landslide for the Prime Minister. Who knows whether

Freddie exercised his electoral right in June 1970, when he was twenty-three. Never that fussed about politics in the first place, he had too many other things on his mind by then.

'It's probably true to say that Freddie's father, strongly committed to the Parsi faith, didn't find it easy that Freddie took the path he did,' said future fellow bandmate Brian May, with customary sweet and diplomatic understatement.[8]

☿

There was more to it. The real cause of angst between Freddie and his domineering father ran much deeper. Teetering on the brink of depression brought on by guilt over his sexuality, he could never bring himself to confess to his parents that he was gay. Or was he? Not even Freddie really knew.

'You can imagine his torment,' sighed Jim Hutton, over dinner in Ireland. 'Freddie told me he thought his father suspected, long before he got his head round it himself. But even then, Freddie wasn't sure. His first experiences had been with boys at boarding school, but I'm sure most boarding-school boys go through the phase. With Freddie, there was stuff with girls as well. He was someone who liked to decide things, and for certain things to be cut and dried. Was he this, or was he that? The not knowing, he said, was the hell of it. Tell you the truth, there were several points in his life before he and I got together, when he probably could have settled with a woman. So you're asking me if he was bisexual, but I couldn't tell you that. What Freddie would say was that he was *sexual*. His sex drive was incredible, almost like an addiction. He couldn't get enough. He didn't understand why he was like it, and said he'd never tried to understand. He just accepted it. As a gift from God, he would joke, even though he said he didn't really believe in any kind of god.'

As Freddie himself said, 'It would destroy all the mystery if I always explained everything about myself. To actually come out with it and go into huge detail about all those things, to be honest, is a bit beneath me. I have maybe a wider sexual taste than most people, but that's as far as I'm going to go.'

Given the way that homosexuals were regarded in the Zoroastrian Parsi culture and religion, Freddie clearly feared that his family would disown him. He was terrified that he would be thrown out and warned never to darken their door again. Which would mean that he would no longer have contact with the mother he worshipped, the thought of which 'just made him want to die':

'Freddie told me he'd lived in a fantasy world as a child, and that everything was all right up until puberty,' said Jim. Once that happened, the hormones kicking in, you know, and sex started dominating his life. He couldn't explain it. He found it difficult to look his mother in the eye after that. I knew where he was coming from, as my own experience had been similar. It was the thing he woke up thinking about, it obsessed him all day long, and it was the thing that got him to sleep at night. He couldn't *not* do it. "I don't know, darling," he'd say to me, "they say a man thinks about sex every five minutes or five seconds or whichever it is, but that must be hundreds or thousands of times a day. Who counted and how many did they ask? The thing is that once you *start* thinking about it, trying *not* to think about it just makes you think about it even more." I suppose, looking back, that my sex drive was less than Freddie's. A bit ... gentler, perhaps, I don't know. Not to get too personal. But then there would come a time when we had no sex life at all. It didn't matter to me. Freddie was over it by then. He had other things to worry about. We still loved each other.'

In those days, most parents didn't tell their children the so-called 'facts of life', but left them to find out by themselves. Given that Freddie couldn't have discussed even straight sex with his mother or father, the idea of trying to talk to them about homosexuality, especially his own, was unthinkable. That conversation never took place. Years later, his mother would say that Freddie wouldn't have minded people finding out that he was gay, and that he himself didn't care what anybody thought of him. Even though he cared enough to have kept it a secret all his life?

'At that time,' Jer said, 'society was different. Nowadays it's all so open, isn't it?' The implication being that, had Freddie lived into old age, he too would have come to be more relaxed about people knowing the truth about his sexuality.[9]

Freddie was by no means the first rocker to be beholden to a voracious sex drive. Musical creativity being the key. Professor Steven Pinker, a cognitive and evolutionary psychologist at Harvard University, refers to music as "auditory cheesecake, an exquisite confection crafted to tickle the sensitive spots of at least six of our mental faculties." Research shows that musical men tend also to be endowed with fine physical coordination and above-average intellect and learning ability. Like the male peacock strutting its stuff and fanning its colourful tail feathers, or a songbird swirling a spell with its sweet call, the flamboyant male rock star does not rest upon the laurels of biological virility. He woos hard and fast, with more than aural and visual appeal, attracting admirers on a deeper, more emotional and more volitional level. 'There is so much more *to* him!' the smitten onlooker swoons. In reality, however, as so many have found out to their cost down the years, there is all too often so much less.

☿

Pop-and-rock-obsessed student Freddie had a picture cut from a music magazine stuck to the mirror in his Gladstone Avenue bedroom. To hide a nasty stain that was lying there? Eric Stewart and Graham Gouldman hadn't written that line yet. Had the song existed, Freddie might have interpreted said 'stain' as his own reflection.[10] Never happy with his looks, he'd go so far as to call himself 'ugly'. Despite which he was known as 'Freddie Baby' in class, canteen and corridor, perhaps in ironic response to his annoying declarations of future superstardom. 'So,' his mates would tease him, 'you're going to be bigger than Jimi Hendrix, then, are you?'

'Absolutely,' insisted Freddie. A whole lot bigger than the face on the mirror back home.

It's a contradiction that is common among artists. As gigantic and flamboyant as they appear on stage or screen, they are often gauche, uncomfortable and insecure away from it. They can be shy and tongue-tied. They manufacture those sometimes monstrous extensions of themselves in order to have something to hide behind and via which to express their artistry – as if the real, genuine article is an insufficient vehicle for their alter-ego fabulousness. You don't have to look far to find clues to the person behind the persona. Anyone who ever spent time in close proximity with Freddie became accustomed to watching his hand fly to his mouth whenever he felt the urge to laugh while in the company of strangers, for example, to shield his protruding teeth. Either that, or he'd stretch his philtrum down over his incisors and roll his lips inwards, to hide his teeth that way. Only when he felt he could trust someone was he able to laugh openly in front of them.

☿

Towards the end of 2016, the University of London honoured Freddie on the front cover of their magazine *Your University* to mark the twenty-fifth anniversary of the death of their most celebrated alumnus, and ran a substantial feature about him within. Former fellow fashion design student Mark Malden shared his memories of the day when he and Freddie became the only male students in a class of twenty-eight girls. They fell in together on the spot. It was fascinating to read him describe their lifelong friendship. Malden had reached out to me back in the 1980s, having just read a review of a Queen gig in a Canadian newspaper that had been lifted from the *Daily Mail*, and asked me to help him get in touch with his old college pal. It was interesting to hear him enthusing about the lessons he and Freddie had shared, in subjects such as pattern-making and textile technology. Most of their tutors, he said, were fashion industry professionals – which made all the difference to how they approached the teaching of their various disciplines.

'They encouraged us to do anything we wanted. It was an incredibly creative environment,' he said. 'The teachers were very free and easy, generally speaking – although Freddie did push the boundaries. I remember once that one tutor got annoyed with him because he'd just wander in and out of the class. In an hour he might go out three or four times.'

All too soon, Freddie's obsession with music got the better of him. 'One day, I walked out of class and found Fred leaning against the wall in the corridor with his eyes closed,' said Malden. 'He was playing air guitar and singing "Purple Haze" by Jimi Hendrix. He was going through the whole song, pretending to be on stage. That's how eccentric he was. He had discovered Hendrix and worshipped him like a god. He would take half a day off to go up to town to see Hendrix play at the Marquee Club or in a matinee concert: every penny he had was spent on going to see him.'

As their first year as fashion design students concluded, in a predictable echo of Freddie's inauspicious dismissal from St Peter's School in Panchgani, he was punished for ill-attendance and asked to stand down. 'His parents begged for Freddie to be able to stay in college,' recalled Malden, 'and Fred said he would change to the graphics course and that he'd be a good boy. So he went across the corridor to graphics."

Working half-heartedly towards a diploma in art & graphic design, Freddie was stretching his tenure and buying himself some time. He was already aware, deep inside, that a life at the drafting table was never going to be for him.

Mark was by then singing and playing rhythm guitar in a band called Raw Silk, performing at venues such as Ealing Town Hall. 'My band was one of a number playing at a graduation party . . . I remember seeing Freddie watching all the bands very, very closely. I think he was learning, thinking to himself, "Hmm, that's clever," or "Oh, I don't like that," or "Look at the way they do that." Funnily enough, one of the other bands playing that night was called Smile. Its members included Roger Taylor, Brian May and Tim Staffell who would, with Freddie, eventually become Queen.'

Out of hours, Mark and Freddie would check out other bands together and frequent the local haunts. They saw the Stones together at the disintegrating Eel Pie Island Hotel: an old ballroom haunt during the twenties and thirties that became the hub of rock bands during the sixties. 'It was so much fun, the creativity was incredible because we were all creative nuts.' Freddie's second band Wreckage (his first having been the Hectics at St Peter's) would later perform in the college's 'Noisy Common Room'. That room metamorphosed into UWL's Students Union Bar, and is nowadays known as 'Freddie's Bar', in homage. Mark Malden had left the college by then, but remembered hearing that Freddie had gone and got his hair permed to look like Jimi Hendrix. He had also worn a white suit for the performance, allegedly, and had 'rolled around on stage singing.' It wasn't a great success: he was literally laughed off the stage by the student body. Still, Mark believed he could understand what Freddie was aiming to achieve: 'He was trying to invent someone. He believed that a rock star was somebody who invented a character and then played that character on stage. Imagine the fortitude of someone who can get laughed off the stage by their peers and then to go back and do it again and again until you get it right.'

Neither Mark nor their fellow classmates knew anything about Freddie's background in those days. He did not divulge that he had been born in Zanzibar and educated in India. He told anyone who enquired about his nationality that he was 'Persian', and left it at that. They could think whatever they wanted to think about him, who cared? Friends will be friends, but this pair lost touch for a year or two after Malden moved to Canada for work. The next time they came face to face was in Kensington Market, 'the Hypermarket' as it was known, when Mark came across Freddie and Roger Taylor flogging gear on their second-floor stall of the three-storey 'Ken High' building. Freddie made no mention of his musical ambition, perhaps fearing that he would be ridiculed. But the next time they saw each other was in Ottawa, during Queen's tour of North America.

In 2016, the University founded the Freddie's Fund scholarship in his memory, to be awarded to a UWL student demonstrating outstanding creativity, resilience and ambition. Two years later, just ahead of the release of the *Bohemian Rhapsody* film in October 2018, his old alma mater collaborated with outdoor media specialist Rapport, Twentieth Century Fox, Regency Enterprises and Global Street Art Agency to unveil a huge, hand-painted temporary mural of Freddie's image on their Paragon Building.

Freddie did earn, for the record, his diploma in art & graphic design. He would soon apply his artistic skills to the design of Queen's astrologically influenced heraldic 'coat of arms'.

CHAPTER SIX
HENDRIX

It was in September 1966 that Freddie's greatest creative inspiration first landed in London. Without permission to play, which set a few teeth on edge.

'I couldn't work too much because I didn't have a permit,' said Jimi Hendrix. 'If I was going to stay in England, I had to get enough jobs to have a long permit. So what we had to do was line up a lot of gigs. Chas Chandler . . . helped me find the right sidemen, people who were feeling the same as me.'

Jamming his way around the capital's cooler nightspots – the Bag O' Nails on Soho's Kingly Street, Blaises on Queen's Gate Kensington and 'the Speak', the Speakeasy on Margaret Street near Oxford Circus – the boy born Johnny Allen who along the road had sidestepped into James Marshall then Jimmy James and who eventually rocked up as Jimi, invaded by stealth. Drawing not only adoring music fans but also the cream, literally, of the rock and pop crop, Hendrix took them on at their own game and paralysed them with talent and attitude. Lennon and McCartney, Jagger and Richards, Beck, Page and the jaw-dropped rest trawled nervously in his wake. Eric Clapton was no longer the undisputed guitar hero of the Western world. Not only did Jimi seize and run off with his crown, Eric practically thanked him for it.

A week later, on 1 October, the amiable young African American found himself hanging in the Little Tichfield Street building of

Regent Street Polytechnic.[1] There, he took in a performance by Cream and at last got to meet Clapton, an audience with whom he had made a condition of accepting the invitation to England. Not that he simply shook hands and greeted 'God' nicely. Up he got, during the encore, requesting permission to jam with the band. He then proceeded to deliver a knock-out cover of Howlin' Wolf's 'Killing Floor' on his borrowed axe. He played the instrument with his teeth, behind his head and as if he were fucking its brains out. Wiggling his tongue and grinding his gear, he screwed the whole room. Imperious rock critics would later pontificate to the point of coming on like complete prats about the electric guitar as technophallus, the thrilling fusion of man and instrument that enabled the artist to showcase both musical virtuosity and sexual potency and all that. *¿Qué?*

Contrary to legend, isn't it always, much of Jimi's act was nothing new. He was only elaborating on what R&B heroes Aaron Thibeaux 'T-Bone' Walker and Eddie 'Guitar Slim' Jones had perfected years earlier. It was from T-Bone that Jimi borrowed that crazy teeth-playing thing, and the nutcase behind-the-back-playing thing. Guitar Slim, he of the demonic stage act and sorry demise, had been the original master of distortion. Never mind: the occasion went down in history as the night Jimi drove old Slowhand down. As Clapton had it, he'd met his match. Rival Jeff Beck, at the time pre-Yardbirds, compared what he had just seen to a bomb exploding.

'(Hendrix) just blew the place wide open, and I went away from there thinking that I ought to find something else to do, go back to panel-beating or something,' Beck said. 'Then I got to know him and found out he wasn't the immovable force, that we could talk music, and he became a great source of inspiration. He was doing things so up front, so wild and unchained, and that's sort of what I wanted to do. But being British, and the product of these poxy little schools I used to go to, I couldn't do what he did.'

Former Animals bassist turned Hendrix manager Chas Chandler would later remember that Clapton's hands were shaking so hard backstage after the show, he couldn't hold a match to light his cigarette. Hardly surprising: he had been humiliated, upstaged and eclipsed by an upstart. A Yank, at that. Despite which, he'd fallen head over the heels for him. All that poor Eric could manage in response to questions about Jimi was that he had been 'floored by his technique and choice of things to play.'

Not long after the performance, Jimi gave a modest, good-natured interview to eighteen-year-old future radio DJ Steve Barker for *West One*, the polytechnic's student magazine, in which he revealed the sources of his own inspiration: three Mississippi blues-men guitarists, singers and songwriters by the indelible names of Elmore James, Muddy Waters and Robert Johnson. He harked back to having first picked up the guitar as a child in his hometown, Seattle, Washington; about doing time in the US Army, and about going '... down south, and all the cats down there were playing blues.' He had toured the chitlin' circuit[2] and recorded with Little Richard, Sam Cooke, Jackie Wilson, the Isley Brothers, the Supremes and the rest before moving on to pay dues in the dives of Greenwich Village.

Keith Richards' squeeze Linda Keith, a twenty-year-old British former *Vogue* magazine assistant turned photographic model who later broke her boyfriend's Stone heart, first saw Jimi in May 1966 at New York's newest nightspot, the Cheetah Club.[3] He was playing with the Squires featuring Curtis Knight. No one had a clue who Jimi was.

'I couldn't believe nobody had picked up on him, because he'd obviously been around,' Linda would recall. 'He was astonishing – the moods he could bring to music, his charisma, his skill and stage presence. Yet nobody was leaping about with excitement.'[4]

Linda invited Jimi over to her apartment on 63rd Street, where she played him a promo copy of throaty blues singer-songwriter Tim Rose's new record 'Hey Joe'. Jimi didn't have a guitar at that point, having had to pawn the one he'd owned, so Linda lent him Keith Richards' white Fender Stratocaster (Keith never got it back).

He got his own band together, Jimmy James and the Blue Flames. Linda took her best friend Sheila and the latter's husband, Rolling Stones manager Andrew Oldham, to watch them perform. It didn't go well. Both artist and potential representative left empty-handed. But Linda, for whom Jimi wrote the instrumental 'Send My Love to Linda' and, in 1970, 'See Me Linda, Hear Me, I'm Playing the Blues', and whom Richards and fellow Stone Brian Jones immortalised in their song 'Ruby Tuesday', was hooked on Jimi. That August, she invited the Animals' bass player Bryan 'Chas' Chandler to hear the dynamite young guitarist play one of his regular afternoon slots at Café Wha?[5] There was left-handed Jimi holding his right-handed guitar upside-down and playing a blistering set. His shock of Afro hair was performing a gig of its own.

'I was determined that he should be noticed, get a record deal and blow everybody's mind,' said Linda. 'I knew it was all there, so I went for it.'

Chandler went all-out to secure a record deal for Jimi. There were no takers. Confident in the brilliance of his find and undeterred by failure, Chas talked his charge into coming to England and taking his chances there. The pair took up residence at 34 Montagu Square in Marylebone, a wood-panelled, blue-velvet-draped ground-floor and basement apartment with a 'kinky multi-mirror bathroom' that belonging to Ringo Starr, who had acquired it because it was close to the Abbey Road recording studios. It would later be occupied briefly by John and Yoko Lennon.[6] The plan was to immerse Jimi in the London club scene and allow him make his mark organically. Predictably, every audience was gobsmacked, while every A-list artist wanted to be him. Yet still no recording deal was forthcoming. In desperation, Chas sought the advice of Animals manager Mike Jeffery, a shady type with a background of bodies and blood. This was despite his suspicions that Jeffery had cheated the Animals out of the lion's share of their earnings, fobbing them off with the excuse that he had invested it on their behalf in a company called Yameta registered in the tax-haven Bahamas.

In a blink, Jimi had copied the 'power trio' concept and had joined forces with thrashing drummer Mitch Mitchell and melodic bassist Noel Redding to launch the Jimi Hendrix Experience. They forged a brand of improv blues rock that would never be outshone. It still amuses me, and it sure must have tickled them, to think that, only nine months earlier, they had been guns for hire on the session-musician circuit and had made what is believed to be their first recording backing one Freddie Lennon on his December 1965 single 'That's My Life (My Love and My Home)'. The then fifty-three-year-old Liverpudlian seaman being the long, lost, wayward father of Beatle John.

'Hendrix was basically the most amazing rock guitarist anyone had ever seen,' affirms Keith Altham, the respected rock journalist, author and broadcaster who later became the personal publicist of some of the UK's biggest acts, the Who, the Rolling Stones, Van Morrison and Marc Bolan among them. On record as having conceived the infamous stunt in which Jimi set his guitar ablaze, Keith was the last writer ever to interview him: at the Cumberland Hotel in London's Marble Arch, five days before his death.

'I was surprised at first to learn that he was Freddie Mercury's hero and inspiration. Jimi was first and foremost a guitarist, while Freddie's great strengths were his vocals and songwriting,' says Keith. 'But then I thought about it, and I got it. It is, of course, about showmanship. About creating impact and seducing an audience. Jimi had all of that in abundance. *That* was what Freddie learned from him.'

As for Jimi, it was all about the music: 'Music makes me high on stage, and that's the truth,' he said. It's almost like being addicted to music. You see, onstage I forget everything, even the pain.'

Keith was only too aware that Jimi was no bona fide original. 'Most of what he did, he stole,' he confirms. 'From the Mississippi bluesmen to the Who's Pete Townshend, Jimi pilfered techniques and tricks like a magpie, and made all those things his own. He borrowed from black musicians who had already recorded but who had not made that jump into the white culture in order to gather a wider audience. For that, Jimi was criticised for having "sold out". The irony. It was crazy: his whole background was black music!

'I was with him in Monterey in 1967,' Keith recalls, referring to the three-day live music event staged in California in June that year. The precursor of modern festivals, it featured, among others, Ravi Shankar, Otis Redding, Janis Joplin, the Who and the Jimi Hendrix Experience, whose appearance Paul McCartney personally had secured. 'I sat on the plane with him for twelve hours, got off in New York, spent a few days there with him and Eric Burdon (the Animals' vocalist), then flew to San Francisco and on to Monterey. The festival is remembered as having belonged to Jimi, and I suppose it was his in some ways, although for me it was Janis Joplin's. I was absolutely mesmerised by her. I'd never heard a white woman sing like the best of the black blues artists the way she did. But she was let down by her band, Big Brother and the Holding Company, who were not great.

'I remember Janis watching Jimi and screaming at Pete Townshend, "He's stealing your act!" That's what Jimi did. He stole the best bits from everyone else's performance. He was completely shameless about it, too, as if to say, "Well, what else are you supposed to do!"

'It *was* me who came up with the idea of him setting light to his guitar. But Jerry Lee Lewis had done it before us, torching a whole piano – in 1958 at the New York Paramount Theater during "Great Balls of Fire" before abusing Chuck Berry, who was about to come on and close the show, with the line "Follow *that*, nigger."'

But Jimi's stage antics, insists Keith, were nothing compared to his incredible sense of humour:

'He was funny. *Really* funny. He did an incredible Mick Jagger impersonation. He could be scathing of other acts, but only in private. Not viciously, I've got to say. He didn't have to be vindictive. He knew how good he was, and how poor some of the others were in comparison. He did like Clapton, though. Eric was the big exception, the one British guitarist he admired and had been desperate to meet.'

'We had science fiction in common. He loved the novel *Stranger in a Strange Land* by Robert A. Heinlein,[7] and he loved *MAD* magazine, the American humour comic. I borrowed his copy on the plane, but then I lost it, and he was so upset. That was about the level of his intellect. He wasn't illiterate, exactly, but he was pretty basic, having not had an extensive education. He talked to me about how tough his childhood had been, but in a detached way, matter-of-fact. He wasn't complaining about it, nor blaming anybody. He simply said that it had taught him values. How to appreciate the material advantages he had now, and the lifestyle he'd come to enjoy. Which by most people's standards got pretty excessive as time ticked on.'

Contractual wranglings, double-crossings, sellings down the Swanee, grievances and lawsuits had long been par for the course in rock'n'roll. As for Jimi, so it would eventually be for Queen – during the early days of their career, at least. Freddie would have known nothing at the time of the off-shore tax-evading set-ups and skulduggery going on behind the Hendrix scene. He probably wouldn't have given two hoots. All he cared about were the artist and his sensational art. No fan of the business of music, and with his own rueful stories to tell, Freddie would not have been in the least surprised to learn later what roguery had gone on behind Jimi's back. Queen fans with a fervent interest in their idols' commercial affairs will find the comparison fascinating.

Redding and Mitchell signed a production contract with Chandler and Jeffery. Come 1 December 1966, however, only Jimi's name appeared on the four-year management contract with Jeffery: proof, when it was needed, that Noel and Mitch were never more than employees, despite all Jimi's personal reassurances to them about equal shares. Not even Chandler was included to begin with, but got himself added after the fact. Mike signed Jimi to Track Records in the UK, upping the ante with a complicated Warner

Bros. deal in America only weeks into 1967 in which the label found itself owning not the artist, as they might reasonably have expected, but merely the services of the Nassau, Bahamas-based Yameta Trust Company Ltd: an offshore holding company formed that year by Jeffery through his London lawyer John Hillman. A tax dodge, effectively, though how this was supposed to benefit Hendrix, an American citizen, was never explained. Yameta would provide recordings of Jimi and of the Jimi Hendrix Experience from the master tapes of which the company retained ownership in perpetuity. It's hard to believe that Warners, home of the Everly Brothers and Peter, Paul and Mary so not just any old push-over bunch, went for it – given the tradition in the those-were-the-days music business for the record label, not the artist or his management, to own the masters of all songs created and recorded during the record deal in question. Not even acts like the Stones or the Fabs owned their own masters. Adding insult to injury, Jeffery went in for the kill with soundtrack-recording exclusion clauses, and also demanded – and got – a hefty budget for promotion and publicity. Such benefits were never normally extended to untried artists just baby-stepping out with a nice little debut album.

So it began, with Jeffery hell-bent on selling Hendrix back to America with juggernaut tours, ever-increasing audiences, lucre-spinning promotional appearances and a moneybags sideline in merchandise. All looked good from the outside in, but there was trouble at t'mill. Not only was Jimi bored with the guitar-igniting, amp-demolishing antics, and up to here with shredding out the same old songs night after night. He'd had it with touring altogether. Which was not exactly good news, as this was where the hard cash was generated, record companies in those days being notoriously slow about coughing up. Jimi had also grown to resent his producer Chandler's control over his music. Jimi wanted to work with other musicians, not just Redding and Mitchell in the somewhat past-it trio format. Chas and Jimi fell out over the latter's drug-taking, as well as Jimi's insistence on the presence of a huge and ever-swelling entourage that was bleeding him dry. Chas quit in the end, in a fit of pique, returning to the UK but clinging to his legal share of his artist. By August 1969, Noel Redding had also quit, Jimi was ensconced in a rented upstate New York home with his loafed-up liggers, and a whole lot of shaking with other musos was going on. Some of whom were with him when he got up to play at the Woodstock Music and Art Fair at breakfast-time on the final day, at which point fewer than ten per cent of the guestimated four hundred thousand ravers in attendance were left. Despite which, Jimi's rendition of the US national anthem 'The Star-Spangled Banner', complete with screeching feedback and distortion simulating the sounds of war, stole what was left of the show. It was of course misinterpreted as his personal denunciation of the conflict in Vietnam. It has since come to be regarded as one of the all-time greatest performances in rock history.

Jimi would not tour again for another eight months, oblivious of his own extravagant expenditure – on cars, guitars, blah-blah-blahs and ha-ha-has; on studio hours, loopies and groupies. Mike Jeffery, who had fallen for his own image as flamboyant rock manager, joined in with the drugging and did his share of the squandering. No wonder the money was running out. The monumental forking-out for Jimi's own recording facility, Electric Ladyland, tipped them over the edge. Jeffery is said to have gone to Mafia contacts for a hefty loan. It wasn't the first time the manager had got between the sheets with mobsters. Issues with the US taxman loomed large. Fortunes were owed. Jimi needed to get out there and tour again in order for Mike to balance the books, but he was in no rush. He continued to experiment, with new producers now as well as alternative musicians. He launched a new line-up, the Band of Gypsys, who twice performed at New York's Fillmore East over New Year 1970. Jeffery got shot of the musos and insisted that Jimi roll the old show back on the road. Was there or wasn't there a signed insurance policy on Jimi's life before he got going on the latest tour? Opinion remains divided. Either way, Jeffery was terrified that Jimi was going to abandon him come December, when their contract was due to expire – even though Mike retained hefty interests in Jimi's career, the New York recording studio and his film rights. Out on tour that autumn, a bedraggled, narc-fuelled Jimi fell short at the Isle of Wight Festival in front of his biggest-ever audience, some six hundred thousand fans, and was so off his head at a performance in Denmark that the show had to be pulled two numbers in. There was scribble all over the architecture. Look out, here comes the godfather and the taxman. Run for cover? He would if he could. But would Jeffery have gone so far as to get his golden goose slaughtered?

'When he was headlining bills, his money went up dramatically, and Jeffery bled him dry,' says Keith Altham. 'Mike was siphoning huge chunks of the earnings into that offshore company where he also had his former charges the Animals' money. The overview is that Jimi was cheated and double-crossed throughout his brief four-year career because he was too weak. He wanted everyone to be happy. He couldn't stand confrontation. He was a nice guy and a brilliant musician, in the Louis Armstrong/Charlie Parker/Miles Davis vein. There was only one of those guys in their categories, and there was only one of Jimi. But he couldn't stand up for himself. Somebody would say, "Sign here," and he'd go, "Oh ok." No argument. No pausing to read the small print. He trusted people too easily, and they let him down.'

As for Queen, things kicked off for them when they were spotted by a couple of engineers from Soho's Trident Studios while the band were testing De Lane Lea Studios' equipment and showcasing the facilities to prospective clients in return for free recording time. Roy Thomas Baker and John Anthony enthused about the band to their Trident bosses Barry and Norman Sheffield, who were toying with the idea of launching their own record label. Barry attended their gig at London's Forest Hill Hospital on 24 March 1972, and was beyond impressed. The brothers offered them a deal that May. Queen nit-picked the contract, demanded that management be included, and argued their corner over clauses pertaining to recording and production. Contractual terms were not agreed until that November, by which time the band had finished recording their first album. Although the Sheffields guided Queen's career until 1975, backed them financially and were instrumental in their signing to EMI, the band felt let down and mistreated by them. The relationship soured, and ended in acrimony. Freddie composed Queen's 'Death on Two Legs' about the feud. Norman Sheffield sued for defamation and won an out-of-court settlement, but the publicity exposed to the world that the song was about him. He wrote a book, *Life on Two Legs: Set the Record Straight*, published in 2013, giving his side of the story. He died of throat cancer in 2014. Jim Beach of law firm Harbottle and Lewis took over Queen's management in 1978, having previously acted for them as a lawyer. He retains the position to this day.

At least, as far as Queen were concerned, there wasn't murder in the mix, as there may have been for Hendrix. When Jimi was found dead at the Samarkand Hotel in West London's Notting Hill on 18 September 1970, foul play was widely suspected. Many fans and music writers still believe that his life did not end accidentally, despite the lack of evidence. According to James 'Tappy' Wright, one of his former roadies, manager Mike Jeffrey confessed to having forced Jimi to swallow sleeping pills washed down with red wine, so that he could cash in on his protégé's $2 million insurance policy and pay off his debts to the Mob. In his book *Rock Roadie*, published in 2009, Wright insists that Jeffery described Jimi as 'worth more to him dead than alive.' The cause of death was given as barbiturate intoxication and inhalation of vomit.

'Would Mike Jeffery have had him killed for the insurance money, to settle his debts?' muses Keith Altham. 'I don't believe so, no. I don't think for a moment that he was murdered. His death was an accident. His girlfriend Monika Dannemann not calling the ambulance quickly enough after she found him is the more likely explanation. I think the conspiracy theory has risen out of the fact that she changed her story so many times in the ensuing years. Whether she woke up during the night, went out for a packet of cigarettes, came back, found him in a pool of red wine vomit or what, we'll never know. Taking her time to dial 999 couldn't have helped matters. She was an odd individual. A former German figure skater who had latched onto Jimi and convinced herself he was going to marry her. Was he ever going to marry anyone? We'll never know. She suffered from mental instability of some sort, that was for sure. I saw this for myself during the last-ever interview I did with Jimi for a BBC radio documentary, part of the *Scene and Heard* series, because she was there.'

How does he feel about that occasion now?

'Kind of spooked, really,' says Altham. 'I heard the whole interview again a few years ago when I was quizzed by a journalist for Jimi's forty-third anniversary. I'd shovelled all the emotion from the shock of his death away. I was forced to relive it and confront it that day. The intimacy of that recording, made in what was in those days a very sleazy hotel – no more than a pick-up joint – really got to me. There were the girls milling around, swishing and mumbling: Monika and Devon Wilson, an American groupie who'd been involved with Jimi for years. There were the sounds of them padding about the room, and the clinking of bottles and glasses. Between them, they kept Jimi's Mateus Rosé topped up. And more besides.'

Manic Devon, often dismissed as a cling-on, was one of Jimi's closest friends. She made herself indispensable, scoring girls and drugs for her womanising junkie main man. She had once, more than once, had Miles Davis and Clapton and Jagger. She had sucked the blood from Mick's sliced finger while a mesmerised Jimi looked on. Hendrix is reckoned to have written the song 'Dolly Dagger' about her. She died a few months after her old lover's demise, in February 1971. She went over the side of an eighth-floor balcony at New York's notorious Chelsea Hotel.[8] Jumped or pushed? Whatever, tbh. You could call it a fitting end.

In 1973, Mike Jeffery was killed in the Nantes mid-air collision over France en route back to Heathrow. No trace of him was found. His secrets went with him.

☿

16 December 1966 was the most pivotal moment of Freddie's life. That was the night when twenty-four-year-old Jimi made his TV debut on *Ready Steady Go!* The appearance marked the release of the Experience's first UK single, their cover of 'Hey Joe'. Freddie tuned in and was stunned by everything about their frontman: his virtuosity, his in-your-face virility, his ethnicity, his charisma, his charm. His image, his flair and, dear God, his *hair*. Jimi sounded like he'd been plucked fully formed from the Mississippi Delta. But the music and the performance were not the only qualities that seduced this gobsmacked, buck-toothed fan.

'Hendrix really had everything any rock'n'roll star should have,' Freddie later enthused. 'He'd just make an entrance and the whole place would be on fire. He was living out everything I wanted to be.'

Even better, it was complicated. This electrifying performer was hailed as a musical genius by the rock community, which by default was white. At the same time, Jimi served to highlight the social contradictions of the black community, particularly in terms of music. Before Hendrix, black jazz, R&B and other artists put together an act that incorporated the guitar as part of a line-up's overall sound without dominating it. It was white artists who perfected and promoted the art of the guitar solo, because of which the rock genre was regarded as their exclusive domain. Hendrix was the first to straddle the two realms, ultimately making rock guitar his own. He came to symbolise a phenomenon that sixties America found uncomfortable and difficult to embrace: a black man worshipped by white youth, especially white males, for having mastered what had hitherto been a white male pursuit: the awe-inspiring art of rock guitar-soloing.

It is likely that Freddie identified on multiple levels with the prodigy who'd had it hard back home, and who'd had to move to London to prove and establish himself. A black man in a white world, Jimi performed on stage with a pair of white bandmates to predominantly white audiences. For white European groupies, he was the ultimate black American sex symbol, and he rose to the occasion. His pals were mostly white, as were his girlfriends. He dressed not as one might have imagined he would or 'should' have, but like a Haight-Ashbury hippie with a twist, in velvet loons, military jackets, brocades, silks and scarves. Freddie took to the look immediately, reinventing himself from the outside in. Desperate to emulate Jimi's musicianship as well as to look like him, Freddie went so far as to get himself a second-hand guitar, which his college pal Tim Staffell re-fretted and modified to suit Freddie's needs. Freddie purchased some manuals and tried to teach himself to play. All too soon, he realised that he was barking up the wrong instrument. He was never going to be a guitar hero. He reverted to his piano, resolving to get as good as he could.

Was Freddie also able to understand Jimi instinctively, at a level he probably couldn't have explained in words? Did he home in on the things they had in common? Or was the appeal confined to Hendrix's musical talent born of a deprived and dysfunctional childhood and of frustration, anger and yearning – all of which touched a sensitive nerve? Freddie was amazed to learn down the line that, for all the adulation from fans and respect from his peers, Jimi had never in his life felt good enough; that he lamented his failings as a singer; that he longed to improve, but didn't know how; that he was desperate to learn other instruments and to read and write music, but never mastered either skill; that he chastised himself for his inability to replicate on his Fender Stratocaster the sounds that he was hearing in his head. Jimi would live for only four more years. He died at the age of twenty-seven. Freddie, four years younger and by that time a member of an embryonic Queen, still struggling and still dreaming of his own rock stardom, was devastated. How could this have happened? Jimi had only just opened his own recording studio. He had just played the Isle of Wight Festival. Although an open verdict was recorded and the murder conspiracy theory persists, the cause of death was most likely inhalation of vomit following accidental overdose of the sedative Vesparax washed down with excess booze. His girlfriend Monika, to whom the medication belonged, later committed suicide.

With no other way of paying their respects on the day Jimi died, Freddie and Queen drummer Roger Taylor shut up shop early at their Kensington Market stall. Late that afternoon, helpless and hopeless during a band rehearsal at Imperial College, Brian, Roger and Freddie resorted to performing a private tribute to their fallen idol, jamming his hits 'Purple Haze', 'Foxy Lady' and 'Voodoo Chile'.

☿

'What may come as a surprise to many of his black detractors was that Jimi Hendrix not only knew that he was black, but what that blackness meant in the context of American history,' commented African American Studies scholar Marcus K. Adams. 'What Jimi refused to do was allow the notion of blackness as defined by others to determine his music. Jimi was neither an activist nor a black separatist, and his central focus, as always, was music, which he saw as being without colour. Responding to a question during an interview about the difference in music and race in England versus America in *Jimi Hendrix – The Uncut Story*, Jimi answers by stating, "I could play louder over there (in England). I could really get myself together over there. There wasn't as many hang-ups as there was in America. You know, mental hang-ups."'

Often dismissed as a racial stereotype – a hypersexual black male high on drugs 24/7 instead of respected as a serious musician – all Jimi cared about was playing the blues.

'Race isn't a problem in my world,' he said. 'I don't look at things in terms of races. I look at things in terms of people.'

From his days learning to play the guitar while growing up in Seattle, Washington, to playing on the chitlin' circuit, before James Marshall had even thought of becoming Jimi Hendrix, reasoned Adams, he always played the blues. 'By refusing to be stereotyped for playing his music, he symbolizes the contradictions on race and ethnicity that continue to be a burden to both blacks and whites.'

That *Ready Steady Go!* performance by the Jimi Hendrix Experience was Freddie's lightbulb. Everything that Freddie would become during the seventies crystallised in that moment. He was so obsessed that he took to following Jimi around the country, at one point attending no fewer than nine gigs in a row. Desperate for dosh to cover travel, subsistence and entrance tickets, he and fellow art student Mark Malden resorted to nude modelling for life-drawing classes at five pounds a go. Freddie rolled his eyes, dropped his towel and thought of the fivers. He stashed them diligently. He was also raking in a part-time pittance at nearby Heathrow airport, working in the catering department there to supplement his income. As soon as he had saved enough, he made a beeline for the army surplus and second-hand stores to find himself an RAF greatcoat, his desire inspired by Jimi's military wear. At the time, it was all the rage. Such overcoats still fetch a couple of hundred quid today. Grey wool, full-length and double-breasted, with eight shiny brass buttons arranged in two rows down the front, he must have cut a dash in it. Freddie sported the splendid garment in January 1967 when he rocked up to see Jimi at the Bag O'Nails. The venue was on the snug side. He must have hoped that he would be noticed by his idol. Who knows whether the pair came face to face. Unlikely, perhaps, but the obsession was sealed. Freddie took to sketching and painting portraits of Jimi, both in class for his coursework and at home for fun. He'd even draw his full-lipped, fright-haired image on classroom walls. He wrote his college thesis about Jimi, he said, later selling it from his and Roger's market stall. If indeed that thesis ever existed, who purchased it? How much did they pay for it, and what happened to it? Wouldn't you think that someone would have come forward by now? What kind of money might it be worth today?

Nearly twenty years after Jimi's death, Freddie would pay tribute to him in the lyrics of Queen song 'The Miracle' on their 1989 album of that name. Although the track was credited to all four members of the band, it was primarily the work of Freddie and bassist John Deacon. This was Freddie, teetering in the twilight, not only paying homage to the artist who had inspired his career but hailing him as a wonder of the world.

'I liked and respected Jimi enormously,' reflects Keith Altham. 'He was a true musician, the kind who doesn't have any say in the matter. If he were still alive, he would still be doing it. Yes, even at almost eighty years of age. I have no doubt. He was prepared to use anything and everything to get there. Once there, he was determined to stay on top. All Jimi worried about was that people were coming to see him because he was a freak show, rather than to listen to his music. Because fans did flock to witness his greatest-showman act. "They're there for the glitter, the gold and the jewellery," he said to me. He just wanted them to come and hear him play. The only thing he truly craved was respect as a musician. He lived for music. He would have gone on to play with different bands and line-ups, I'm sure, and he would have moved into more experimental work. If only he'd lived long enough.'

In April 1967, Keith was with the Jimi Hendrix Experience during the UK package tour that featured the Walker Brothers, Cat Stevens and Engelbert Humperdink. 'Scott Walker came to me one night in absolute despair. "What am I *doing*, Keith?" he said, on the brink of tears. "What am I doing playing this crappy pop stuff when there are people out there like Hendrix? I've got to get into experimental work!"

'What Jimi did peripherally was only publicity stunts. Somebody would come up with this or that, they sounded like good ideas, so he did 'em. People can dismiss publicity all they like. Jimi was clever enough to realise its worth. You can be the greatest talent on earth, but if nobody knows about you, you're finished before you've even started. You've got to get their attention first, before you do anything else. And that is what he did. He was up for literally anything that Chas Chandler or I could come up with. Hence, if you want to get into the headlines, set light to your own guitar.'

'We made it, man, because we did our own thing,' said Jimi. 'We had our beautiful rock-blues-country-funky-freaky sound, and it was really turning people on. I felt like we were turning the whole world on to this new thing.'

Keith Altham insists that Jimi would have kept searching in other directions, forever on the lookout for something new: 'He'd have kept on doing that. He would have continued to take risks,' he says. 'He was a pusher of boundaries. For Scott Walker, Hendrix was a catalyst for change. He became that, too, for Freddie Mercury. Freddie was not only inspired by Jimi, he caught his ball and he ran with it. It's no surprise, when you think about it, that Jimi was the musical love of Freddie's life.'

☿

CHAPTER SEVEN
LEADER

During my first interview with Freddie and Brian in 1984, at the
Queen Productions offices in Notting Hill's Pembridge Road,
Freddie mentioned in passing that he had once played piano in a
school band. He must have regretted it the moment he said it as I
seized on it, pestering him with questions that he didn't want to
answer. He fobbed off his piano-playing ability with the dismissal
that he'd 'only done up to whatever the grade was' (Grade IV
Theory and Practical), could 'barely sight-read,' and admitted that
he played by ear. I slipped in a frivolous question about him getting
his old group to reform. For their twenty-fifth anniversary that
year, say. A charity bash, I ventured, in aid of his old school? It
could never have happened. Not only because four of the five
Hectics had been only borderline musical in the first place, and had
long ago deflected their momentary fame'n'glory gaze in the direction of more sustainable careers; but because Freddie, as we know,
never looked back. Switched-off, tongue-tied and apparently
content to leave most of the talking to Brian, he withered me a look
as if to say, '*please.*' I asked only in jest, trained as I was to heat-seek
a headline. The more outlandish or ridiculous the enquiry, went the
thinking, the less likely you were to get a direct answer but you
could well wind up with something worthwhile. There was no
sensation to be had that day. But it was worth a try. Freddie shuf-
fled silently in his cushioned window seat. He drew his knees to his

chest and wrapped his arms around them. I wasn't aware at that young age of the implications of body language, but I can usually read the signs now. In simulating this classic posture of being hugged, Freddie activated the sensation in his brain of being comforted. He was not only holding his thoughts and feelings in, he was taking precautions to keep me out. He felt either bored, irritated or threatened. Possibly all three. He was putting a barrier between us, indicating uncertainty and insecurity. I had alluded to something that evoked memories he did not want to recall, from a past he did not care or did not want to revisit.

Disengaging from the interview, Freddie stared through the window into the middle distance. Could a misty view of the outside world have appeared to him more manageable than the contents of his mind and memory? I have often thought back to that day, and have always wondered about it. Brian, who was to become a friend and supporter over the years to come, continued to do most of the talking.

Given that Freddie was a brilliant performer with breathtaking presence, as well as a superlative songwriter who needed no assistance from anybody, why didn't he opt for a solo career in the Bowie or Elton mould? What made him go full Jagger/Davies/Plant, fronting a band instead of going it alone? Again, the answer is Hendrix.

'Freddie's greatest inspiration was not a solo artist,' points out Simon Napier-Bell. 'Jimi had a band, the Jimi Hendrix Experience, and it was vital to him. He couldn't play the sort of set he played with just any musicians; these guys were the frame he needed for his picture, the throbbing backdrop to his sometimes quite sparse rhythmic playing, or his long periods of feedback and extended sounds. Anyone aspiring to be a new Hendrix would straight away think "band".'

Napier-Bell is a legendary figure in the international music business who has spent his life not only managing artists' careers but also enhancing their lives. He has written songs for them, produced them, masterminded their promotion and made global superstars of them. Having nurtured the Yardbirds, Eric Clapton, Jeff Beck, Marc Bolan, Japan, Wham!, George Michael, Sinéad O'Connor and more, he can tell you in a drink the kind of artist best suited to solo pursuits and the type who will never make it without a band behind him.

'Freddie was buck-toothed and gay,' he says. 'He needed dark glasses, a protective setting, a comforting suit of armour, a frame, a band. "*I Am* the Champion" would never have clicked with audiences the way "We Are the Champions" did. Freddie knew that he needed to fake it, that he had to be one of a male gang, in order to hide his fragility. No "real man" strides the stage like a macho strongman the way Freddie did. He doesn't need to. Strong men stay in the background, quietly confident. Weak men fool you with butch bravado. Little dogs bark loudly. Big dogs stay cool. None of Freddie's biggest hits would have worked as well outside a band setting.'

Solo male artists, Simon adds, are comparatively rare, for complex biological reasons:

'Males bond and rampage: together! In groups. Girls, on the other hand, are at their most attractive when they're alone and fragile. They are seduce-able. Or rape-able. Hence the solo girl image being more common than the solo male image. Men always find courage in numbers. Shared responsibility is effectively nil responsibility. Football crowds, armies, bully boys, gang bangs. For a fragile man, the best way to avoid being bullied is to be adopted by one of these gangs; to become their mascot, their joker; to sing for them in return for their protection; to mesmerise them with your bravado and cleverness. Whether you're Donald Trump or Freddie Mercury, you're damaged goods trying to find a niche in which you can frighten away the cruel world around you. And that is why Freddie Mercury could never have sustained as a successful solo artist.'

From his short-lived school group founded more than sixty years ago to the twenty years he spent as a member of Queen, passing through various embryonic line-ups in between, Freddie was never destined to be a one-man band. Most schoolboy combos burn and fade. There are obvious exceptions. John Lennon founded the Quarrymen with classmates in 1956, only three years before Freddie was pulling his Hectics together. John named his group after his Liverpool school, Quarry Bank High, an establishment he loathed with every corpuscle. He met Paul McCartney at a church fete in July 1957. With George Harrison and Ringo Starr on board, they floored the world.

Many rock fans believe that Mick Jagger and Keith Richards got together at school. Not exactly: both attended Dartford's Wentworth Primary, but didn't hook up while they were there. It didn't happen until the former was an eighteen-year-old London School of Economics student, the latter at the easel at Sidcup Art College. A chance conversation on the station platform sixty years ago led to Keith joining Little Boy Blue and the Blue Boys, the group that Jagger fronted. It folded when Mick'n'Keef met Brian Jones and Ian Stewart. 'The Rolling Stones' still has a cooler ring to it.

U2's magic happened in 1976 when teenage drummer Larry Mullen Jr. advertised for musicians on the noticeboard of his Mount Temple, Dublin high school. Paul 'Bono' Hewson, David 'the Edge' Evans and Adam Clayton responded.

The Red Hot Chili Peppers flared to life at LA's Fairfax High School in 1983. Advancing in those early days as 'Tony Flow and the Miraculously Majestic Masters of Mayhem', they made their capsicum leap after signing with EMI.

The Radiohead boys merged at Abingdon School, Oxfordshire in 1986 as On a Friday. Signing a six-album EMI deal in 1991, they took their new name from a track on Talking Heads' 1986 album *True Stories*.

And Green Day were a bunch of fourteen-year-olds at Pinole Valley High School, California, whose third album *Dookie* went overnight-huge in 1994, shovelling up punk to the mainstream. It seems a pity, though it's a pipe dream, that the Hectics couldn't have done it too.

☿

Jimi Hendrix was not the only reason why Freddie opted to be part of a band. In April 1969, he met David Bowie. The Bromley schoolboy who would later kid the world that he, too, had gone to art school (though he hadn't) was at the time a struggling musician who could barely give it away. Three months younger than Freddie, David Jones was a schoolboy saxophonist who had got into jazz at the behest of his doomed half-brother Terry. He joined his best friend George Underwood in the Konrads to play fetes and functions, and left school in July 1963 with a single O level in art. With the help of his teacher Owen Frampton, father of singer Peter, he became a trainee visualiser at a West End studio. But he 'realised very early on that I was never going to make much money from art. So I went into music. We all knew that was where the serious dough was.'[1]

The Konrads came and went. David and George reinvented themselves as Dave's Red & Blues, then as the Hooker Brothers and as the King Bees, by which time David was Davie. That was in 1964, when he first met Marc Bolan. Davie joined folk-soul-blues outfit the Manish Boys from Maidstone. They went nowhere sharpish. He joined the Lower Third, a Margate Mod squad, who knew him as Davy. After their single 'You've Got a Habit of Leaving' failed to chart, David quit to study mime at Sadler's Wells, but still got up with the band for a while. He changed his name one last time. Moving through managers and musical styles, he was at one point part of the Buzz, and then the Riot Squad. Billing themselves as 'The Complete Musical Entertainers', the latter performed twenty shows around the UK during spring 1967, parading pop, parody, burlesque and tableaux. That same year, aged twenty, David released his Anthony Newley-esque novelty single 'The Laughing Gnome', the one that would return to haunt him. There were also his eponymous debut album and a further single, 'Love You till Tuesday', the latter a reworking of a track on his LP. Packed with clashing themes and influences of every kind of music he had heard in his life, that album seemed to be trying to be all things to all people. Like the singles, it flopped spectacularly. David fell in with young American producer Tony Visconti. The pair would soon be sharing a Beckenham, Kent home while Tony produced Marc Bolan. Marc's star rose ahead of David's, for which Bowie never forgave him and was determined to pay him back. The Brooklyn Boy would become his producer eventually. David slept with his mime teacher Lindsay Kemp while maintaining several girlfriends – tweenage temptress Dana Gillespie, fashion and set designer Natasha Korniloff, singer-songwriter Lesley Duncan, ballet student Hermione Farthingale – and lived a life of bi abandon. But his career was in a cul de sac. Manager of the day Ken Pitt suggested he try cabaret, but Visconti wasn't having it. Apple, the Beatles' label, sent him packing. He failed auditions for nude stage musical *Hair!* and for the film *The Virgin Soldiers* (although the producers backhanded him a walk-on). Exhausted, desperate and boracic, he went blagging for work at a London printing and photocopy shop. He formed a trio, Turquoise, who performed Brel alongside Bowie, and went out as Feathers with Hermione and guitarist John Hutchinson, he who played guitar on the original *Space Oddity* in February 1969. He supported Marc Bolan's Tyrannosaurus Rex and Lithuanian sitar player Vytas Serelis on a tour of the UK . . . as a *mime* artist, with a kooky routine depicting the Chinese invasion of Tibet. Bolan must have felt threatened by David to a degree, because he didn't allow him to sing on that tour. David co-launched a folk club in the back room of the Three Tuns pub on Beckenham High Street and carried on gigging, convinced that his moment would come. In April that year, at a lunchtime gig at Ealing Technical College and School of Art, he first set eyes on Freddie Mercury.

Although that gig is usually recorded as a David Bowie solo effort, there exists tangible proof that the folk performance was by

'David Bowie & Hutch' – aka the aforementioned John Hutchinson. In 2013, London auction house Bonhams offered a lot in their Entertainment Memorabilia category comprising not only the original contract for the gig, but also a letter penned by Bowie. The booking agents were G&S Entertainments in North London, the engagement was for an hour-long lunchtime show, 12:30-1:30, and the fee was £17 – of which the booker claimed a fiver, just under thirty per cent. It was an extortionate cut by any era's standards. The Bonhams lot sold for £3,500.

Freddie, anyway, was in on it. Not only did he attend the performance, he cut class to rock up early and made himself useful as a stand-in roadie to David and John. He fetched, carried and helped to set up the duo's equipment before positioning himself to take full advantage of the short show. Of all the joints in all the towns in all Blighty that David had played, he would remember Ealing College . . . because of Freddie.

I knew David in the early days. I was a gauche Bromley kid, and he was a rising, falling but determined to make it at any cost star. My friends and I doorstepped him after school at his Beckenham home, Haddon Hall. His wife Angie would dish out signed black and white publicity shots and pack us off home to our mothers. A classmate and I were invited in for tea with him one afternoon. We gasped at his silver bedroom ceiling and Christmas-coloured sitting room. We were enchanted by his lemon silk kimono, his black nail polish, his long, slender feet, which were on the blue side and looked a little like freshly caught herrings. I became a music writer because of him. In later years, after interviewing him on the road several times, we became friends. It happened only because he was by then living in New York, pre-second wife Iman; because I was frequently on the East Coast on assignment; and because David was partial to hanging with 'people from home'. We had Margate in common: a modest seaside resort in south-east England to which my Welsh-born paternal grandparents had retired and where I spent virtually every school half-term and holiday. David's grandparents had married there, and lived there for a while. His 'Nan' had been a nurse at the town's Royal Seabathing Hospital. When I happened to mention over lunch at Indochine, a chic French-Vietnamese Downtown restaurant and favourite hang-out of his, that I had been commissioned to write a biography of Freddie Mercury, he lent me his house on Mustique.

Really? Scoffers, it happened. The pictures tell the story. My eldest daughter Mia and I stayed in David's Caribbean home, in those days known as Britannia Bay House. I slept in his bed. I awoke every day to the view from his balcony of St Vincent, fifteen minutes and a thousand US dollars away by six-seater Aero Commander 500 – the very view that he had constructed his house to enjoy. I wrote the first draft of my first book about Freddie there. Why? Because David invited me to. Why would he? Because he was, he said, 'So fucking fond of Freddie Mercury.'

'Not that he was "Mercury" when I met him,' said David. 'Nothing like. None of the name or the character, only all of the attitude. I did a gig at Ealing Tech, the college where he was doing art. I'd never set eyes on him before, he was just this scrawny little toerag bending over backwards to get in with me 'n' Hutch. Made himself busy. Plugged in some leads, moved some crap. Not long after, I bumped into him again, in Ken Market. He recognised me first, and came over. He was working for one of the guys there, selling boots. Quite nice ones, actually, they came up well over your ankle in the direction of your knee, and had platforms. Sounds a bit poncey, doesn't it? But I was into all that. They were cool. The daisy roots du jour had my name on 'em.[2] "Space Oddity" was a hit by then, not before time. It had taken me ten sodding years to become an overnight sensation, I was fucking exhausted. I "had potential" written all over me according to the rotters who fell over each other to pour Technicolor shit all over me. Thanks to Auntie Beeb, I'd done it.[3] But I was still skint. Still scraping it together. I never found out how he did it, but Freddie swung it for me to get a pair of them boots for nothing. Not counting "Under Pressure" – you can't count that – I still owe him a favour. So please, have a month in my gaff on dear old Freddie, why don't you. I never did manage to get her down there. I guess it's not gonna happen now.'[4]

Might there have been more to their friendship than he was saying? Who could call themselves a journalist, had they not asked?

'Did I *shag* him, you mean?' David chortled, grinning lasciviously. 'Doesn't it always boil down to that. Let's just say that he was out and about, and I was out and about. Up, down, in out, shakin' it all about. Doin' the pokey cokey and turnin' it round. Same city. Same hangouts. Our parts crossed. Should I say, *paths*.'[5]

☿

Knocking around London and beyond with his old college mate Tim Staffell, Freddie soon got to meet the other members of Smile, the outfit Tim had been playing with lately. Their tall, gangly guitarist was an egghead by the somewhat unprofessorial name of Brian May. Neither he nor Freddie could work out how they had never come across each other before, given that they lived only streets from each other in Feltham, and that Brian had played in other local bands. A clever and cherished only child, Brian had started to play guitar at the age of six, and had built his own instrument with the help of his father from bits of a mahogany fireplace surround and pieces found lying around their home. He plucked its strings with silver sixpenny pieces. He was also now studying maths, physics and astronomy at London's Imperial College. He and Tim had earlier been in a band called 1984, and had even, in May 1967, supported Freddie's idol Jimi Hendrix at Brian's alma mater. A member of the entertainments committee there, May and cohorts selected a string of acts to soundtrack the Imperial College ball. America, Spooky Tooth and Steamhammer also performed, in various settings around the building. Jimi cost them a thousand pounds. The ticket price exceeded one pound each, and the students' union turned a profit.

'We (1984) were playing in a room at the bottom, and Jimi was on in the main hall so, yes, in a sense, we supported him,' recalled May in 2015. 'We were stood in the little corridor backstage between the stage and Jimi's dressing room – which was actually the jazz club room where Roger Taylor and I first played together, strangely enough. Just kind of clumped outside waiting for him. Jimi came out of the dressing room and said: "Where's the stage, man?" We just pointed, starstruck. He was the coolest guy on earth.' Jimi started playing *Foxy Lady*, and the hall was enthralled. '(He was) just widdling his finger on the string very, very, very slowly, building up a feedback note,' said Brian. 'He'd just smile and laugh and move it around. He was wicked. Always that twinkle in his eye. It took a long time – then suddenly he was ready, and he was at full volume, and he just rolled into that fantastic riff.'[6]

But May was on a trajectory at the time that appeared not to leave room for a full-time career in rock music. He was the first to admit that 1984 tended not to specialise in original material, but played covers of the Stones and Yardbirds variety.

'I was never that happy about it,' admitted Brian. 'I left because I wanted to do something where we wrote our own material.' He went, and the group disintegrated. He and Staffell eventually found each other, enlisted a keyboard player, and got themselves a drummer the old-fashioned way: by advertising on the college noticeboard. The successful candidate was Roger Meddows Taylor, a blue-eyed blond from Truro who had given his all in local Cornish group Johnny Quale and the Reaction, later shortened and tightened to The Reaction. Meddows Taylor himself had sung lead vocals. Now in the capital to study Dentistry at the London Hospital Medical School, he had asked his Shepherd's Bush flatmate Les Brown, an old mate from back home and, like Brian, also at Imperial, to keep his eyeballs peeled for signs of bands who needed a drummer. Now that Brian and Tim were composing their own songs, they needed a new identity. That was Smile, a cacophony of metal, monster and minstrel that sounded different right from the start.

As Brian said in 1977, when Queen were well underway, he could play his audience cassettes of Smile that featured 'the same general structures as what we're doing today.' That was the beginning. After Brian's graduation in October 1968, he elected to remain at Imperial to study for his PhD while working as a post-graduate tutor. This meant that he could keep the band going on the side. It wasn't so cut and dried for lead singer Tim or keyboardist Chris Smith, both Ealing College undergraduates; nor for Roger Taylor, who threw in the sickle probe halfway through his degree and pledged his troth to Smile instead of perfecting the grins of patients. The band supported Pink Floyd at Imperial. They supported Family, Yes and T. Rex too. In February 1969, they dumped their keyboardist, and took part in a charity concert performance at the Royal Albert Hall. It was at about this time that Tim started showing up at rehearsals with his friend Freddie Bulsara in tow. The moment would later be remembered as a kind of magic, a variation on the theme of love at first sight. Freddie was wild about the sound coming out of these guys. They, in turn, were mesmerised by his look, his demeanour and his witty, pretty, pithy personality.

Ah, hindsight. How it bends and reshapes time. To listen to this story told and retold, these dudes had just met the love of their lives. Well, it's never as simple as that. Never as complicated.

The tenner-a-week 'Kasbah' art stall that Freddie had been running with Roger Taylor expanded into gladrags. Glammed-up moth-eaten tat, mostly. Eventually, he found himself on another stall selling those boots that Bowie loved. Val Finn remembers it well. As twenty-one-year-old Valerie Doyle from Dublin 'with a dyed-blonde afro' and the cheek of the world, she was Freddie's closest friend for a while during 1970 and 1971. She has never before spoken to any journalist or author, nor shared these memories.

'I worked on a stall called Noddy's Nipples in Ken Market,' she tells me, 'selling belts and bags, stuff from the Boer War, cowboy hats, fringed jackets, holsters, much of which would go as stagewear for all the bands coming in. Freddie's stall was on the corner. There was a bit of a gap between stalls, then two steps, and I used to sit there. Freddie started coming over to sit with me. He could keep a clear eye on his stall from there. Whenever a customer came up, he'd get up and go over to serve them.

'We just loved it in the market. It was a very special time. We both adored Jimi Hendrix, Janis Joplin – he was mad about her – Stephen Stills, Cat Stevens and others. Loads of artists used to come in, and Freddie was in his element. He was such a beautiful human being. Kind, loving, sensitive and gentle. He was the easiest person in the world to love. I am seventy-one, a mother of three adult sons and a grandmother now, and I've never met anyone else quite like him. Even though we were young – Freddie would have been twenty-five or so, while I was four years younger – we were rather spiritual and deep-thinking for our age. We both read *Siddhartha*, the novel by Hermann Hesse with a theme of spiritual journeys and self-discovery. We would spend hours talking about our own journeys, and where we were heading. Life and music. Those were our favourite topics of conversation.'

Freddie and his baby-doll blonde girlfriend Mary Austin would frequent Val's tiny attic flat on Old Brompton Road nearby, where the three of them slouched on her bed and listened to records.

'Mary was very nice,' says Val, 'a gentle soul. She didn't have a lot to say, but she was always really comfortable with us. Freddie was the chatterbox, he never stopped. I told them about my life before I met them, I'd had my share of adventures by then. When I'd first come from Dublin, my friends and I used to hang with a band from Belfast called Heir Apparent who were signed by Chas Chandler, Jimi Hendrix's manager. The band were sucked into this fabulous world, and they took us with them. I'd travelled with girlfriends to Morocco, where I met Jimi in a casbah and smoked a joint. I had lived in Amsterdam and Malaga. In London, I danced with Keith Moon at the Speakeasy: he stripped naked on the dance floor right in front of me, as Jimi and Eric Clapton looked on. There was a lot of craziness. Inhibitions were let down. I remember it as an incredible time.'

When famous artists wandered into Kensington Market, Val would often know them personally. Freddie was impressed.

'Roy Wood came in one day, and asked Freddie to look after his guitar while he went shopping. Freddie took it in his stride, he wasn't starstruck. He used to sing along with whatever music happened to be playing when he sat with me on the stall. But I had no real idea of what he was capable of as an artist at that point. It was around then that I got deeply into meditation. I went and found myself a teacher. "The world is completely lost," I told Freddie one day, and announced that I was leaving. He was amazed. He couldn't believe that I was going to go and leave him. He didn't want to be left. He was a soul man, and I was his soul sister. There was a pure love between us. We knew each other so well that we'd never even asked each other our surnames. I didn't realise until years later that he had changed his name from Bulsara to Mercury. I suppose I just assumed that it was always that. We didn't ask each other about our families, it just never came up. He didn't say anything about Zanzibar or India. Considering that we were all so interested in Indian teachings and spirituality, it does seem a bit strange now that he didn't tell me that.'

Freddie wasn't glam or made-up in those days, Val recalls: 'He was just Freddie, slim and plain. His beauty was the feeling you got when he spoke to you. You felt his presence, which is impossible to describe.'

Along with countless others from many countries, Val became a follower of teenaged Indian-American guru Prem Rawat, who spoke at Glastonbury Fayre in June 1971 and subsequently all over the world. After joining one of his ashrams in Ealing Broadway, she achieved enlightenment, she says. She wishes with all her heart that Freddie had too.

'I attended his first big gig at Imperial College in July 1970, at Freddie's invitation. He had to have me there. He was terribly anxious, and said to me, "Keep a place beside you for me, will you?

I'm so nervous." He had bracelets up his arm, and was wearing velvet jeans. He looked beautiful. I was blown away by his performance. I had no idea where that huge voice came from, I'd never heard it before. He came straight over afterwards. He was shaking, but delighted. I held his hand, and told him he was great. I felt that he really needed to hear that from me.

'In a way, for the time that it lasted, I couldn't have been closer to anyone than I was to him, nor he to me. And then I went off, and the friendship just drifted away. You know how it is. The next I knew of Freddie was when I heard Queen on the radio.'

Did she ever try to contact him? 'No. I never did. I felt that I'd left that world. He was on a different track now, and so was I. We'd had our moment. I had gone off in search of truth, peace and happiness. His ego had kicked in, and it got too big. Do I feel that Freddie's ego destroyed him? Yes! He fell for it all. He wasn't to know that fame and fortune was just an illusion, that none of it was real. He took on identities that were not really him. His life as Queen frontman took him from simple beauty to shocking awfulness. I don't blame the band. I met them a number of times, and I liked them. We've all got to do something useful with our lives, and I'm sure they believed that what they were doing was creative and meaningful. But you also have to be very strong to survive in that world. Showbusiness, the music industry, whatever you want to call it: it's full of traps.'

Could Freddie have saved himself, I ask her. 'He could have. Of course he could have. All he needed was somebody to grab him and say, "Come on, let's get away from all this." Somebody to guide him back home – to *himself*, I mean. Because home is the true, inner self. I knew that the real Freddie was still in there. It's about the child within, who never leaves us. Freddie needed to return to his inner child. He didn't recognise that, and he didn't ever return. It was the biggest mistake of his life.'

What if Freddie had stayed with Mary Austin? 'I wish he had! Then again, do I? I don't think she could have been what he needed her to be. She was lost in the fantasy as well. She fell into his new world along with him. Then Freddie happened to get very rich, and she hung around to have all that too, instead of going off, finding herself and living her true life, after he decided that he was gay – which I never saw, by the way. That just wasn't him during the days when we knew each other and spent time together every day. Mary didn't have much enlightenment. I've watched interviews with her since, enough to know that my instinct about her was right. But she was kind.

'When I went to see *Bohemian Rhapsody*, I took my two grand-daughters, who were thirteen and fifteen at the time. I cried and cried. By the end of the film, they had their arms around me, but they couldn't console me. Why was I sobbing so hard? Because I'd *known* this guy. He was such a beautiful human being when I knew him, and to think that this world made such a mess of him and freaked him out the way it did. It was like watching someone you love being bullied and beaten up. It broke my heart.

'I had experienced for myself what the world of sex and drugs and rock'n'roll is all about. It's basically why I got out. There was too much disaster in the rock world. Too many casualties. I felt that Freddie was completely corrupted. He didn't deserve to be, he was more than that. He walked into the quicksand. It happened to a lot of people in the business. Freddie was very vulnerable, I knew that right from the start. A lot of musicians were. They were on the same trail. I found myself thinking that it was like wandering into a supermarket and being able to have anything you wanted, anything at all. You could have it all, but you could never leave. Industry folk were not there to save you, they were just looking out for themselves.

'Freddie got totally lost in all that. It wasn't a good life that he led, once Queen were successful. How I wished I had been there for him instead of going off to have my own life back in Ireland, in Texas and all those other places. It might sound naïve, but I wish it with all my heart. I wish that I had been able to save him.'

☿

CHAPTER EIGHT

QUEEN

But all that was to come. Before Queen had even been thought of, let alone conceived, Freddie was still intent on making himself indispensable to the members of Smile. He brazenly offered them styling tips and tricks and even started accompanying them on the road. A single deal came their way via Mercury Records' European head honcho Lou Reizner, who had negotiated David Bowie's deal in America. In June 1969, the label booked Smile into Trident Studios in Soho's St Anne's Court. Thus began the 'Sheffield Brothers years', a tangled, tortuous, ultimately litigious period in pre-Queen and early Queen history that their movie deftly avoided. Never excavate the uncomfortable previous. Steer clear of gashing open old wounds.

Smile gurned, made nice, recorded diligently. They waited patiently. Time ticked, but still nothing changed. They spent the summer performing a string of gigs booked by the Rondo agency. Mercury Records did get around to releasing *Earth/Step on Me* that August, but in America. With zero publicity or promotion to boost its chances, it evaporated. Other sessions in further-flung studios were booked. An EP was made, but it never saw the light. Those recordings would not be unearthed until a decade and a half later, by which time Queen were superstars. Come the end of 1969, the band were frustrated and on the verge of calling time. Brian had his PhD to return to. Roger knew the drill, and could easily have taken up his saliva ejector again. Tim realised that he no longer even liked the kind of music Smile were making, and quit to join a new line-up, Humpy Bong. He needn't have bothered. Within a single single and a fleeting television appearance, the bong had humped its last. Tim went off and made a name for himself in animation. Mercury Records, deciding that a band could not be a band without their lead singer, cancelled Smile's contract. The grimaces set in.

Now that West London's Barnes was the place to be, Brian, Tim, Roger and a pair of pals from Liverpool band Ibex installed them-selves in a damp Ferry Road bedsit. The rest of the band soon checked in, using the dump as a base from which to seek a London record deal. Working his way into their circle, dropping in on their rehearsals and pitching up at their gigs, Freddie got on their good side. The band eventually started allowing him to get on stage and sing with guitarist Mike Bersin. Their road manager Ken Testi recalled a quite astonishing, almost full-fledged performer:

'He gave the same kind of performance he did at the peak of his career,' Testi said. 'He was a star before he was a star . . . he'd strut around the stage like a proud peacock.'

Freddie travelled with the band back to Liverpool, dossing on floors and making himself useful. As enthusiastic and hard-working as Ibex were, no deal was forthcoming. Original members drifted away and were replaced. The new improved line-up played just one gig. Which went down in history for all the wrong reasons . . . and a single right one. Freddie's recently acquired habit of lifting and twirling his mic stand in the manner of a drum major four-fingering a baton came unstuck on this occasion. The microphone was attached to a heavy, unwieldy stand. When Freddie grabbed and attempted to swing the thing, its lower half fell off. Freddie didn't bat an eye, he just carried on strutting and twirling the top half. Freddie's trademark 'sawn-off mic stand' was born.

It was but a minor aspect of Freddie's inherent showmanship. All who witnessed his performances, even in those early days, agreed that he was a natural. More remarkable was the fact that his stage persona was so bizarrely at odds with his off-duty self. How did he summon the courage to go out there in a sunburst blaze of confidence and arouse the gigsters with such swagger and shameless exhibitionism when he was otherwise, away from the lights, a cringing wimp? Whence came the Jekyll and Hydeness? Friends and fellow musicians who were used to him skulking around kitchens, dressing rooms and backstage cubbyholes were inclined to snigger behind his back as he wrestled, elbowed and kneed his way into his skimpy hand-sewn stage gear. No one could have called him classically good-looking, not by any stretch. Freddie was embarrassed by his swarthy skin. He grew a thick fringe to cover his dark eyes. He was still hiding his goofy teeth behind his hand.

In the end, he grew tired of Liverpool, of all the hacking to and fro. He'd had his fill of destitution, of tossing and turning on filthy floors. He left the band and meandered back to the bursting bedsit. Where Brian May and Roger Taylor continued to linger, a band without a voice. The answer – Freddie – was hiding right there, in plain earshot.

Back to Gladstone Avenue Freddie would lope once a week, to lap up hot, home-cooked dhansak – perhaps his only substantial meal four times a month – and touch base with his kin.[1] Compromising questions were sidestepped. His mother Jer would hover protectively, ready to intervene when things flared between Freddie and his father. He lugged his portfolio around the London agencies, bagged himself an agent and sat around waiting for design work to flood in. It didn't. His heart wasn't in it. All he could think of was finding a new band to join, or about starting his own. Resuming contact with some of his old Ibex cohorts, he reinvented the band as Wreckage. How satisfying to deliver their first gig at Freddie's old art college, where he found himself cheered by a boisterous crowd down from 'Ken High'. Brian and Roger were in the audience too. They stood pinching themselves. Not that the band were much cop, by available accounts. They were eclipsed by their front man, who was full of it. Freddie Bulsara? Never knew he had it in him . . .

The gig's success was enough to land Wreckage a date at Imperial College, with rugby club bookings to follow. Maybe Brian and Roger had dismissed him too soon. Freddie, meanwhile, soon grew tired of his musicians' inability and indifference. He wrecked Wreckage with his withdrawal, got up to audition for Sour Milk Sea, played a few gigs, ponced about as a rock star in waiting, and waited patiently. He must have realised that the dawning was not far off.

☿

Brian May's assertion that Queen's first official gig took place on 18 July 1970 is challenged by superfan and collaborator Jim Jenkins. According to the lifelong aficionado, whose recollections and expertise have often been called upon by the band's organisation themselves, it happened on 27 June 1970. 'Roger Taylor's mum arranged the gig earlier in the year, and placed an ad in the local press,' Jenkins confirms. 'The group booked were Smile, of whom Roger was a founder member. Another ad appeared in the press during May, the month before the gig . . . Smile called it a day, as Tim Staffell left the group. This gave the opportunity for Freddie Bulsara to persuade Roger and Brian May he could be their new singer.' Roger didn't want to let his mother down, Jenkins explained, so they decided to go with Freddie on lead vocals.

The next crucial step was the changing of their name to Queen. Suggested by Freddie, disliked by the others, it worked.

As for a bass player: a few came and went before the band settled on Leicester-born electronics wizz John Deacon, who officially joined the band on 1 March 1971. This would later lead to quibbling over when exactly the band should commemorate their fiftieth anniversary. Having formed in May 1970, they celebrated in 2020 after having been together for fifty years. As John came on board almost twelve months later, 2021 marks fifty years of the classic line-up. Except that John hasn't been a performing, recording member of the band since he stood down in 1997. Whatever the dates, Jenkins says, 'From Truro to Knebworth (the band's last-ever gig with Freddie as frontman) was a journey like no other.'

Their rise, when it came, was sensational. There would be seven hundred and four live performances by Brian, Roger and John with Freddie at the helm over a period of sixteen years. Signing their EMI deal in 1973, they released their debut single 'Keep Yourself Alive' and first album *Queen* within months. By the end of their UK tour supporting Mott the Hoople, they were launching their own official fan club. The following year they delivered 'Seven Seas of Rhye', the *Queen II* album, and embarked on their first headlining UK tour. Off they went to America with Mott, and released the 'Killer Queen' single and yet another album, *Sheer Heart Attack*. They 'broke America' and didn't look back. The US welcomed them on their first headline tour in 1975. They made for Japan and Queenmania, on a scale not witnessed since the Beatles. The appearance of Freddie's triumph 'Bohemian Rhapsody' on 31 October 1975 gave Britain what would come to be regarded as a 'second national anthem', and fixed Freddie for all time in the nation's hearts. The albums and the anthems kept coming. The tours got more adventurous, taking Queen into parts of the world that had never previously welcomed a rock band. They relocated to Munich, to work at Musicland Studios. They scored their first number one in America with 'Crazy Little Thing Called Love'. They later mangled their reputation there with their defiant 'I Want to Break Free' single from 1984's *The Works* album, and its 'offensive' promotional video. The single was, however, a huge hit in both Europe and South America, where it was taken up as a theme song of the fight against oppression.

Freddie, Brian, Roger and John dipped a toe in solo work in tandem with their band commitments. They were blacklisted by the

Musicians' Union for disregarding the United Nations' condemnation of South Africa's apartheid regime to perform in Bophuthatswana's Sun City resort, an independent state where gambling, topless revues and other banned forms of entertainment could be enjoyed. They were ignored for Bob Geldof's December 1984 chart-topping 'Do They Know it's Christmas?' single, but were the undisputed stars of Live Aid during the July 1985 global jukebox extravaganza. When they embarked on their *Magic* tour of Europe in 1986, no one had a clue it would be their last.

☿

It has always felt as though as though they lasted so much longer. Probably because Queen, the loss of Freddie notwithstanding, have never gone away. The show must go on, sang the man, and naturally it did. Coming to terms over time with the imminent demise of their beloved friend and bandmate, at least Brian and Roger were able to reach a mutual conclusion that the only fitting way to honour him was to carry on.

'He was incredibly brave,' said Roger in a television interview. 'Obviously he knew, and we all knew at that time. But the best thing is just to get on with life.'

'The one thing he wanted to do was keep on working in the studio,' Roger also remarked. 'He was absolutely determined to keep the group going and keep working, and that actually kept him going for a long time.'

Freddie himself set the precedent, working until he could literally no longer stand. 1991's *Innuendo* album was his final collaboration with Queen. The video for its eighth track 'These Are the Days of Our Lives', a ballad in the 'Love of My Life' vein and written primarily by Roger with contributions from the others, reveals graphically how shockingly frail Freddie had become towards the end. It was filmed in May, six months ahead of his death. The track was released as an American single on Freddie's forty-fifth birthday, 5 September 1991. It also appeared as a double A-side with

'Bohemian Rhapsody' in the UK and Ireland on 9 December that year, a fortnight after Freddie's passing. 'These Are the Days of Our Lives' debuted at number one in the UK and reigned for five weeks. It took the BRIT Award for British Single of the Year in 1992.

Three years later they released their fifteenth album *Made In Heaven*, their last with tracks featuring Freddie. He had promised to leave them as much music as possible to be going on with, and recorded until he could no longer do so during his final months.

'He just kept saying, "Write me more. Write me stuff," Brian told the *Daily Telegraph* in 2013. He described *Made in Heaven* as 'a real labour of love,' and said that it had 'so much beauty in it.' '"I want to just sing this and do it and when I am gone, you can finish it off," Freddie said. He had no fear, really,' added Brian.

The last vocal performance of his life was the album's track 'Mother Love'. Co-written by Brian and Freddie, it came at a time when the band were shacked up at Mountain Studios in Montreux more or less around the clock, ready to jump to attention whenever Freddie felt well enough to sing. It was during the laying-down of this track that Freddie's strength deserted him dramatically. He gave in to respite. Taking his leave, he promised to return to the studio as soon as he was able. He never did. He flew home to London on 10 November and took to his bed. Two weeks later, he was dead. That's Brian's voice singing the final verse, not Freddie's.

Not until 2004 did Queen begin a collaboration with former Bad Company/Free/the Firm/the Law frontman Paul Rodgers, as Q+PR (sometimes written as QPR). It sustained until 2009, during which time the band clocked up two world tours, a 2008 studio album, *The Cosmos Rocks* (featuring fourteen tracks co-composed by Brian, Roger and Paul, it was Queen's first album of original material since *Made in Heaven* thirteen years earlier), a pair of live albums and three live DVDs. Two years later, the remaining members of Queen teamed up with *American Idol* contestant Adam Lambert as Q+AL (QAL), lasting from 2011 to the present day.

They toured the world in 2014/15 and 2017/18, and advanced on the *Rhapsody* tour in 2019/20, with later dates postponed due to the coronavirus pandemic. All the tours have been blazingly successful. Brian and Roger have always been adamant that the best way to preserve Freddie's memory was simply to keep going. They have never sought to replace him with alternative singers, they have simply done their best to honour his memory and legacy. Their ongoing love and respect for Freddie is clear from their many interviews down the years; as is their gratitude for his inspiration and dedication.

Could his bandmates, then, have been the true loves of Freddie's life? Tempting though it is to imagine closeness and eternal confidence-keeping between the boys, Freddie shared only the tip of his iceberg with them. He kept a certain distance and maintained his mystery, even back in those early, pre-rich days on the road when they were still obliged to bunch up and share hotel rooms. Nor did Freddie confide in them about his private life. Brian once observed that the 'hot chicks' who used to pitch up backstage and beyond to hang with Freddie had somehow evolved into 'hot guys'. He was amused to note that, by the time Freddie got round to addressing the situation with them, the rest of the band had of course worked out what was going on. There was not, nor would there ever be, an announcement that he was now officially homosexual. Whatever trip he was on, it was up to him. Likewise, he extended them equal privacy. Four bandmates equalled four sets of complicated home lives. The girlfriends and mistresses, wives, ex-wives and endless children of Brian, Roger and John, set against Freddie's own frenetic lifestyle, was a soap to rival anything on television. Even Brian, the 'Sensible One', played away from home behind first wife Chrissie's back with an actual soap queen, former *EastEnders* actress Anita Dobson. Back and forth he went, unable to make up his mind between his women and trying desperately not to break the hearts of Jimmy, Louisa and Emily, his brood. Even after he had left his family for Anita, there was an affair with his married secretary Julie Glover, wife of showbiz agent John, that led to an ultimatum from Miss Dobson. He put a ring on it in November 2000. At last count there were some seven grandchildren, and apparently cordial relationships all round.

Roger was the obvious playboy, the 'Girl-In-Every-Port One'. I clearly remember his cavortings with PR girl Roxy on the road, while he was still involved with gorgeous French brunette Dominique Beyrand, a former PA of Virgin boss Richard Branson. Roger and Dominique lived together for twelve years, and had two children, Felix and Rory. Then Roger met Debbie Leng, the sexy model who made her name as television's saucy 'Cadbury's Flake girl'. When Roger married Dominique in January 1988, it was Freddie and Mary who signed the register. He then went home to Debbie, the couple having already set up home together. Roger was later cornered into giving an explanation: he had done it to protect the legal and financial interests of his ex-partner as well as his children, he said. The admission made a mockery of the marriage vows, but still. He and Debbie stayed together for fifteen years, and had three children together, Tiger Lily, Rufus and Lola. In 2010, he married effervescent South African Sarina Potgieter.

John the 'Quiet One' Deacon was always the most committed family man. He married his only wife, Polish-born Veronica Tetzlaff, in January 1975. She gave him five sons and a daughter, Luke, Cameron, Robert, Joshua, Michael and Laura. After Freddie's death in 1991, John retired from the band four years later, then went off the rails. He began to frequent the London strip club SophistiCats in the early 2000s, overdosing on grande marque champagne and taking up with British lapdancer and glamour model Emma Shelley, whose stage name was 'Pushbar' (*Pushbar!*) She was some twenty-five years his junior, surprise, surprise. John even forked out for a Mercedes and a £320,000 flat for her. He danced her around high-profile London restaurants such as Nobu.

But bands are not families.

'Even though we spend years of intense time together creating albums in recording studios, preparing for tours in disused theatres, church halls or rehearsal studios, and in radio and TV stations doing promo,' mused a musician who must remain nameless. 'And even though we're jumping on and off planes and boats and trains together, and are in and out of hotels and venues together, there has to be time off from each other on a regular basis. You've got to be able to rub along in a band, especially at the outset when money is tight and when you're living in each other's pockets. At that point, you are young, carefree and winging it, with no responsibilities. Beyond that, a band's existence is riddled with contradiction. We might share the contents of our hearts and lay our souls bare when we're writing and recording, and turning our imaginations and exchanges into songs. But we also fight like cats and dogs over every aspect of existence. Good bands do, at least. It still doesn't entitle you to invade a bandmate's privacy, or to expect him or her to share every last bumwipe with you. As a band, you are obliged to present a united, at least cordial if not bosom-friendly front, because the paying public have to believe in you as a focused entity if they are to be enticed into buying your music. Behind closed doors, a private life away from each other is absolutely vital, if you are to succeed at keeping the thing going for as long as it takes to pay your mortgage off and put by for a rainy day.'

There has to be downtime. There needs to be room to breathe, away from the fray, and opportunity to persist as individuals. During the crazy years, when Freddie's interests were glaringly at odds with those of the rest of the band and most of their entourage, he took to staying in separate hotels away from the others. His health issues, when they arose, were a burden to Freddie and only him until the signs became too obvious to dismiss. At that point, he knew that he owed it to them to explain. The future of the entire band being in jeopardy, Freddie reluctantly came to terms with having to come clean.

As Brian revealed in an interview with *The Times*, '(Freddie) said, "I suppose you realise that I'm dealing with this illness." Of course, we all knew, but we didn't want to. "You probably gather that I'm dealing with this thing and I don't want to talk about it, and I don't want our lives to change, but that's the situation," he added. And then he would move on.'

According to Roger, interrogated by *Rolling Stone* magazine in 2014, 'He decided to just invite us all over to the house for a meeting. "You probably realize what my problem is," Freddie said. "Well, that's it and I don't want it to make a difference. I don't want it to be known. I don't want to talk about it. I just want to get on and work until I fucking well drop. I'd like you to support me in this."'

Just as they always had, from a distance or point-blank, it's what they did.

CHAPTER NINE

SECRETS

Are homosexuals born or made? Do inherited traits – 'pre-wiring' – or life experiences – acquired influences – play the greater role in human sexual orientation? Why, in the 2020s, are we still asking the nature-nurture question? Because the debate as to whether or not sexuality is dictated by genes has raged long and hard, but largely inconclusively. Biomedical scientists racing to prove the existence of a 'gay gene' even 'confirmed' at one point that they had located it. The announcement, along with their triumph, proved premature.

In 2019, a major analysis of the genetics of same-sex sexual behaviour funded by the U.S. National Institute of Health and other participants concluded that, while genetics and therefore biology play an important part, the drive to seek same-sex experiences is influenced by perhaps thousands of genes, not just one.[1] Researchers identified five genetic variants present in the full human genome that appear to be involved. Those five comprise less than one per cent of the genetic influences. Two of the five variants found were discovered only in males, and one was discovered only in females. One of the male variants could be related to sense of smell, which is involved in sexual attraction. The other male variant is associated with male pattern balding, and is found near genes involved in male sex determination. The study found that all genetic effects probably account for around thirty-two per cent of a person's inclination to seek same-sex sexual activity. Emotional, social and environmental factors having been found to be just as influential, it is therefore impossible to determine the orientation of an individual based on genes alone.

Particularly sensitive is the discovery that engagement in same-sex sexual behaviour has genetic correlations with mental health issues, such as major depressive disorder or schizophrenia, and with traits like risk-taking, cannabis use, inclination to experiment, and loneliness. The scientists who led the 2019 investigation insist that their study does *not* suggest that same-sex sexual activity causes or can be caused by these conditions or characteristics. They underline that depression or bipolar disorder could just as easily be the result of homophobic discrimination and the stress it can cause.

'(Same-sex behaviour) is written into our genes and it's part of our environment,' stated geneticist Benjamin Neale, one of the chief researchers on the study's international team of top geneticists, psychologists and sociologists. 'I hope that the science can be used to educate people a little bit more about how natural and normal same-sex behaviour is . . . this is part of our species, and it's part of who we are.'

The study is highly controversial because evidence that genes influence same-sex behaviour could prompt anti-gay activists to demand gene editing or embryo selection, even though such intervention is as yet medically impossible. It is also feared that evidence of genes playing merely a partial role in sexuality could boost the argument of those who maintain the belief that homosexuality is a choice, and who even support extreme measures to 'cure' it, such as conversion therapy. Before expressing outrage at such statements, we should remind ourselves of the many men still living today who are old enough to recall that, for much of their own young lives, homosexuality was still regarded as a psychiatric disorder.

Universal understanding of human behaviour and sexuality has never been more vital. While awareness and changes in the law in many countries have led to increased social acceptance, the

LGBTQ community still faces many challenges. Any scientific investigation that supports them can only be viewed as positive.

Robbee Wedow, a member of the study's research team and a postdoctoral research fellow at the Broad Institute of MIT and Harvard, came to terms with his own homosexuality via a path not dissimilar to Freddie's.

'I grew up in a highly religious evangelical family,' he said, 'being confused about not being attracted to women and being attracted to men, being convinced it was a sin and that I would go to hell.' For the longest time, he admitted, 'I definitely tried to pray it away, tried to like girls, tried to have girlfriends. This wasn't something I, of all people, would have chosen. There must be some sort of biological background . . . saying "Sorry, you can't study this" reinforces it as something that should be stigmatised.'

What were Freddie's views on sexuality? Did he understand it as a fundamental part of his identity? Did he fathom it as by no means limited to the ability to reproduce, but as the factor which defines how we see ourselves and how we relate physically to others? Could he have had any idea that orientation is the result of a combination of biological, hormonal, emotional and environmental factors; did he get that many things contribute to it, and that contributing factors may differ from person to person? Had he come to accept that his homosexuality (or possible bisexuality) was not caused by the way he was parented, nor by anything that might have happened to him when he was young? Or was his sexuality instinctive, not something he analysed in any great depth, and certainly not an aspect of himself that he ever felt obliged to explain? Did he just shrug, accept what and who he perceived himself to be, and go with the flow? We are never likely to know, because he never discussed it publicly. It might have amused him no end to think that we would still be getting our knickers in a twist over it, thirty years beyond his death. He might forgive us our long-term fascination, given that matters gender- and sexuality-related have never before been more relevant.

Freddie's sensitive nature and self-contained personality were assaulted on all fronts. His own family's culture and religion actively demonised same-sex behaviour. Aware of the pressure to conform, find himself a respectable female with the requisite child-bearing attributes, settle down and deliver greatly desired grandchildren, he must have concluded that he had no choice but to suppress his natural inclinations and resign himself to do what was expected of him.

Girls were always attracted to Freddie, and he to them. His first serious girlfriend was fellow Ealing College art student Rosemary Pearson. The striking strawberry blonde became a professional artist and lecturer in art theory at the University of Sheffield. As twice-married mother-of-four Dr Rose Rose, she did not go public about her love affair with Freddie until thirteen years after his death. She was, she explained, trying to come to terms with her feelings about her relationships with two gay men (having also discovered that her second husband was homosexual). A boarding school survivor like Freddie, Rosemary was his girlfriend for about a year from 1969 until 1970, during the Smile episode. The Freddie she knew was the class clown, an affectionate and 'cuddly' partner, a passionate lover and an exuberant drama queen. She admitted to having been hopelessly in love with him, and to her denial of that fact for more than thirty years.

'I think Freddie did love me,' she said in 2004.[2] 'But for me it was too ambiguous, he was androgynous. He liked to think of himself as both genders, and talked about it. He certainly kept telling me how much he loved me, he was true to me, he didn't look at any other women. But we couldn't carry on. I said, "Your mind is somewhere else, you're too different, you've got this urge to do something."'

Freddie's insatiable curiosity made Rosemary feel inadequate. She described herself as having been a 'linchpin', a 'bridge between his fantasy world and his real world': 'If I took him over the bridge, I feared he wouldn't be mine anymore. I'd make excuses about introducing him to (her twenty-five years older homosexual doctor friend) Patrick Woodcock, and we'd have terrible rows about it.[3] I didn't completely understand it. I think I did know he was gay, though I don't think he was seeing anyone else. I felt I was either the person who made it happen or I would have to walk away.'

'The Queen thing', as she referred to the experiment that became the band, 'grew out of his personality. He was finding his feet. People sent him up about his persona. I thought they were insensitive. I thought the theatrical persona, the gayness, was an add-on, and I was drawn to his otherness.' She revealed that Freddie told her about his attraction towards certain men. She said he would confide in her that he might be gay while they were in bed together, having just made love. Rose was naturally offended. It made her feel inferior. Her suspicions crystallised into firm realisation when at last she caved into his urgent demands to meet her gay friends. Patrick Woodcock's Pimlico dinner parties featured future luminaries David Hockney, the painter, the artist and future film director Derek Jarman, and any number of flamboyant performance artists.

'I thought, Freddie is my boyfriend and where am I?' she said. 'If I had handed him to the artists, he would have been immediately taken over because he wanted to be taken over. Obviously I'd lose him. It would have been like, "Here's a nice young man for you," as if I was procuring. I didn't feel that was my role. Eventually I went round to Freddie's flat one Saturday afternoon and told him it was over. He sobbed like a little child. I left, and never saw him again.' Rosemary did not follow Freddie's career or listen to his music. She avoided Queen's videos and television documentaries about them and Freddie. She did her damnedest to put him out of her mind and life.

'I haven't acknowledged until now the massive impact knowing Freddie had on me,' she said in 2019. 'For me, he was the ultimate model of how to follow your dream. The experience of loving him left me feeling rejected and uncertain, but in the end, it gave me the impetus to be my own person, to try and do what he had done.'

☿

Freddie's young devotion to another female lover took him much further than his relationship with Rosemary Pearson. It led to a six-year love affair and all the way to the promise of marriage. When Mary Austin was twenty-three and she and Freddie had been together for four years, he presented her with a giant box on Christmas morning. 'Inside was another box, then another, and so it went on,' said Mary. 'It was like one of his playful games. Eventually, I found a lovely jade ring inside the last, small box. I looked at it and was speechless. I remember thinking, "I don't understand what's going on." It wasn't what I'd expected at all. So I asked him, "Which hand should I put this on?" And he said, "Ring finger, left hand." And then he said, "Because, will you marry me?"

'I was shocked,' Mary admitted. It just so wasn't what I was expecting. I just whispered, "Yes. I will."'

But theirs was a fantasy destroyed by the reality of his urges. The oft-revisited scene that was milked to high heaven in the film still rips at the heart. The cosy pair co-habit for six blissful years until Freddie's musical career lifts off – at which point his social circle expands, he spends more and more time away from his beloved, and eventually starts staying out all night. Changes in the rhythm of their relationship lead to the tragic, make-or-break moment when Mary anticipates that Freddie is about to dump her for another woman. She challenges him, and he blurts to her that he thinks he is bisexual. Mary contradicts this by telling him what he thinks he already knows . . . that he is gay.

Do we buy that she 'gave him permission' to go off and be a fully-liberated homosexual – which he would still be forced to conceal from his parents and sister, his fans, the general public and above all the Zoroastrian Parsi community? Did she really bestow the wings with which he could fly to his realm of freedom and self-expression? Or was her 'gift' to Freddie in fact the key to Pandora's box of wickedness and an unwitting 'tool of revenge', conveying him to a wretched dimension of promiscuity, addiction and abuse?

Freddie was not the first gay male to strive to live a straight life, pledging his troth to a woman and ultimately shattering her heart. Leaving antiquity and the classicists aside, there are countless modern examples to raise a brow. Take Irish poet, playwright, author and all-round decadent Oscar Wilde, who married Constance Lloyd in 1884 and fathered two sons. He later fell in love with precocious journalist and art dealer Robert Ross, with whom he experienced 'Greek love'. Wilde went on to indulge in the love that dare not speak its name with the Marquess of Queensberry's son Lord Alfred 'Bosie' Douglas, which dragged him off the rails and landed him behind bars.

American composer and songwriter Cole Porter surrendered to a lavender marriage with rich Kentucky-born divorcée Linda Lee Thomas in 1919. His wife was eight years his senior, and well aware of his gay and bisexual proclivities. For her, the marriage provided social status; for him, a respectable (and vital) heterosexual front. They remained devotedly together until her death in 1954.

Fifties rocker 'Little' Richard Penniman, the 'Architect of Rock'n'Roll', dressed up in his mother's clothes and make-up as a boy. He was brutally punished by his father for it, and was ejected from the family home when he was fifteen. A self-confessed voyeur, he married Ernestine Harvin in 1959 and 'enjoyed normal sex' for the four years they spent together. He later confessed to having 'always' been gay, but retracted the statement after his religious conversion to denounce the activities of homosexuals and transgender people as 'unnatural affection' that 'goes against the way God wants you to live.'

Bisexual theatre and film director and producer Tony Richardson married actress Vanessa Redgrave in 1962. They had two daughters, actresses Natasha and Joely. He was terminally unfaithful, contracted HIV and died from AIDS complications in 1991, the same year as Freddie.

Singer-songwriter Barry Manilow married his high school sweetheart Susan Deixler when he was twenty-one. They divorced two years later due to his 'artistic commitments'. At seventy-three, he shocked his predominantly female fanbase with the revelation that he had always been gay. He declared a forty-year relationship with his manager Garry Kief, whom he married in 2014, once same-sex marriage in California had been legalised.

DJ Kenny Everett, a close friend of Freddie's until they fell out, never speaking again after Christmas 1980 (so Kenny was *not* one of the last people ever to speak to Freddie) married former backing singer turned psychic Audrey 'Lady Lee' Middleton in June 1966. Lee told me herself that she turned a blind eye to his 'homosexual cavortings'. After they went their separate ways, she married *The Sweeney* actor John Alkin, and they relaunched themselves as spiritual healers. Kenny stopped denying that he was gay during the 1980s, despite rumours about his relationship with his top-heavy television sidekick Cleo Rocos. He died aged fifty from AIDS-related illness four years after Freddie, in 1995.

And Sir Elton John, who was devoted to Freddie right to the end, became betrothed to secretary Linda Woodrow during the late 1960s. Their wedding was called off. He entered a long relationship with his hot-headed Scottish manager John Reid, who would also manage Freddie and Queen. The couple collapsed in 1970, but Reid remained Elton's manager until 1998. In 1984, Elton married German sound engineer Renate Blauel in Australia. Marital bliss faded fast. Elton hooked up with David Furnish in 1993. They were among the first to have a civil partnership in 2005, on the day the new Act went live. When gay marriage became legal in 2014, they were married at Windsor on the ninth anniversary of their civil partnership. The couple had two sons via a surrogate. Zachary was born in 2010. Elijah joined them three years later.

Food for thought. Freddie declared throughout his life that Mary was the only one for him; that she was his 'common-law wife'; that he could never love another as much as he loved her. He relied totally on her, he said, and he was leaving everything to her. Did he ever consider a lavender splicing? If Freddie loved Mary so deeply that there would never be anyone else for him, not in any true and lasting sense, might they not have been able to establish common ground that could have given Mary the marriage and children she wanted while leaving room for Freddie to indulge himself with men on the side?

Shocking? Many among the British upper middle classes, the aristocracy and royalty have lived that way for centuries, long-suffering wives turning blind eyes to their husbands' 'weaknesses' – mostly fostered in the first place at boarding school, and which had all too often commenced with kinds of abuse.

And what about the phenomenon known as MSM: men who have sex with men (or males who have sex with males), on the rise since the 1990s? While some are gay or bisexual, pan– or omni-sexual, many are straight, and even married with children. MSM being a behaviour rather than an identity. Many such men seek out casual sex with other males online. Their interpretation – excuse? – is that they are primarily or exclusively attracted to women. Many insist that they have no sexual attraction to men beyond their desire to have sex with them. They define 'sexual attraction' as a combin-ation of physical and emotional desirability, and assess that their interest in women comprises both. Their interest in men, on the other hand, they explain as purely or mainly sexual, and not in the least romantic or emotional. Some say that they are not drawn toward male bodies the way they are drawn to the female form. Some admit that the only physical part of the male that interests them is the penis. These men report that they do not find men handsome or attractive, but they do find the male member desir-able. They sometimes self-limit their same-sex activity, or dismiss it as inferior to the sex they engage in with women. In order to justify it? Are they able in this way to reassure themselves of their 'normal', 'healthy' sexual interest in women, and brush off the sex they have with men as incidental or aberrational? Whatever, they seem to be able to identify as straight or heterosexual, even though their hetero-sexuality is not exclusive.

So it's fluid, and not defined. A degree of same-sex desire and behaviour does not necessarily compromise their identity. While some agree that their behaviour might more accurately be described as bisexual, they tend to maintain an unthreatened straight or heterosexual public identity while accepting the reality only in private. There is, 'they' say, 'a lack of social incentives' to come out as bisexual. They probably *are* bisexual, but resist admission because of the stigma that persists. Not to mention the fact that their female partners might not go a bundle on it. To the outside world, they are heterosexual. They are bisexual only in private with other men. What they get up to with other chaps is but a temporary fantasy. They get to have it both ways while their wives are none the wiser. Hmm. How would they react if they discovered that their wives were playing dirty in comparable ways?

Wait. Isn't this what Freddie opted for when he broke it off with Mary to avail himself of the fancy-free homosexual smorgasbord? He never let her go, after all. When they dismantled their bijou home and called time on coupledom, he bought her a flat, round the corner from his. She could see into his place from her bathroom, and he could almost see into hers. He found her a job in his organisation, so that she would still be around, managing his life and being at his beck and call. She would continue to travel with him. She would be whatever he needed her to be. She was on his payroll, and was provided for by him, for the rest of his life and ultimately of hers. He made no secret of the fact that he was leaving her, in his will, his lavish home and the lion's share of his wealth. He gave her the responsibility of dealing with his very remains beyond his death, which Mary herself admitted was asking too much. He kept her only unto him, as the vow goes. Why not marry her, then, and be done? Philip Schofield's wife Stephanie did not desert her husband of twenty-seven years when the TV presenter came out in February 2020. Why not? They had grown up together. They had raised two daughters. He declared on live television that they had never had any secrets from each other. It is likely that Steph had known about Phil's true orientation all along. Showbiz rumour (unsubstantiated) has it that he only came clean in public when he did because a blackmail attempt had been made, and because a national newspaper was on the verge of outing him.

Different times. Mary was not the kind of woman who could have gone for that. She could not have listened to Freddie making solemn promises in full knowledge of the fact that he would not be keeping them, and that her husband would proceed to live a double life. She was candid about her acceptance of the situation. Had they stayed together, she reasoned, it would literally have threatened her life.

'If he hadn't been such a decent human being and told me, I wouldn't be here,' she told the *Daily Mail* in 2013. 'If he had gone along living a bisexual life without telling me, I would have contracted AIDS and died.'

As for Freddie, his succinct statements about his former lover said it all.

'There have only been two individuals who have given back as much love to me as I gave to them,' he said. 'Mary, with whom I had a long affair, and our cat, Jerry.'

'My bond with Mary seems to grow and grow. If I go first, I'm going to leave everything to her. Nobody else gets a penny, except my cats.'

'I might have all the problems in the world, but I have Mary and that gets me through. I still see her every day, and I am fond of her now as I have ever been. I'll love her until I draw my last breath. We'll probably grow old together.'[4]

The irony being that Freddie compromised himself to live a double life anyway. He was never honest with his family about his lifestyle. He never in his life came out as gay. While his passion flared for many a dashing bruiser who caught his eye, his liaisons could never accurately be described as full-blown 'relationships'. There was always Mary, or the thought of her, hovering physically nearby or in his mind's eye like an image of the holy Mother of God above an altar. His 'Old Faithful', forever there for him, when all else failed. Not until well into the 1980s when he entered his 'eternal triangle' period and juggled affairs with Irish hairdresser Jim Hutton, German restauranteur Winnie Kirchberger and Austrian sex-bomb actress Barbara Valentin, was his pure love for Mary ever in jeopardy.

☿

Peter Freestone, that other benign, devoted stalwart in Freddie's life, made fascinating observations about his boss's many partnerships with other males. He also explained his desperate need for conflict.

'He never met what you could call an "equal partner",' Phoebe told me. 'All of his men were less than him, if you get my meaning. He had a secret fantasy about meeting his match. I wonder whether, in reality, that could ever have been possible. Freddie's men were all menial compared to him. Well, there are not too many superstars in the world, are there. It is very rare for them to meet each other and form relationships. When it happens, there is the danger of them cancelling each other out. I'm thinking of the likes of Richard Burton and Elizabeth Taylor, whose love was doomed.

'Part of Freddie would have loved to have a partner to look up to. In reality, that was never going to happen. Just going by the kind of places he frequented after hours, for a start. There weren't the opportunities. Plus, of course, Freddie had his inhibitions and insecurities. He was what he was, a wonderful songwriter, singer and performer. A great showman. He was the first to say that he wasn't a great intellect. He had no interest in politics. He hardly bothered with current affairs. His world was a bubble, in many respects. Those of us who shared it, for the briefest moment or for many years, had to learn to dance around him. Our lives worked according to his rhythms and needs. It couldn't have lasted, otherwise.'

So there were the names dredged up along the way. The record company executives, such as Ronnie Fisher and David Minns,

Freddie's first true male love; and, according to former Queen manager John Reid, the one for whom Freddie wrote and composed 'Love of My Life' in 1975. Did he? Others have long maintained that the song was written for Mary. Freddie himself would never say. David was Freddie's first serious if secret boyfriend, whom he saw in tandem with Mary during the final year of their affair. Freddie even purchased a flat for David and himself to live in together. It is rumoured that he also penned 'You Take My Breath Away' and 'Good Old Fashioned Lover Boy' about 'Minnsie', his 'dearest', who knew Freddie as a 'dreadful tart' and as 'Mercles'.

American Joe Fanelli came along post-Minns, in 1978. The thirty-two-year-old rock star and the twenty-seven year-old professional chef fell for each other hard and fast. But Joe eventually grew tired of all the skulking around and Freddie's insistence that they must keep their relationship secret. They fell out of touch for several years, crossing paths from time to time as Joe continued to work in London restaurants, and Freddie continued to renew Joe's visa each year so that he was able to stay and work in the UK. Joe went on to become Freddie's personal chef, and took up residence at Garden Lodge. Reckoned to be the only member of his inner circle who was able to handle Freddie's panic attacks, Joe stepped up as one of Freddie's nurses when he came home from Switzerland to die. Joe was diagnosed HIV positive in 1990, and died in 1992, the year after Freddie.

Grinning blond DHL courier Tony Bastin came along in 1979, and Freddie was smitten. They began an on-off and often long-distance affair that lasted for around two years.

'Tony was not Freddie's type at all,' reflected Peter Freestone. 'Freddie liked chunky and hunky and a relatively blank slate, someone upon whom he could leave his mark. He liked the stability of a permanent partner as a secure base from which he could continue to play the field.' Freddie's lovers tended to have unsophisticated roots, he added.

'Although a country boy himself, which he was loath to admit, he had an acquired sophistication which always rubbed off on his lovers and raised their expectations.'

Still, Tony as good as moved into Freddie's Stafford Terrace flat, and even installed Oscar, his cat. He also started travelling with Freddie as often as possible, or joining him at a handful of destinations when the band were on tour. Freddie flew him first class and spoiled him with beautiful presents. No wonder he developed a taste for the high life. He grew blasé, however, to Freddie's chagrin. When Freddie learned that Bastin had started seeing a 'slim, young blond' behind his back, he was devastated. He summoned Tony to the US, ended the relationship to his face and put him on the next flight back. Bastin was told in no uncertain terms to strip Freddie's flat of his belongings but to leave the cat. Tony later died of AIDS at the age of thirty-five, just before Christmas 1986.

It was a pattern that was to repeat over and over throughout Freddie's chequered romantic career.

'Freddie was often let down badly in relationships and became extremely cautious about who he got involved with emotionally,' said his close friend, the journalist David Wigg. 'Once they'd got the Cartier bracelet or the car ... you know. They weren't very clever, these "friends" of his. It happens a lot with these people. The entourage have inflated egos, sometimes bigger than the ego of the star they serve. They start to believe that they can do it too, forgetting the fact that they haven't an ounce of talent themselves, and are only where they are because of who's paying them.'

Could the betrayals explain Freddie's on-going penchant for zipless sex with an endless string of partners, while saving his affection and emotional commitment for the handful of friends he could genuinely trust?

So then came Vince the barman, whom Freddie met in Los Angeles. A tall, chunky hunk with a flop of dark hair, he could not have been more Freddie's type. But he wasn't about to give up his job and lifestyle to follow a rock star about on tour like a lackey.

Freddie was soon demanding of Vince that he drop the bar work and come away with him on tour, but Vince said no. 'I'm not prepared to give up my life for what could be six months before you tell me it's over and ship me back,' he said. Sorry, Freddie. They all liked Vince a lot, but he was the one who got away.

Looking back on their short-lived affair, Vince remarked, 'At that time, I had a Harley Davidson and I think that's what made him interested . . . I had seen Freddie in a video, and I said to my friend, "God, that guy is really hot!" . . . three weeks later I'm in bed with him. I just couldn't believe it! I was a biker man at that time. It was macho and we didn't wear shirts behind the bar, we were bare-chested and kinda buff . . . He was very special, very tender, very caring. Freddie was the highlight of my life, definitely.'

Body-builder Peter Morgan joined Freddie in Buenos Aires during Queen's outing to South America in 1981. Mildly famous thanks to his stint as a former Mr UK, Morgan had also enjoyed a starring role in one of the first gay videos. Things were punchy between them. He and Freddie were always falling out. The relationship collapsed when Freddie discovered that his beau had been two-timing him with a significantly younger man. Freddie dumped him and that was that.

He met stocky, mouthy Bill Reid from New Jersey in a New York bar in 1982. It might have been murderous. This was Freddie's most turbulent affair, punctuated by violent attacks and outbursts which more than once left Freddie almost hospitalised. Smashed-up hotel rooms, munched flesh and broken glass were the hallmarks of their brief relationship. The day that Queen were scheduled to appear on American's late-night television show *Saturday Night Live* that September, Freddie had fought so vociferously with Reid the night before that he awoke to find that his voice had deserted him. Peter Freestone shut him in a bathroom with a bottle of Olbas oil and tried to steam his voice back. Of all Freddie's lovers, Reid was the most obvious proof that Freddie depended on conflict to be able to go out and deliver his best performance. As Peter

Freestone put it, he needed to 'sing angry', and Bill Reid was as angry and as ugly as it got. Peter also said that Bill was the reason why Freddie went off New York; and even, perhaps, why Freddie gave up on trying to maintain relationships, settling instead for what he described as 'the safer option' of 'a different guy after every show.' Reid also lost out to AIDS eventually.

As did Winnie Kirchberger and Jim Hutton, who beyond all others came closest to being the true male loves of Freddie's life. But would they rival Mary?

CHAPTER TEN

MARY

Mary Austin had no reason to suspect any dilemma or complication when she and Freddie started going out together, as they called it in those days. He did not let slip his confusion or divulge his struggle for identity. Nor did he share the reason why his art school girlfriend Rosemary Pearson had finished with him. He gave the impression, to pretty, blonde, ethereal, wouldn't-say-boo teenage Mary of being a straight male seeking a committed romantic relationship with a female of about the same age and with similar interests. This was obviously Mary's expectation too. It was the basis upon which their long, devoted but ultimately cursed love affair was founded.

We know that Freddie was not frank with his new girlfriend about his sexuality, thanks to all that she has said down the years about the manner in which it dawned on her, and the way their partnership disintegrated. Mary's worst nightmare, once Queen had begun forging a path to fame and fortune, was that Freddie would leave her for another woman. It was only towards the end that she began to grow uneasy. Call it an inkling. We know that she responded to her boyfriend's tortured confession that he believed himself to be bisexual with that heartbreaking hunch that he must be gay. What on earth could he have said to that? What was her reaction? Neither of them said anything, remembered Mary. There was nothing *to* say. They simply hugged, in sad acceptance of what had to happen next.

Freddie did not tell Mary about the cinema date that he and Rosemary had gone on the previous year, to see director Ken Russell's breakthrough picture *Women in Love*. An adaptation of D. H. Lawrence's controversial 1920 novel, it charts the lives and loves of a pair of sisters, Ursula and Gudrun, whose male romantic partners Rupert and Gerald grow intellectually and physically attracted to one another. The novel's raw excavation of human sexuality, in particular its exploration of bisexuality, outraged post-Great War society. Its shock factor was compounded by the widely held assumption that Lawrence had written the novel to confront his own confusion. The 1969 four Academy Award-nominated screen adaptation, for which Glenda Jackson as Gudrun bagged the Best Actress Oscar, was one of the first studio films to feature full-frontal male nudity, notably during the scene in which Oliver Reed's Gerald and Alan Bates's Rupert wrestle, naked and sweat-soaked, before a blazing log fire.

Freddie, recalled Rosemary, was wildly turned on by the male-on-male grapple. He couldn't eradicate it from his head. It exacerbated his obsession with the notion that he might be homosexual himself. He went on and on about it, even as he made love to her, 'wondering what it would be like with a man.' Rosemary's self-esteem was crushed, which we get. This was certainly a contributing factor in her decision to end their relationship in 1970.[1]

There was more. When the story's two couples repair to an Alpine inn for Christmas, Gudrun becomes enchanted by Loerke, a gay German sculptor. She becomes increasingly fascinated by his assertion that the creation of art depends on brutality. This may well have sparked, in Freddie, the realisation that conflict could be exactly what he needed to boost his ability to perform live. He would go on, in years to come, to generate conflict with partner after partner, in order to create the requisite energy to go out on stage and give his all.

Can conflict really enhance creativity? Sujin Lee, Associate Professor of Organisational Behaviour at the Korea Advanced

Institute of Science and Technology, certainly found so. In her 2015 Paper *The Combined Effect of Relationship Conflict and the Relational Self on Creativity*, she concluded that helping people to see themselves in relation to others, especially during episodes of conflict, made them crystalise their goals and strive to achieve them by more creative means. 'This is because most people want harmonious relationships with those around them, and when obstacles to achieving that harmony appear, they become more determined to overcome them,' she said. Freddie clearly found conflict inspirational to the point of being the sine qua non of preparation for his spectacular performances.

'It was almost as though Freddie needed these surges of passion to start his creative juices flowing,' observed Peter Freestone. 'That either because of the high pressure of work, he finished relationships, or conversely engineered dramatic rows when he needed the extra boost.'

Emotional conflict certainly appears to have enhanced his creativity.

Women in Love, the novel and the film, also prompted discussion regarding the existence of 'two kinds of love', and whether an individual is able to feel and consummate both equally. Alan Bates's character Rupert tells his wife Ursula that she is enough for love of a woman, but that there is another eternal love and bond for a man; the suggestion being that he had fallen for Gerald, who later stalks off alone to end his life among the mountains. The dilemma – whether it is possible to love both a woman and a man at the same time, which may well have been triggered by this film – was to preoccupy Freddie for the rest of his life.[2]

Brian May saw Mary first, at an Imperial College gig in 1970. He asked her out and they dated once or twice. Did they hook up, hang out, go steady? Was there a crush? Did she carry a torch for him? None of it. The Brian and Mary show never got off the ground.

Freddie clocked all this, saw that physics was sparking no chemistry, and began pestering his bandmate until the latter caved in and agreed to introduce them. Freddie was smitten as good as immediately. Mary took her time to warm up, pretending to play the field. She seemed determined to avoid the attentions of this unusual guy with the hots for her. Which reveals much about her shyness and lack of self-confidence. Freddie was undeterred. He kept trying. When he invited her to celebrate his twenty-fourth birthday with him on 5 September that year, she pretended she was busy. She later elaborated to journalist David Wigg that she was just 'trying to be cool':

'Not because there was any real reason I couldn't go. But Freddie wasn't put off. We went out the next day instead. He wanted to go and see Mott the Hoople at the Marquee Club in Soho. Freddie didn't have much money then, and so we just did normal things like any other young people. There were no fancy dinners – they came later, when he hit the big time.'

In common with Freddie, Mary hailed from a humble home. Her father was a wallpaper trimmer, her mother a cleaner. Both parents were deaf and mute. She had been a trainee secretary when she found her job at Biba, a small fashion boutique which would grow into a world-famous emporium and dominate the look of the 1970s. What was her role there? This has never been quite clear. Whether salesgirl or secretary, executive assistant or manageress, she worked for the coolest clothes and lifestyle store in London, selling the pop-garb mode of the moment that she herself wore. She and Freddie had similar personalities. They displayed the bare minimum of themselves, allowing the observer to work out the rest. Projecting as low-key friendly and happy-go-lucky, they could both be somewhat frivolous and materialistic. It contradicted hidden depths. Recognising each other in the first moment, theirs was a meeting of souls who quickly became entwined. There was also the relief that they both had awful teeth: while Freddie's top front set protruded goofily, Mary's top middle two incisors had a crunched-on-a-peach-stone broken look that distorted her mouth and made a graveyard of her smile. She would get them fixed in years to come: her teeth in photographs taken during Freddie's heyday look perfect. He probably footed the bill. Nothing would ever have been too good for his Mary. As far as he was concerned, he had found the perfect girlfriend. They didn't come better. She offered the ideal relationship to which he aspired. He must have imagined them settling down with a couple of kids running in the yard, and growing old together. He decided that they had known each other for eternity.

The glorious paradox about him being that, despite his taste for hunky men, there was never a time when Freddie did not adore gorgeous women. He relished the fairer sex. He soaked up their glamour and femininity. He loved the timbre of a woman's voice, the gleam of her skin, the lustrousness of her hair; her scent, her make-up, her swishiness; her coquettish, vibrant, vampish ways; her little-girliness; her demanding, pouting petulance. As he matured, he came to favour and identify with females who were the opposite of Mary: flamboyant actresses and singers; loud gals inclined to swank, boast and flaunt. We're talking Anita Dobson, queen of the Queen Vic, who dallied with Brian May and eventually married him;[3] showgirl Elaine Paige, she of *Evita, Cats, Chess* and *Sunset Boulevard* fame; and Austrian-born German film star Barbara Valentin, of whom much more later. There was also Diana Moseley, his strong, no-nonsense costume designer and party person, like Freddie a total perfectionist; and la Superba, Montserrat Caballé, one of the finest and most interpretative operatic sopranos of the twentieth century. Though her flare had softened with age, her great dignity and elegance never failed to floor Freddie. He was a juvenile in her presence, a playful pup at the pumps on her feet.

Which begs another question: what if you fancy being a boy today, a girl tomorrow? How do we know he didn't? We do know that Freddie adored the cross-dressing experience of 'I Want to Break Free'. The song, a track on *The Works* album, was written for Queen by John Deacon in 1983 and released the following year. When we think of that track, is it the song that we hear first or the video that we see? The camp David Mallet-directed dragfest featured all four band members got up as women in a hilarious parody of that most cherished of British television institutions, *Coronation Street.* Freddie, wielding a vacuum cleaner, played a strumpet hausfrau in stockings and suspenders, black leather mini skirt, tight pink top and pointy black brassiere. He also sported a bouffant, striking eye make-up and a thick moustache. Brian did downbeat housewife in dressing gown and curlers, while Roger went for teen-temptress schoolgirl and John disapproved as Granny. A Dionysian section featured Freddie prancing, writhing and giving it all that with dancers from the Royal Ballet. Hugely popular among homegrown fans, 'Break Free' was banned by MTV in America. The single died a death there. Worse, Queen's reputation was never fully restored in the States until after Freddie's passing. Perhaps they shouldn't have demanded its release there after all.

All kinds of messages have been read into 'Break Free' down the years. Did Freddie (or John) want out of the band? Was one or other (or all) of them desperate to walk away from their current personal relationship(s)? Could Freddie, frustrated by all the skulking, have been dying to come out as gay and be done? Could the song even have been about breaking free from AIDS – which by the mid-1980s had become a global pandemic? Was it symbolic of Freddie being way ahead of his time (again), albeit imprisoned by the mores and expectations of a culture and a past to which he did not relate?

Abandonment to a life of rock'n'roll is so often an excuse. It at times appears to justify an existence of excess and reckless hedonism, the self-centred ridiculousness of which you are to be pitied for because, poor thing, you are only a *rock star* . . . 'Well, dear, what on earth do you expect, he's *one of those* . . .' The implication being that, were you not a rock star, you would be castigated and cast asunder for such scandalous behaviour. 'Typical rock star' is one of the best oxymorons ever coined. What rock star worth his NaCl was ever 'typical'? No two of the greatest among them have ever been alike.

Rock'n'roll is a law unto itself. Which is the point of it. It breaks its own rules: the music, the spectacle, the surrealism. In terms of the expression of extremes of imagination, innermost thoughts and darkest dreams, nothing comes close – to the point that we identify 'rock stars' in all kinds of other professions too. What was John McEnroe if not the Freddie Mercury of tennis? What was Formula 1 world champion Lewis Hamilton with all his pole positions and podium finishes? How about the wild men of football – Ronaldo, Maradona, Paul Gascoigne, Vinnie Jones, George Best? What was stirring in the synapses of architect Antoni Gaudí when he conceived La Sagrada Família, the still unfinished, eccentric Roman Catholic Basilica in Barcelona on which he toiled for forty-three years? Had Salvador Dalí been a musician, might he not have been a Freddie Mercury? Had Freddie grown up to be what he set out to be – an artist – might he not have been as preposterous and as strange as the Spanish surrealist? Dalí, who hosted anything-goes orgies, wore diamanté-studded socks he claimed were a gift from Elvis Presley. He created a cylindrical hologram of Vincent Furnier, aka glam rocker Alice Cooper. He was also inclined to proclaim the superiority of his own art form over that of Freddie and his ilk. The eye, postured the artist (infamous for having sliced open an eyeball in *Un Chien Andalou*, the 1929 silent film he made with Luis Buñuel) tends to triumph over the ear. The ephemerality of music was, in Dalí's withering view, but a poor relation to the majestic endurance of painting.

'And yet some of his works seem to celebrate music,' points out Dalí historian Paul Chimera. 'He himself was seen in at least one photograph appearing to be playing the piano. And Dalí was known to spontaneously break out in dance and song. I can confirm the latter, as, at one of my two meetings with him at the St Regis Hotel in New York, he suddenly began singing a song about the Virgin Mary!'[4]

☿

Which brings us back to Freddie's own Madonna. It was a catastrophe, it really was. At least for Miss Austin. His gasp-inducing bequest to her, a 'mere' former girlfriend, was in fact a blatant act of propitiation.

Young as she was, Freddie perceived in Mary even during the earliest days all the requisite qualities for her to serve as his rock. There's no suggestion that he coerced her, but he did make it difficult for her to walk away. Spinning the impossible dream of the one true, perfect love, he made her his for all time. From then on, whenever he felt his life of rock'n'roll excess spiralling out of control; whenever he felt unable to cope with the rigours of touring, recording and juggling his motorway pile-up of a love life, for which read 'sex life'; whenever he felt he needed to get a grip, he would simply reach for his Mary. Unquestioning, allowance-making, forgiving, she was the mother figure who knew him, and who accepted him warts and all.

'Mary Austin was Freddie's mum, in a way,' music publicist Bernard Doherty told me.

'She was there for him every moment of the day, putting her own life on hold to do so. Where he went, she went. She hardly ever left his side. No wonder he was devoted to her. She evidently filled that great hole that was left by what his parents should have been to him when he was small. Instead, they stuck him on a ship and sent him to school thousands of miles away. He was eight years old. Can you imagine? In his deepest psyche, he would never have resolved that. Then there was Mary. "Mother Mary comes to me," sang McCartney on "Let It Be" in 1970. Coincidentally, the year Freddie and Mary met. It could have been their theme tune, with its matriarchal Blessed Virgin Mary connotation. Mary was the Mary in that song. She was pure. Not even Freddie was sleeping with her in the end . . .'[5]

It wasn't long before they moved in together. Their first home was a tiny bedsit on Victoria Road, off Kensington High Street, a leisurely stroll from their places of work, which cost them ten pounds per week. They went up in the world two years later, to a proper self-contained flat at almost double the price. The downside was rising damp, but they put up with it. They had fun setting up home together and created a cosy nest. Visitors recalled Freddie receiving them in his dressing gown and slippers and pouring them endless cups of tea while they sat chatting and putting the world to rights.

'All my lovers asked me why they couldn't replace Mary, but it's simply impossible,' Freddie once said. 'The only friend I've got is Mary, and I don't want anybody else. To me, she was my common-law wife. To me, it was a marriage.

'We believe in each other. That's enough for me. I couldn't fall in love with a man the same way as I have with Mary.'

'I used to learn things about our relationship through interviews he did. Mainly for David Wigg at the *Express*,' said Mary in a television documentary. 'It took a long while for me to really fall in love with this man. But once there, I could never turn away from him. His pain became my pain. His joy became my joy.'

Wiggie himself was fond of describing them as 'brother and sister', though even he on occasion gave in to romantic spin. 'The only person he felt truly comfortable with was Mary,' he said. 'Who was, I think, the truest love of his life.'

☿

Rock'n'roll, fame, fortune, go anywhere, do anyone, world your lobster or no: had the love of my life turned out to be gay, bi or whatever variation on the theme, and craved a different lifestyle from what I was equipped or inclined to share, you wouldn't have seen me for dust. Why didn't Mary walk away and begin again elsewhere? Why, if Freddie felt so guilty at having 'misled' her that he decided to be morally and financially responsible for her welfare, didn't he grant her a generous settlement, buy her a house beyond the fringes of the capital or in some far-flung corner of anywhere else, and help her to make a fresh start? Surely, had she really been the love of his life, he would have loved her and left her and let her go. She was only twenty-five when their romantic relationship ended. I have never understood why she remained in his life and became another of his yes-people. She evolved into a kind of Mrs Danvers: an imperious and disapproving gatekeeper, staring down her nose at the frothy darlings who dawned and drifted, tightening her lips and rolling her eyes at Freddie's increasingly aberrant antics, putting up with all who flitted through his life ... I'll say it again, *why*? Was she hoping against hope for the time when Freddie would have had his fill and called time on the madness? Did she dream of getting him back when he was done with 'all that', and of having him all to herself? Did she long for the corner-turning, after which they could settle down and grow old together as man and wife at Garden Lodge, the house she had found and helped fashion into the perfect home for him, only to see it hijacked and taken for granted by Freddie's louche band of boys? Forget the lack of sex (who even cares, by then?) Was she playing the long game, confident of ultimate triumph?

I'll tell you what she hadn't banked on: the chance that Freddie might meet another woman, whose claim on his heart would be more than a match for hers. Nor had she expected that Freddie might find his way to a significant man – *men*, even – whose hold on her only beloved would prove too muscular to escape. She can't have allowed herself to fear the worst: that Freddie's reckless, death-defying lifestyle would cause him to succumb eventually to HIV; that she would never again get her one true love to herself; and that she would be forced to share the blessing of his death with those with inferior claims on him. 'Old Faithful', so she was. Since he died, she has gone up in the world. Meet 'Freddie Mercury's widow.'

A video clip on YouTube features Freddie and Mary on a riverside terrace in Budapest in July 1986, on what turned out to be

Queen's final tour. In a fetching fluorescent yellow tracksuit against a backdrop of twinkling lights over the dark Danube, Freddie stands between red-T-shirted Mary and an unnamed Hungarian as he attempts to commit to memory the words of folk song *Tavaszi Szél Vizet Áraszt* ('The Spring Wind Makes Waters Flood'), that he planned to sing at Queen's historic gig there. More haunting hymn than folk number, the peasant ditty is the first song learned by Hungarian children in kindergarten and is held dear throughout life. Freddie knows instinctively how significant a moment in the show this is going to be. He is determined to get it right. As he twists his tongue around the unfamiliar lyrics and gargles the awkward syllables to fit the tune, he glances frequently at Mary for approval. She gazes back at him in silent adoration. The moment, captured for posterity, says everything about their relationship. Elsewhere in the clip, Mary is seen following Freddie about in an art shop, making notes in a spiral-bound reporters' notebook, taking down details of pictures and *objets* that he selects for purchase.

I think of her back in the eighties, at most of the Queen gigs I attended. I remember her in a pair of daffodil rock-chick leggings – was the colour yellow significant between them? – and stilt-like heels, coming on like a rocker's moll; berating some interloper (as I saw her do) with the haughty brush-off 'I am Freddie Mercury's girlfriend.' She kept her distance from Her Britannic Majesty's press corps, dismissing us with 'I'm not a celebrity, I don't give interviews.' She would give a fair few after Freddie's death, almost all of them to David Wigg. She felt safe with him, because Freddie had. In the meantime, she rose to the role of imperatrix over the king of Queen's empire, and was matriarch to his second family: a largely homosexual entourage of friends, most of whom were on Freddie's payroll. The inner circle were also resident at Garden Lodge: Peter 'Phoebe' Freestone, Freddie's Guy Friday and right-hand man; Joe 'Liza' Fanelli, Freddie's former lover turned personal chef; and Jim Hutton, the barber from County Carlow, Ireland, who first met Freddie at the Copacabana gay club and who became his live-in lover and gardener. More of whom soon.

Mary may not have lived in the house during Freddie's lifetime, but she certainly ran the show. The boys blew hot and cold about her, failing to understand her place in their Freddie's heart. She had tried but failed to get him to commit to her in other ways, even suggesting at one point that they have a child together. Freddie's retort was predictable, that he would rather have another cat. He did adore his moggies. She would resign herself to relationships with other men, none of which succeeded in the long term. In 1981 she met songwriter and musician Jo Burt, who had played with the Troggs, Tom Robinson, Black Sabbath, Bob Geldof, Sweet and more. He was soon installed at the Kensington apartment bought for Mary by Freddie. Through her, Jo got to know him. Freddie flew them both to New York for his thirty-fifth birthday celebrations – that legendary party planned to span a weekend but which dragged out over three drunken and debauched weeks. Burt went on to play fretless bass guitar on three tracks intended for Freddie's 1985 solo album *Mr. Bad Guy*, recorded at Musicland in Munich. One of them made the cut.

'For five years we were in each other's pockets,' said Burt of Freddie in November 2018. 'We regularly had Sunday lunch together. His were slightly more crazy as it was post-Saturday night clubbing and there would often be all kinds of people, remnants from the previous night's partying, round at his place. Musically, we had a huge amount in common, but he was a lot richer than I was! He would play rough mixes after being in the studio and would ask what I thought.'

Freddie moved around quite quietly, said Burt: 'There was no big entourage or tipped-off paparazzi. He had a chauffeur who was also a bodyguard, and they pretty much went everywhere together. He was never really stopped in the street, although he never really went out much during the day, he was a night-time person. If he were to shop, he would often do it privately. On one occasion I was

The Mercury Space Program,
Zanzibar: the inspiration
for Freddie's cosmic new name?

'32 Londoners on the London Eye'
… a revolving initiative celebrating
luminaries from elsewhere who made
their name and consolidated their
fame in England's capital city.

They met over Noddy's Nipples in
Kensington Market … Val Finn,
née Valerie Doyle, Freddie's closest
friend 1970-'71.

Chhatrapati Shivaji Maharaj Terminus,
Mumbai's magnificent railway
station from which Freddie made his
long train journeys to school.

Jimi Hendrix, Freddie's greatest
creative inspiration.

Freddie's bandmates Roger Taylor
and Brian May, at Brian's alma
mater Imperial College London,
5th March 2013, unveiling a PRS
plaque commemorating their
first-ever gig as Queen.

'Venus in Furs' ... Freddie had eyes only for his
Mary (until biology got the better of him).

She got her teeth fixed. He never did. Always his 'Old Faithful',
Mary Austin was never his bride.

Freddie's loyal barber boyfriend Jim Hutton, right, reminiscing
with his old Garden Lodge housemate Peter Freestone at the author's
book launch, the Groucho Club, London, 1997.

War Baby: beautiful Barbara Valentin
in her teens.

Starlet with looks to melt Elvis:
Barbara on the threshold of
her movie career.

Busenwunder ('Busty Babe'):
La Valentin in her heyday.

Freddie and Barbara, the old married
couple of Munich.

Even the stars have their stars. For Freddie, there was none but Montserrat Caballé.

'Barcelona', his duet with 'Montsy', was Freddie's proudest achievement.

David Wigg, celebrated showbiz journalist and Freddie's trusted friend.

Freddie's friends Peter Straker and Paul Gambaccini at the Savoy Hotel's Mercury Phoenix Trust fundraiser, in honour of what would have been Freddie's 65th birthday, September 2011.

The earliest loves of Freddie's life: Freddie's sister Kashmira and his mother Jer with the author, the Savoy Hotel, London, September 2011.

Reunion: the author with Queen's favourite lensman Richard Young and Peter Freestone, Shezan, Knightsbridge, June 2019.

Reunion 2: Peter Freestone and the author, London.

Her again, with Sir Timothy
Miles Bindon Rice and Brian Harold
May CBE, Chichester, Sussex,
March 2013.

'We Will Rock You', the stage
musical that rocked the world.
Dominion Theatre, London.

The door to Garden Lodge,
Freddie's Kensington home, as it
used to look each year on his
Anniversary. With grateful thanks to
Debbie and Trevor Jones.

'Just throw me in the lake
when I'm gone ...' Freddie's statue,
Montreux, Switzerland.

'I'm just a singer with a song …' ('In My Defence', 1986)

with him when diamond merchants flew in to see him at the hotel where we were staying.'

Jo-and-Mary's Cristal went flat. Their demise spelled the end of both Jo's friendship with Freddie and their musical collaboration. Mary moved on to painter and interior designer Piers Cameron, which must have felt more like it, as together they started a family. Freddie was chuffed to accept the role of godfather to their first-born, Richard, and doted on the little boy. Their second son, Jamie, was born soon after Freddie died. When her thing with Cameron collapsed, Mary explained that it was doomed to failure because her new partner had always felt overshadowed by the love of her life. 'Freddie had widened the tapestry of my life so much,' she said. 'There was no way I'd want to desert him ever.'[8]

She married businessman Nicholas Holford on Long Island in 1998, seven years after Freddie died, with only her sons as witnesses.

'I think Nick was very brave to take me on, really,' she told Wiggie. 'I come with a lot of baggage, a huge chapter in my life. At first because of the past and the broken affairs, I wasn't entirely sure about marriage. Then someone said, "You don't know until you try." But as life unfolds, I can now be happy with him. I can appreciate what I had and what I now have, and move on. I was getting there, but I think I could only have moved on by meeting somebody.'

'When I met Nick everything came around a lot quicker. I wanted some stability for myself and the children. I felt that this man could give us that – stability in a loving family way. I'd lost my family really when Freddie died.'

As Mr and Mrs Holford, they managed five years.

☿

I have sometimes imagined Mary drifting around the wooden minstrels' gallery at Garden Lodge. Tiptoeing down the wide, sweeping staircase and across the polished parquet as if she doesn't own the place. An uneasy ghost, she picks her way among the Dalís, the pre-Raphaelites and the Victorians in their gilded frames, the antique *meubles*, the silver *objets*, the Tiffany lamp, the Lalique vases and Japanese porcelain. She pauses at the door of the elegant dining room, eyes glinting at the memory of flames in the cold candelabra, where Freddie would host grand Christmas dinners past. She treads, silent and shoeless, over the black and white tiles of the kitchen floor, tapping lacquered nails against the oxblood cabinets. Echoes of aching laughter bulge the walls. She strains to hear. She glides through silk kimonos, glances around for the costume worn by Montserrat in a production of Donizetti's opera *Lucrezia Borgia*, remembers that it was returned to Montsy after Freddie died. Her mouth flickers, a Mona Lisa moment. Moving past the clutch of platinum and gold discs on the landing, she inclines her head around the door of the master bedroom suite with its rainbow-lit ceiling. Freddie's bedside treasures, even the bottles of Eau Dynamisante and his favourite Roger & Gallet soaps in the bathroom, some used, some still boxed, have lain untouched for years. Thick seams of dust have settled over his things like city snowfall. In death, at last, he belonged to her.

☿

Freddie left each of the three men of his household £500,000 with which to buy their own home. This was a considerable amount in 1991. In order for the legal process of probate to be completed, those still living in the property were required to vacate it. They had to leave within weeks. There were no fond farewells. They felt that there would never be a reunion, nor any welcome return – and time proved them right. Both Peter Freestone and Jim Hutton would fret that they had trunks and boxes crammed with their own personal possessions stored in the loft at Garden Lodge, which they feared they would never be allowed to collect. Sure enough, they never saw them again. They are most likely still there.

148

'I lost somebody who I thought was my eternal love,' Mary told David Wigg in 2000. 'When he died I felt we'd had a marriage. We'd lived our vows. We'd done it for better for worse, for richer for poorer. In sickness and in health. You could never have let go of Freddie unless he died. Even then it was difficult.'

How does Mary feel today, at seventy? Was her love for Freddie and the life he gave her worth it? Were it possible to rewind, what would she change?

'I lost my family, really, when Freddie died,' she said, expressing sentiments she had voiced before. 'He was everything to me, apart from my sons. He was like no one I have met before.'

Love of his life? He thought she was. *She* thought she was. There was more and less to it.

CHAPTER ELEVEN

JIM

'I sometimes wonder whether I ever did know the real Freddie Mercury,' Jim Hutton admitted in 1996.

I had married earlier that year. My former husband and I were spending part of our extended honeymoon at Delphi, a picturesque lodge and salmon fishery near Leenane in County Galway. When I drove the hundred-and-sixty-odd miles south-east across Ireland to visit Jim at home in Bennekerry, County Carlow, we hadn't seen each other for nine years. The man whom Jim had called his 'lover', his 'boyfriend', his 'husband', his 'best friend' and 'the most extraordinary thing that ever happened to me', and for whom he'd relinquished his own life, had been dead for half a decade. It was nearly as long as Freddie and Jim had been together. For Jim, the process of coming to terms with the cataclysmic effect of his loss was only just beginning. 'It has taken me quite a while to gather my strength and face up to it,' he said. 'I haven't been ready to accept Freddie's passing. I've been clinging to his memory and not letting him be dead, if I'm honest. It was making me odd. Even though I'd lost everything – my partner, my home, my income, my lifestyle, my friends, my future – and although I'd watched Freddie slipping away right in front of me, so I knew better than anyone that there was no hope for him, a part of me was hanging on to the idea that it could all be just a bad dream. I wanted so much to wake up and find him lying there next to me that I started to let the fantasy become my reality.'

There prevail some distorted and mistaken views about Jim's six-year relationship with Freddie. *Bohemian Rhapsody* the film is partly to blame, for having portrayed him as a plain-speaking waiter who spurns Freddie's advances at one of his extravagant parties in 1985. Freddie is then shown tracking Jim down to his modest home, after which he whisks him off to Wembley Stadium to witness Queen's Live Aid performance, calling on Freddie's parents en route to introduce his 'new man' to Mum and Dad. Mr and Mrs Bulsara, true to form, behave in a kindly, welcoming manner. The clear message is one of happiness and relief that their beloved son has found somebody to love, albeit another man. Their approving nods and smiles indicate acceptance of Freddie's admission to them that he is gay.

None of which happened.

Because Freddie never came out. He steadfastly refused to confirm or deny who he was for the sake of privacy and dignity, both his family's and his own. He was outed posthumously. He was declared a gay icon only after his death.

The other problem was Jim's own 1994 memoir, *Mercury and Me*, ghostwritten by respected Fleet Street journalist Tim Wapshott. In fairness to Tim, he stands up to be counted and puts his name on the line. Literally, on the book's front cover. We can therefore be in no doubt that Jim did not write the book himself. What I knew already from some of its content – before I set off from Delphi to see him that first time, and before our encounters developed into the friendship that brought him to London to attend my own book launch – was that Jim's memoir stopped short of the whole truth. For example, there is nothing in it about his own background. Yes, the ungrammatical title is *Mercury and Me*, so we know before we start that its subject matter is confined to a specific period of time and is by no means broad. But there should at least be something of Jim's childhood and earlier life, to set the story in context. I mentioned this to him when we talked, but he was reluctant to be drawn. 'We'll leave my family out of it,' he said. 'This has nothing to do with them.' Only years later did it occur to me that he didn't want to draw attention to them and was protecting their identity for the same reasons as Freddie had protected his own family. During a time and in a culture in which all forms of nonmarital sex were regarded as heinous; when access to contraception was restricted, politicised, and contrary to Catholic doctrine; and while 'homosexual acts' remained criminal offences, it was grossly shaming to an Irish Catholic family to have a son who was gay. Same-sex sexual activity would not be decriminalised in the state until 1993, more than a quarter of a century after England. As 'the only gay in the village' back home, Jim's future had looked bleak. He had even submitted to vocational training in the church at one point, an episode that echoed the experiences of Irish actor Gabriel Byrne, revealed with terrible eloquence in his 2020 memoir *Walking with Ghosts*. The juxtaposition of Jim's early life and his contrasting years as a rocker's partner would have made unputdownable reading. But there is none of that. He shares nothing about how he felt as he came to terms with his orientation. We are left to assume that he withdrew to London to live and work, where he could explore his sexuality openly and legally. On page one, we are in London, in 1983. Jim is thirty-four years old, and about to meet Freddie. He never takes us home with him. The most we get of his other personal life is in 1988, when 'I returned to Ireland for a fortnight to see my family. While I was away, Freddie got bored and flew to Munich for a few days with Phoebe and Peter Straker.'

Having gleaned elsewhere that he had been born Séamus Hutton, 'Séamus' being the Irish equivalent of James, I applied to the Civil Registration Service in Dublin for a copy of his birth certificate to confirm this. But it wasn't the case. Seven days after he was born, Jim was registered as 'James' in the district of Carlow. Not only that, but he hadn't, as he'd told me, been born in Carlow Town. The certificate states that his mother Annie and 'vanman' father Thomas welcomed him at their home in Palatine. He wouldn't have been the only gay in the village. In a tiny hamlet like that, he would have stood out like a sore thumb.

I hope he knew a little of the fascinating history of the place of his birth. Three miles or so from Carlow and less from Bennekerry where Jim would eventually settle, Palatine derived its name from a colony of German refugees who were driven from their native country during the reign of France's King Louis XIV. Seven thousand Protestant Lutherans from the Lower Palatinate on the middle Rhine (south-west Germany, four hours or so north-west of Munich) were rescued by ships sent by Queen Anne. Some of them stayed in England, some sailed on to North America, and the rest went to Ireland. Most of the Palatine families settled in County Limerick; others in Kerry, Tipperary and Wexford. Twenty families landed in County Carlow in about 1711. Their settlement was known as Palantinestown. These hardworking people were mostly farmers, carpenters, blacksmiths, bakers, masons and shoemakers. From Ireland, they emigrated to other parts of the English-speaking world, including Canada, Australia and New Zealand. The only signs that they were ever in the vicinity are some sweet old stone cottages and the name of the hamlet where Jim was born.

Few could have predicted Ireland's volte face vis-à-vis its attitudes towards LGBT rights. From having been the least accepting and the most resistant, the country became the most liberal within a generation. It was one of the first to legalise same-sex marriage, in May 2015. Two years later, the state appointed openly gay Leo Varadkar as its head of government (Taoiseach).

☿

Jim's book is also nebulous about what exactly happened on the day Freddie died. He gives a precise, detailed account of having carried Freddie to the toilet at around 6 a.m., after which he took him back to bed and heard a sound 'like one of Freddie's bones breaking'. Freddie 'screamed out in pain,' Jim said, 'and went into a convulsion.' Did this happen? No one else in Freddie's close support group reported it. Jim then recounts how he called out to Freddie's chef Joe, who was elsewhere in the house. Joe, acknowledges Jim, was excellent at handling Freddie during his anxiety attacks. They calmed him down together until he fell asleep, then phoned Gordon Atkinson, Freddie's GP. The doctor arrived to administer morphine. Heavily pregnant Mary Austin visited mid-morning, Jim says. Elton John turned up to see his friend that afternoon, at which point Jim took himself off to Holland Park for a break and a change of air. He returned to find Freddie's close friend Dave Clark sitting beside the bed, massaging Freddie's hand. Freddie seemed to have slipped into semi-consciousness. Dr Atkinson left, early that evening. Jim handed Freddie his cat Delilah to stroke, and Freddie indicated that he needed the bathroom again. Jim ran downstairs to fetch Peter Freestone, to help him carry Freddie to the toilet. Alas, they were too late. Dave, said Jim, appeared not to have noticed that Freddie had urinated. He and Phoebe began stripping the bedclothes, and asked Dave to step out of the room for a minute so that they could change Freddie into fresh T-shirt and boxers. Jim remembers feeling Freddie trying to lift his left leg. 'It was,' said Jim, 'the last thing he did.

'I slipped my arm under Freddie's neck, kissed him and then held him. His eyes were still open. I can remember very clearly the expression on his face – and when I go to sleep every night it's still there in front of me. He looked radiant. One minute he was a boy with a gaunt, sad little face, and the next he was a picture of ecstasy.'

Had time confused his memory a little? A quarter of a century later, the former leader and drummer of the Dave Clark Five granted an interview to the *Daily Express* in which he revealed that he was the only one in the room when Freddie let go, and therefore that *he* was the last person to see him alive.

Peter Freestone, in his 1998 intimate memoir, shares a variation on Jim's version of events.

'As Joe escorted Dr Atkinson through the garden and thence out into the Mews, Dave Clark came downstairs and asked Jim and I to go upstairs to help Freddie to the lavatory. We were pleased and surprised that Freddie had been able to ask to be relieved,' said Peter. 'While Freddie was clinically bed-bound, he was proud to the end that as far as he was concerned, he wasn't.

'When we got to his bedside and started to move him, we found that nature had taken its course. In the process of making him comfortable again, both Jim and I noticed that he wasn't breathing.'

The time was about 6.45 p.m., recalled Peter. His kneejerk reaction was to have someone chase after the recently departed doctor. 'Although Joe's running out into Logan Mews alerted the press to something going on, Joe managed to stop Gordon and brought him back inside. Gordon immediately came up to Freddie's bedroom where he pronounced Freddie dead and certified the time as being twelve minutes to seven.'

At Rutland Terrace, Bennekerry, the comfortable home that Freddie's money had bought, Jim and I ate homemade vegetable soup and white bread rolls together at his kitchen table. We later strolled in the garden at dusk, admiring his unusual lavender-coloured 'Blue Moon' hybrid tea roses with their large, fragrant heads. Freddie apparently adored this special variety. Jim had planted and cultivated these himself, in memory of his late partner. It was as we stood inhaling their scent that Jim revisited the moment of Freddie's passing.

'I wasn't there,' he said frankly, shaking his head. 'The fact is, I *wanted* to be there. Maybe I felt I needed to validate myself, my importance in Freddie's life, by being with him at the exact moment he crossed over. Because I wasn't far away. I was in the house, but not in the room. It seemed symbolic, and was perhaps another example of me needing him more than him needing me. Maybe I did force my needs onto him. The wedding rings and so on, the calling each other "husband", all the "I love yous". Freddie was the first to say it, if you want to know, and of course I leapt at that and grabbed it, because it was all I wanted. To be his one and only, you know. It took me a long time to work out that whenever Freddie said, "I love you", he wasn't telling you, he was *asking* you. He was needy of love and affection for himself, not expressing to me that I meant the world to him and that he couldn't imagine his life without me.

'I did behave like a spoilt eejit sometimes, I don't mind telling you. Because I think I had worked out deep down that what we were was a bit of an act, as far as Freddie was concerned. People used to make bitchy remarks. They went over my head, most of the time. I'm a simple man, I've never pretended to be anything else. I've always been open. I was the one destined for a life in the church. I trained to join an order of brothers, but had to quit after my head was turned by one of my teachers. When someone called Freddie and me a "masquerade", I didn't even know how to spell it or what it meant. I had to look it up. I managed to find a dictionary in the house. Freddie wasn't really a book person, I barely saw him read anything apart from catalogues from auction houses or Tiffany and Cartier and those places, looking at things he wanted to buy. But yes, I looked up "masquerade", and I was very hurt. Even though I have to face the fact now that they were probably right.

'Freddie might have been kidding himself when he called me "my man", you know? Or making fun of me. I always felt he did it in a jokey way, quite camp, which he was, and which caused more than a few rucks between us. He was always joking around with his friend Peter Straker, and I know that quite a lot of it was at my expense. Freddie was always quick to row, like he enjoyed it. He had to win, too. Every time. I never did get used to his mood swings, and it did get me down at times.

'So only Dave Clark was in Freddie's bedroom when he actually died. I can admit that now. I can admit it to myself. I bigged myself up. You have to ask why. After Freddie died, I was no one. I didn't matter to any of them. It's probably the reason why I did the book in the end, to establish myself officially as having been his partner, and the part that I played. But it was only that. A *part*. I was like one of Freddie Mercury's chorus line. However hard I tried to kid myself, I was not the love of his life.'

If Freddie's relationship with Mary was a fantasy, what he had with Jim was an illusion.

'I was only one aspect of what he needed in life,' Jim said. 'I know now that no single individual could have met all his needs. There were so many of us. Mary, Phoebe, Joe, Peter Straker, Barbara Valentin, Dave Clark, Elton John and the rest. Every one of us brought something to Freddie's life that he depended on. We *all* fulfilled his needs. We were like his court jesters, as I heard people say more than once. I resented it. I resented *them*. I get it now. I need to admit to it, now, to be able to move on and have a life of my own.'

What did Jim think might have happened had Freddie not contracted AIDS, and had he lived out his natural life span? Would their relationship have lasted? Would they have grown old together?

'I doubt it,' admitted Jim, sadly. 'I was there for a purpose. The sexual relationship we had, which I knew full well had not been exclusive, had pretty much run its course by the time Freddie became ill. I cast myself as someone important in his life, when really I was only the same as everybody else. All of us who lived at Garden Lodge – Phoebe the personal assistant, Joe the cook, me the gardener and the handyman and the fella who looked after the fish, as well as the others who came in each day, Terry the driver and Mary the . . . ' he hesitates . . . 'whatever you want to call her . . . were equally important to him. I was no more special than they were. I think, deep down, that I knew this at the time. I must have done, because whenever his family came round, for a Sunday dinner or a tea or something, I was obliged to leave the house, go to my shed and be just "the gardener", "the pond guy". If I'd been Freddie's true life partner, he would have been proud of me. He would have introduced me and shown me off. He would never have done that to me. I would never have done that to him, that's for sure. He had no idea how much it hurt me, being treated like that.

'I didn't *want* to know that was all I was, because of the way it made me look: a fool.'

Why didn't Jim stand up to Freddie, assert his own dignity and rights, and insist on being introduced to Freddie's parents, sister, brother-in-law and their children as Freddie's other half?

'Because he would have gone berserk,' Jim said quietly. 'He would have exploded, and that would've been it. I'd have been out of Garden Lodge like a one-way boomerang, no way back. I was living with him in *his* house, on *his* money, on *his* terms, to *his* time-table. In the end, I was even on his payroll. A hired hand. It was *all* about him, I don't kid myself. He would not have stood for that kind of demand from me. I was afraid he would overreact, and kick me out. I loved him. He was the one for me. I didn't want it to end.'

Jim thinks back to the final months of 1991, when Freddie had resigned himself to his fate.

'He had no fight left in him by then. I suppose if he'd still been healthy, still able to run around lording it and having the lifestyle he loved, I don't doubt that I'd have been paid something and sent off. That was Freddie's way. I have to accept that. I do find myself wishing now that I'd done my book with someone who had known Freddie personally, and who had understood his ways. No disrespect to the author. The book we did is the book we did. I wasn't always able to express what I wanted to say in my own words. I'm a simple man, as I told you. I don't understand publishers, publicity people, journalists. All these types have expectations. I had to bring out a version of myself, which is what you read in the book. I'm not denying the book. I told my story. It's just that the Freddie and Jim you read about there is not the whole story.'

Jim first met Freddie in 1983 at the Copacabana in Earls Court. Popular among members of the emerging clone scene, 'the Copa' was London's first public nightclub for the gay community. It was situated a short stroll across the Cromwell Road and from Logan

Place, a significant factor for Freddie when trying to decide where to buy a house. The venue later became Club 180, and subsequently a branch of Wagamama. The Copa had an upstairs bar on three levels with an extensive garden, called Harpoon Louis, later known as Harpos and then as Banana Max. Nearby on Old Brompton Road was the Coleherne pub, a notorious leather bar during the 1970s and another favourite haunt of Freddie's. Its regular crowd included film director Derek Jarman, actors Ian McKellen and Rupert Everett, DJ Kenny Everett and ballet dancer Rudolph Nureyev. The homosexual handkerchief code was common practise among its clientele, giving rise to the venue's nickname, the 'Cloneherne'. Next to the pub, they danced in a basement club widely known as 'the best disco in town', the Catacombs.

Jim was seeing someone else at the time of that initial Copa encounter. He refused Freddie's invitation to a drink. They stumbled across each other again two years later, at Heaven nightclub underneath the arches at Charing Cross station. Freddie was out on the prowl with partners in crime Peter Straker and Joe Fanelli. Jim, who was at the time employed as a £70-a-week barber at the Savoy Hotel along the Strand, and had digs an hour away in Sutton, Surrey, later found himself back at Freddie's 12 Stafford Terrace, Kensington flat. Where Freddie wasted no time in getting the cocaine out. Jim wasn't into it, and declined.

'Cocaine, the rock star's ruin,' muses manager Simon Napier-Bell. 'Like heroin, it kills, but it does so by stealth. It doesn't just eat into their flesh, it consumes an artist's creativity while silently guzzling his money. Cocaine and sex is the lethal combination, but it's the one they all fall for. Put those two things together and anything goes.' Which was clearly what Freddie had in mind.

He and Jim fell into bed, but were too wasted to rise to the occasion. Jim recalled that they settled for a kiss and a cuddle, and that he took his leave at around noon the next day. Although they exchanged telephone numbers, he did not expect to hear from Freddie again. Nor did he . . . until several months later.

Unbeknown to Jim, Freddie was, at that time, living as a tax exile in Munich. Having followed the likes of John Barry, Tom Jones, David Bowie, Rod Stewart and Pink Floyd out of the country into off-shore enclaves, Queen had now decided to spend most of their time away from home to avoid the crippling tax rates on top earners then in place. Freddie would return to London sporadically for work engagements and the odd weekend. Jim was none the wiser about Freddie's complicated personal life. He assumed that he, like himself, was footloose and fancy-free. Freddie did not divulge that he was embroiled in two intense relationships back in Germany, one with a man, the other with a woman. The first was bluff restauranteur Winnie Kirchberger. The second was Austrian film star Barbara Valentin.

Jim had written off his Mercurial experience and put it behind him when Freddie called out of the blue and invited him to a dinner party at his flat. When Jim arrived, he was dismayed to find his host buzzing on coke again, and up for anything. Another excursion to Heaven ensued, the guests departing en masse. They included Peter Freestone and former John Reid sidekick turned Freddie's personal manager Paul Prenter, whom Jim had disliked at first glare. Jim and Freddie picked up where they had paused.

Since the pair had last seen each other, Freddie and Queen had completed sensational sell-out tours of Australia, New Zealand and Japan. They had been down to Brazil to headline the huge Rock in Rio festival, and Freddie had recorded and released his first solo album *Mr. Bad Guy*. Jim, in marked and almost embarrassing contrast, had sheared a few heads of hair and got plastered in a handful of seedy clubs. If he feared that he would never live up to the larger-than-life rock star with the world at his feet, he was not wrong. What in God's name did Freddie see in him, they all wanted to know: a below-average Joe with a run-of-the-mill job and an unremarkable lifestyle? It occurred to Jim at that point that Freddie had asked him barely anything about himself, his family, his own life. He would be taken aback to learn that Freddie found him attractive because he was the dead spit of one of his favourite screen idols, the *Gunsmoke* TV actor and *Deliverance* star Burt Reynolds. All too soon, to his immense and mounting bafflement, Jim started to receive calls directing him to ticket desks at Heathrow airport, whence he would fly into the arms of his world-famous beau for bizarre weekends in the capital of Bavaria.

☿

If Jim Hutton fell in love, it was with the whole package. Not merely the man, but mostly the mythology. The music, the reputation, the wealth, the luxurious lifestyle. What was not to like? A fair amount, according to Jim, who was not what you could call fazed by stardom, having trimmed many a rock lock in his time. Even Bowie's blond bits. Mild-mannered and undemonstrative, sexually reserved, reluctant to draw attention to himself – which was surprising, given that Jim had grown up the seventh of ten kids in a council house, and had known from toddlerhood to speak up or be ignored – he found himself shaken by Freddie's mood swings, his voracious sex drive, his outrageous flirting with other men when they were out, his tendency to engineer spectacular fall-outs and break-ups so that he could control the make-ups, his manipulative habits and childish insistence on always getting his own way. It was that child in Freddie who succeeded in melting him. Jim's eyes flared as he remembered the Freddie he adored. 'The baby browns, the slight but muscular body, his sensitivity, his enthusiasm, his deep insecurity. I was hooked,' Jim said. 'He had me. I was crushed when I discovered that Freddie only wanted me out in Munich to make this other guy jealous. A German called Winnie Kirchberger, who had a restaurant, and who was almost identical to me.'

Barbara Valentin, Freddie's female companion in Munich, spoke of Jim as Freddie's 'puppet on a string':

'Freddie treated him badly,' she said. 'He'd bring him over from London, then send him home again, sometimes all in one day. I heard many sad stories during that time. Jim would cry very often. I'd say to him, "Just resist. Say no for once. Don't let yourself be used."'

"Yes, but I love him," Jim would say. For that, he was shoved around like a monkey. He'd do anything Freddie said. It was always on Freddie's terms, and Jim came running, every time. Freddie was often mean.'

Given that they were all aware of his propensity to use and abuse others, why did Freddie's lovers keep crawling back for more? What was the hold that he had over Jim? Again, Jim loved the idea of Freddie more than the reality. He had, he admitted, become mesmerised and blinded by Freddie's limelight.

Psychologists call it 'BIRGing': 'basking in reflected glory'. The term describes a tendency to pursue and develop one's connection to highly successful and desirable individuals. Recognised in modern social psychology as one of the most significant motivational drives, it is generated by a need to be regarded in a favourable light by other people. This in turn increases one's self-esteem. Impressive associations – 'friends in high places' – can make a person 'look good'. Just as some people get a kick out of sharing a hometown with a random celebrity, having kids at the same school as someone well-known, when one of their children excels at their exams/in a music performance/out on the playing field or when 'their team' carries home the cup, certain individuals appear to develop a taste for the glow to be derived from an association with success, however tenuous. Even when the achievement in question had nothing to do with them.

'That was me,' Jim admitted. 'It made me feel like *I* was someone, being around Freddie. I was no one going nowhere. I had no prospects. I was in a dead-end job without opportunities to make anything more of myself, you know. Before I met Freddie, I'd never even been to a gig. I go from that sad state of affairs to the first rock concert I ever go to being Live Aid, where the audience was the whole bloody world.'

It did go to his head. Jim's expectations would come to exceed what Freddie was able to offer. He grew hostile towards Mary because she, not he, was paraded about on Freddie's arm from star-studded opening to first night to gala performance as his official partner.

'Jim wanted something more conventional than Freddie was able to offer,' said Peter Freestone. 'We all had our place, and we all knew our place. If you were going to be part of Freddie's life, you had to go into it on his terms. There was compromise eventually, and their relationship deepened during Freddie's final years.'

The mad Munich years were make or break. When the tax exile episode concluded and Freddie's new home Garden Lodge was ready to move into, he had decisions to make. Others were about to be made for him. His beleaguered affair with Winnie Kirchberger having come to a crashing end, Freddie was now juggling two lovers against the reliable backdrop of Old Faithful Mary. Having purchased an apartment with Barbara, Miss Valentin's clear expectation was that she and Freddie would consolidate their relationship and live together between Munich and London. But Freddie had become aware that he was living on borrowed time. It was with Jim, not Barbara, that he moved into Garden Lodge.

'We'd had the best years, the wildest times, and experiences I'd never imagined I'd ever have,' said Jim. 'Looking back, when it was time for him to return from Munich and re-establish his life in London, Freddie must have known he was on the brink, in terms of his health. He didn't say anything, until the time came when he had no choice but to say everything.

'Whatever it was that he had with Barbara, I honestly didn't understand. Then again, there was so much about Freddie that I didn't understand. I stayed with him because I loved him. It's the truth. You hope that somehow things will work out all right, even though deep down you know they're never going to. In the end, you learn that the only thing for it is to live for today. It's what we did. In our own way, for the time that we had, we were happy.'

☿

Jim's problem was that he was neither one thing nor the other. Far from Freddie's equal in terms of talent, experience, worldliness, potential or wealth, he wasn't the cliché gold-digging moneygrabber, either. It's ironic that certain people would have found someone of that nature more acceptable. At least they would have known where they stood. Such crafty, colourless, carnivorous types are ten a penny in the rock business. Wherever you look, Jim was not that. During the early stages of their romance, Jim's pride would not allow him to be paid-for. He would leave himself desperately short of cash for the week just to buy Freddie a double vodka and tonic in a bar. When he gave in to Freddie's demands and relocated to Garden Lodge, he insisted on contributing £50 a week for his keep. It was more than half his weekly wage. The sum would not have covered the cost of a quarter-bottle of Freddie's favourite Louis Roederer Cristal champagne. Instead of seizing the opportunity to become a kept man, he continued to get up, get dressed and go to work as a barber at the Savoy, until such time as Freddie deemed the arrangement impractical. After that, Jim was talked into becoming the gardener with special responsibility for Freddie's valuable koi carp, for which he would receive a salary. Jim's first Christmas present to Freddie, a leather jacket for which he paid in instalments but which Freddie didn't like and barely wore, was eclipsed by the Cartier lighter that Freddie gifted him, along with a casual thousand-pound cheque . . . the same sum that all the staff received. Jim could see where this was going.

Just as he could when Freddie bumped and grinded with racy young specimens during nights out clubbing, which would send Jim into paroxysms of jealous rage. Such scenarios gave Freddie exactly what he wanted: an opportunity to woo back his lover, proving to himself time and again that it was he who called the shots and that he could reel Jim in whenever he wanted. This was obviously abusive behaviour, and Freddie was clearly on a power trip. Jim, the abusee, enabled their toxic relationship by refusing to walk away from it.

'I tried to leave him, so many times,' he insisted. 'He would always make it impossible for me to go. I was afraid to walk, anyway. To have quit would have made me look like a failure. Something in me couldn't face people knowing that it hadn't worked out. They would have pointed the finger at me, and would have said that I wasn't enough for him. I suppose I must have known that he was treating me badly. I shouldn't have let him, but I was powerless to resist.'

Freddie treated Jim as he did because Jim's passivity allowed him to. That didn't make Jim to blame. Nor did it absolve Freddie of guilt. I have wondered, did Freddie deliberately choose less powerful, pushover partners because it meant that he could always have the upper hand? Was he aware that it was because he was 'who he was' that they would always come running, yes, sir, no sir, and forgive him the latest misdemeanour or outrage as soon as he expressed remorse and promised to change his ways ... which he never did? It was Freddie's personality, not Jim's, that set the pace and dictated the progress of their relationship. No matter how often Jim justified the situation to himself, he knew it was a mess.

'There were so many reasons to stay with him,' Jim told me. 'I did feel this deep uneasiness that I could never get to the bottom of. What I wanted with Freddie, I know now, didn't exist. It could not exist. It was a fairy tale. Someone explained to me years later that an abusive partner has to want to change. By staying with him, I gave Freddie permission to abuse me. He had no reason to change because I stuck around. He played on my terrible weakness for him. He knew that he could always get me back.'

In the end, Freddie's illness turned the tables. Jim would be there for him until he drew his final breath. There came the point beyond which Freddie could no longer deny his illness. Could he have forged this relationship with a man he trusted never to desert him in order to guarantee himself a loyal partner to cling to during his final, hopeless days?

'He had Phoebe, he had Joe, he had Mary, all of us,' repeated Jim. 'But we couldn't *all* sleep in the bed with him, could we. Freddie couldn't bear to go to sleep by himself, or to wake up alone, especially during that final year. I promised him that I would be there for him when he fell asleep, and that I would still be there the next morning, when he woke up. I told him I would hold him and that I would never let him go. That was all he needed from me at that stage in his life. It was the least I could do, after all we'd been through. I have no regrets as far as Freddie is concerned. Because I kept my promise.'

☿

Although Jim was diagnosed as HIV positive in 1990, he did not die from AIDS. By 1996, highly active antiretroviral therapy (HAART) had become the standard treatment for HIV sufferers in the UK and elsewhere. The medication that might have saved Freddie's life, if only it had been developed and launched just a few years earlier, kept Jim going for the rest of his. Having been reassured by Freddie, he maintained, that he would be allowed to continue living at Garden Lodge, Jim was devastated when Mary, who had inherited the place, gave him three months' notice to leave. Peter Freestone later set the record straight about whether Freddie wanted Jim to have the house.

'It is something Freddie might have said in a moment, but he was always very particular to write down anything he really wanted to happen, especially in his will,' Peter said. 'Anything verbal doesn't mean anything.'

Commenting on the 'guilt' Freddie had carried since the day he broke Mary's heart, Peter insists that this was not the reason why he left her his house and most of his wealth.

'Freddie taught me love is a quality, not a quantity,' he said. 'You don't use all your love once and then it's gone. Freddie did love Mary, but then he also loved Jim. He loved his friends. Mary was so important to him because she was there when he made the transition to being gay, and she stood by him. Freddie felt huge guilt more than anything, for what he put her through in 1975 when he broke their engagement and told her the truth about himself. But I do think it is significant that, in the end, he gave Mary the house and half of all his future earnings from Queen. That is what he felt for her.'

Had Freddie felt the need to effect any changes to his will, he would have been able to do so almost until his dying day.

'Before Freddie died, he expressed verbally his wish that Jim, Joe and I could stay in Garden Lodge until we were ready to face the "outside world",' said Peter. 'He knew none of us would want to stay forever, and was even then thinking about others before him. It was a very kind thought, but not very practical . . . he left Garden Lodge and all its contents to Mary Austin. This did not include three adult males. So that Freddie's written will could go through probate, it was necessary that we were no longer in the house. We were all given three months to make our arrangements.'[1]

Thanks to Freddie's loyalty and generosity, they were not evicted onto the street with nowhere to go.

With the half a million pounds Freddie had left him – Peter Freestone and Joe Fanelli received the same amount, as clearly stated in the Last Will and Testament, of which I have a copy – Jim purchased a three-bedroom home in Ravenscourt Park. But he was not happy in London without Freddie, and eventually made plans to move home to Ireland. With Freddie's help and financial support, he had designed and built a bungalow next door to the Bennekerry home of his mother Noeleen Ann – who appears on Jim's birth certificate as 'Annie Hutton, formerly Doyle', and who later became known as 'Nan'. But she died a week before he returned. He worked locally with one of his brothers as a handyman and carpenter. A few likely lads came and went, and even another longish-term partner. But the new boy couldn't compete with the memory of Freddie, said Jim. Was it that, or was Jim ruined by Freddie Mercury to the point that no mere mortal could ever be good enough? Whatever, the relationship fell apart. Content, at last, to share his life with a couple of dogs and half a dozen cats, Jim lived out his days in peace.

It was lung cancer that got him. A hopelessly heavy smoker, Jim had been ailing for some while when he died on New Year's Day 2010, nineteen years after Freddie and three days short of his own sixty-first birthday. His funeral mass, celebrated at St Mary's Catholic church in the parish, was attended by a huge crowd: a testament to Jim's and the Hutton family's local popularity. Jim's remaining brothers, sisters, uncles and aunts buried him in the cemetery alongside his parents. 'Barcelona', Freddie's duet with Montserrat Caballé and Jim's favourite piece, was played at the graveside as his coffin was lowered in. Later that evening, a local group called After Dark performed 'Bohemian Rhapsody' in the go-to Barracks bar in Carlow Town, dedicating their rendition of Queen's greatest hit to the memory of 'Gentleman Jim'. No member of Queen nor of the Garden Lodge gang having made the journey to Ireland for the funeral, none of his old friends was there to hear it.

Brian May at least paid tribute from his home in Windlesham, four hundred miles away.

'Jim and Freddie were close for many years, and in modern parlance would have been called civil partners,' he wrote to the followers of his website. 'Jim was a quiet and gentle soul, unimpressed and faintly amused by the machinations of fame, rock and roll, and Queen, and so provided Freddie with a refreshingly different view on life.'

Remembering the life, and not its end.

CHAPTER TWELVE
BARBARA

Which brings us to Barbara. If you believe the film, as I said, she did not exist. There was no trace of her. But she lived, she breathed, and she was larger than life. She was, for a while, a most significant other in Freddie's. Had he not fallen ill, who knows how things might have panned out. They might even have married, which believe it or not was mooted. It was the outcome for which Barbara longed. Her desperation heralded her downfall. But what they had together was perhaps the closest that Freddie ever came to a collision of kindred spirits, sparking an equal and passionate pairing. They had much in common, having survived abuse and abandonment, challenging childhoods and the ravages of war. They had made their way through life on their own terms. Not only had they both flourished and even excelled in the arts, but they had found solace there. Having overcome crippling complications in their personal lives, having won and lost love and having gained strength through disappointment, neither was in the habit of dwelling on the past. What had been, had been. They had moved swiftly on. They were survivors.

When they met, Barbara and Freddie were both living life to the max while not averse to the idea of settling down with somebody to love ... if they found the right one. At forty-one, she was a screen siren on the turn. Freddie, six years her junior, was a global superstar. They say it happens when you least expect it. They understood each other, supported each other and, crucially, had no secrets from each other. There was no legacy of guilt, no elephant in the room, no overhang of ordure. If only for the fact that she enabled him to experience uninhibited freedom in a relationship, she is entitled to recognition and respect. Tolerated to begin with but later dismissed and even treated with contempt by some of Freddie's people, she has been all but rubbed out since her death. When forced to acknowledge her, they'd like us believe that she was less than a footnote, and of no real importance in Freddie's life. How convenient, if that were true.

It isn't.

☿

'More than anything else, with me, Freddie was childlike,' Barbara told me in 1996, the first time I flew to Munich to spend time with her. We hadn't seen each other for a decade. I was pregnant at the time, but I miscarried during my stay. Late one afternoon, after doing the Happy Hour rounds of some of Freddie's favourite haunts with her, I took my leave to go and meet an old friend. One minute I was scanning the rush-hour traffic for a vacant cab. The next I was on my knees in the gutter, the pain so intense that I thought I'd been knifed. I managed to get back to her apartment. Sleeves rolled, no nonsense, she looked after me. Just as she had cleaned up and looked after Freddie, more times than she could remember. We had discussed that side of their relationship at length.

'He brought out the mother in me,' she said. 'He responded to new things the way a little child does. He needed nurturing and constant reassurance, and I was able to give him those things. It was more about that, between us, than about a full-blown romantic, sexual affair. But lots of men are like that with their women, aren't they? Not that most of them would admit it. Many men can't seem to function without a woman to lean on, to do everything for them, and to make them feel important and secure. "*Cherchez la femme*," the French say, and it's true. But what they are really saying is, "*Cherchez Maman.*" I know I was both his woman and his Mummy, for the time that we had. He called me those things. I gave him strength, and he gave me status. Being seen out and about on the arm of the great Freddie Mercury, even though I had of course fame in my own right, in Germany at least, and I'd had many high-profile liaisons, it gave me a lot. A lot. People respected the fact that I was with him. It was equal for us both.

'We gave each other what we both needed at that time in our lives. And of course, the lines become blurred. Being only human, our affection for each other, our dependence on each other, some-times spilled into other experiences. Sex too, yes, this as well. Usually with someone else present between us, yes. This was the way that Freddie liked it, and I gave him whatever he wanted. Because we were there for each other. I would have to say, in every way. What I know for sure is that he couldn't have behaved this way with Mary. She would never have allowed the man Freddie needed to be. She had her fantasy about who he was. She convinced herself that he would be with her if only he was not gay. This was laugh-able. He said himself, many times, that he could never have shown his true self to Mary. She would probably have dropped dead from shock.'

It wasn't hard to see why Freddie was floored by this unique and dazzling woman. She had all the time-honoured attributes said to drive men wild with desire. At fifty-six she was in full bloom; a sombre beauty with an entrancing smile that never quite reached the eyes. She still carried herself like a movie star, as though onto a film set. Wherever we went, heads turned. Her hair, make-up and clothes were camera-ready. She had an energy and an aura that lit up rooms. I was intrigued by her.

If you combined the screen allure of some of Hollywood's most celebrated leading ladies – the fickle severity of Greta Garbo, say; the bewitching vulnerability of Marilyn Monroe; the peachy sass of Jean Harlow, and the curse-y, stormy glamour of Carole Lombard

– you still couldn't get close to what Barbara had. There are shades of Brigitte Bardot in her early publicity photos; a bounciness more redolent of the young Faye Dunaway or even the fledgling Meryl Streep than of Jayne Mansfield, the blowsier beauty with whom she is usually and disparagingly compared.[1]

Barbara met Freddie towards the end of 1981, when Queen returned to Munich to resume recording. The band's association with that city had begun in 1979, with 'Crazy Little Thing Called Love', recorded at Giorgio Moroder's Musicland Studios with their new producer Reinhold Mack. Having lodged briefly in the 'awful' concrete-blocky Arabella-Haus apartment hotel above the studios, where Led Zeppelin, the Rolling Stones and Deep Purple had recorded before them,[2] Freddie moved into the home of his boyfriend Winfried 'Winnie' Kirchberger, a restauranteur who owned and ran the Sebastianseck eaterie on Sebastianplatz. It was to that address that Freddie once had a brand-new, ribbon-wrapped Mercedes Coupé delivered for Winnie's birthday. But their affair was explosive. Each found each other impossible to live with. There were endless explosive break-ups and stormings-out. Freddie relocated to the Stollberg Plaza apartment building at Stollbergstrasse 11, above the Austernkeller: the Oyster Bar. This was in a more upmarket neighbourhood than his previous place. Barbara lived opposite. Some have claimed that Freddie's personal manager Paul Prenter introduced them. Others that they ran into each other naturally, most likely in the oft-frequented 'New York' club. Wherever it was, they quickly fell in together, and became regular drinking partners. This complicated Freddie's chaotic private life even more, especially after Freddie took to staying at Barbara's flat. The other three members of the band were tearing at their follicles at this juncture, frustrated by Freddie's reluctance to focus on work.

Of the three overlapping lovers – Jim, Winnie and Barbara – the actress was by far the most vocal and demanding. Members of Freddie's tribe describe him as having been 'floored' by her and felt that he had 'met his match' – that phrase again. Often dismissed with a sneer as a 'soft-porn star' and model, there was rather more to Barbara than most of them knew. She had appeared in more than seventy films, and rose to prominence in a series of cult pictures by the wunderkind of New German Cinema, Rainer Werner Fassbinder. Her relationship with the director pre-echoed the one she went on to share with Freddie. One of Fassbinder's wives described him as 'a homosexual who also needed a woman'. It established the blueprint, Barbara believed, for what she had come to expect from men. Fassbinder died in 1982 aged thirty-seven from a sleeping-pill and cocaine overdose. His muse was now footloose. She overreacted by indulging in the wildest affair of her life, well aware that Freddie had other lovers. She also knew that he would continue to play the field. One-night stands were his preference. He picked them up on his manic rounds. More than a few wound up in bed with Freddie and Barbara together. Was Freddie pushing the envelope, testing his new girlfriend to see how far he could go? Couldn't Barbara have put her foot down? 'I could have,' she agreed. 'I didn't want to.'

After her death, her daughter Nicola-Babette 'Minki' Reichardt said, 'I know they were in love. I know that my mother was in love with him because she said so. I think their relationship was very close and very intense. They really liked the conflict. They were talking, shouting, arguing, and then they were in their arms again, it was always very lively. I think Freddie was the love of her life.'[3]

Miss Reichardt is also quoted as having said, 'The two were very close to each other, often slept in the same bed, but they did NOT have sex.' But as Barbara told me, her own children were the very last people with whom she would ever have dreamed of discussing her sex life. They were never in the room. No one other than those present could have known what did or didn't go on.

According to Barbara's close German friend Elisabeth Volkmann, 'Freddie loved Barbara. Barbara loved him. And it was a big love between both. If he wouldn't be homosexual, maybe they are married.'

Journalist David Wigg, my friend for more than thirty years, recalled having once walked in on Barbara, Freddie and others happily in bed together, and being invited to undress and join in. The professional reporter made his excuses and left.

As for Peter Freestone, he was the first to go against the grain and confirm to me that Freddie and Barbara had been an item. 'They had the most intense, loving relationship,' he told me. 'I know one hundred percent they shared a bed on numerous occasions.'

Yet still the backlash. There has been a swell of vitriol from young Freddie and Queen fans who for whatever reason refuse to accept the fact that Barbara and Freddie had a full relationship. 'But if Barbara said she had sex with Freddie, she had sex with Freddie,' comments psychotherapist Richard Hughes. 'Why not? Elton had Renate. Imagine the conversations he and Freddie must have had about all that. Then there was Kenny Everett and his wife Lee – *and* Cleo Rocos, his sidekick. Who was gorgeous, artistic, voluptuous, and a total manifestation of what it means to be "Rubenesque". I remember Kenny being absolutely obsessed with her "tits". Nothing wrong with that. Breasts are an obsession for all of us. It's a developmental connection. Needing the mother's breasts for sustenance at the very beginning of life creates a fundamental attachment. In "Object Relations Theory", the infant's relationship with its mother is deemed to determine the child's adult character. The first objects or what are called "part objects" in a young life relate to the mother. The breast that feeds the hungry baby is the "good breast", while the baby who goes hungry relates to the so-called "bad breast". Generally, the mum is the primary caregiver, and this influence is reflected throughout life.'

Barbara was obviously blessed with magnificent breasts.

'I remember thinking, whenever I watched her in interviews, that there was something grotesquely maternal about her,' says Hughes. 'Something of the fifteenth century wet nurse. She was *jolie laide*, wasn't she: that French idea of being essentially ugly but somehow beautifully so. She was ugly in a compelling way, to the point that you couldn't take your eyes off her. She had this huge energy, she was both wet nurse and whore: the kind of woman who just keeps going. Freddie was massively drawn to it, both the concept and the woman.'

No, there was nothing to be gained by lying about having sex with Freddie. He was dead, so how could she benefit from it? Peter Freestone's take was that, as Freddie's personal assistant, he was told absolutely everything, and that Freddie would not have been able to keep such a thing a secret. Yet he readily admits to a period when he *was* kept in the dark by others about developments in Freddie's life. He said that he was so upset by it that he threatened to resign.

'I began to feel an unsettling shift in our relationship,' he said. '... I remember it building up to a moment when after much soul-searching I told Freddie in the middle of 1989 that I thought it was better that I left Garden Lodge ... I was beginning to feel very marginalised in the household.'[4]

Gossip was reaching Peter's ears, he explained, that led him to realise he was not being kept informed about Freddie's hospital appointments and medical treatment. Where once he would have been party to diary dates and arrangements at all times, and even booking such appointments himself on Freddie's behalf, he was now, for reasons unknown, being left out. Although Peter was well aware that Freddie could have contracted AIDS, this had not been spelled out to him. Only through confrontations over time with other members of the household did he discover that Freddie suspected Peter of having leaked details about his health to the press. But Peter was the most honest, trustworthy and reliable person there. Knowing him as I do, this was the last thing he could ever be accused of. The situation persisted for months. It became unbearable. In the end, word reached Freddie that Peter was planning to leave. Matters came to a head, and they had a heart to heart.

It was only then that Freddie admitted to his assistant that he was 'very sick'. He refused to elaborate. And it was only when Freddie told Peter how much he needed him and wanted him to stay that things were ironed out. It still wasn't clear who had been spilling the beans. The culprit's identity would not come to light until after Freddie's death. His cook Joe Fanelli, during his daily workout at the gym, had chatted casually to his friends there about developments at home. One of those 'friends' turned out to be an undercover red-top tabloid reporter.

As Barbara said, she and Freddie had promised each other faithfully not to share the intimacies of their relationship with anybody else. As long as the other still lived, at least. It was for them, and them alone. 'What was between Freddie and me was between Freddie and me,' she said. Why disbelieve her?

☿

I made several visits to the home they bought together, a cosy third-floor apartment on Hans-Sachs-Strasse. South of the city centre and next to the Isar River, the neighbourhood had once housed Munich's Jewish community. It became famous during the eighties as a gay and lesbian enclave. It then fell into disrepair the following decade, after so many gay men there had died. It would rise again thirty years later, and would assume yet another identity. Barbara's lavishly appointed flat had Freddie's stamp all over it. They had selected and purchased its furnishings, artworks and artefacts together. The antique chandelier in particular was very 'him'. Her sideboard was a jumble of freshly polished, silver-framed photographs of Freddie and of the couple together. Several had clearly been taken in the apartment and at locations around Munich, Montreux and at Garden Lodge. There were also portraits of her children and grandchildren. Piles of Queen and Freddie CDs and videos lay untouched, some of them still in their cellophane wrappers. She lacked the courage to listen to or watch them, she said. She feared the emotions they might stir. In her locker in the building's basement, she said, she still had the clothes, shoes and other personal belongings that Freddie had left behind: 'Bags and bags of them.' I wonder what happened to them after Barbara died. She introduced me to Tarzan, her sixteen-year-old 'child' with Freddie – a much-loved and generously fed black cat. After Freddie's death, she would never leave Tarzan in the care of anyone else for more than a couple of days. Freddie's spirit could have somehow passed into him, she thought. 'Freddie felt strongly that our souls do not move from one lifetime to the next. I didn't agree,' she said. 'He is still concerned for me in death. Whether it's Freddie or whether he wants me to feel comforted by the cat, it is for me to care for the cat.' It was the reason why she could never bear to leave the animal for long. She lavished that cat with more attention and love, observed her son Lars, than she ever showed her children or her men. When the pet gave up the ghost in 1999, three years ahead of Barbara, she was inconsolable.

Looking around her crammed and compact home, I wondered how they had ever imagined it could accommodate the two of them. Barbara's personality alone filled the place, let alone all the stuff.

'We were as one when we were together, wherever we were,' she smiled. 'We blended. He filled any space in his special way, yes. But Freddie was not big. This apartment would be perfect for the two of us here. The idea was that we would live between Munich and London. Freddie was restless, he liked to have his bases and to move around. He still had his apartment in New York and would buy a home in Montreux.' The plan didn't work out. Freddie's affair with Munich was on the wane. It broke Barbara's heart that they were unable to live together permanently.

☿

Barbara was a war baby, born in Vienna in December 1940, during a period when Austria was annexed to Nazi Germany. Her father Hans Ledersteger was an Austrian film-industry art director. Her mother Irmgard Alberti was an actress. Barbara's life was troubled from the start. Hans was a womaniser and a drunk. His wife divorced him while Barbara was still little. She grew up in Bruchsal, three hours north-west of Munich. On 1 March 1945, only a few months ahead of the end of the war and when Barbara was four, the city was bombed by the Allies. A thousand citizens perished, and the entire inner city and its Baroque castle were destroyed. A month later, allied forces stormed the ruins and claimed Bruchsal without resistance. Many local women and girls were raped by French colonial troops.

She developed early, sprouting breasts so abundant that men called her 'Busenwunder' ('busty babe'), and treated her like a grown woman ahead of her time. Her mother's third husband Dr Erwin Valentin, an esteemed military doctor considerably older than his spouse, punished his teenaged stepdaughter by making her shovel coal in the cellar. She achieved her Mittlere Reife, the German equivalent of British GCSEs, and left school at sixteen, having had it with education. After her first love affair failed, she tried to take her own life, but was rescued in time. 'I was,' she said, 'in love and, frankly, stupid.'

Barbara moved to Munich before her eighteenth birthday and found herself an agent. An Austrian expatriate in post-war Germany, she became a household name through her many appearances in German-language B movies. Her dramatic personal life dominated headlines. In 1973, she starred in *World on a Wire* (*Welt am Draht*), a television film directed by Fassbinder. She went on to make seven films with him. Her final celluloid appearance was in *The Second Victory*, the 1987 British drama starring Anthony Hopkins and Max von Sydow and directed by Gerald Thomas. Based on the novel by Australian writer Morris West, it was set in Allied-occupied Austria at the end of World War II.

She married three times that she would admit to. There may have been one or two more. All her husbands had been married before. All of them abandoned their wives for her. Her first two, who were older than her, were obviously paternal replacements, she and her birth father having long been estranged. Rolf Lüder, diminutive and ten years her senior, left his marriage for Barbara shortly after they met at a party. They married on her twenty-first birthday, 15 December 1961, settled in Berlin and were blessed with a son they called Lars. Rolf, the smart and handsome owner of a street-cleaning company covering Munich, Berlin and Hanover, was supposedly a millionaire. He was also a wife-beater and a gambler, and blew his fortune at roulette tables while his neglected spouse and child went hungry at home. The marriage disintegrated. Rolf committed suicide four years after their divorce.

In 1967, she married her bristly forty-six-year-old divorce lawyer, Dr Ernst Reichardt, who was almost twice her age. He ran his own firm in Berlin specialising in copyright, intellectual property and matrimonial law. Ernst fathered Nicola-Babette and adopted his stepson. Barbara walked out six years later. Reichardt's replacement, whiskery wannabe screen writer, director and author Helmut Dietl, four years Barbara's junior, also left his wife and kids for her. Six years on, he vanished, and they never spoke again.

There were endless affairs and 'involvements' as Barbara continued to chase happiness. She was by her own admission 'not a good mother. Not a hands-on mother. I was often away working, filming, sometimes for months at a time. I adored my children and I gave them everything, material things, but they were mostly raised by fathers and nannies. I have regrets, of course. But I did what I had to at the time. I was working, I was ambitious, what can I tell you? I put my career first, for better or worse. I was not close to my kids, and I think they have suffered. But I believe they always knew I loved them. There have been times for us to have our discussions, and for explanations to be given. I know that they blame me. I know there are things about the life they lived growing up that they would change, if they could. I was who I was. I regret much. We can only be the kind of parents to our children that our parents were to us, I think, no matter how much we would like it to be different. I often left them, yes, and I am sorry.'

As for her lovers: 'I was very often used – for my looks, my body, rather than for who I was,' she said. 'I didn't know better. I always thought it was love when it was only lust. If they wanted that, then they must love me for myself, was how I looked at it. I was wrong. There were many famous and wealthy men, who I know now wanted the one thing. Never the woman, they wanted Barbara Valentin from the screen. They wanted to own the famous actress. They wanted her for sex. You can imagine, it was all so different with Freddie.'

Lars revived his mother in his introspective 2018 German-language memoir, *Barbara*. He paid tribute to an impulsive, gut-driven woman who was open, talkative, funny, daring, and irrepressibly loud. He tells how vociferous she could be in restaurants if her dinner wasn't served promptly or if the chef had added garlic to her food when she had explicitly asked them not to. She was in the habit of flirting with waiters (as I witnessed), regardless of whether she was in a deluxe restaurant or a cheap-as-chips diner. All who crossed her wished they hadn't. She rarely started arguments but always finished them, whipping out her manicured claws. At home, she was fastidious. Her apartment was perfectly organised, from paperwork and clothes to kitchen equipment. She ironed enthusiastically, even things that didn't need ironing. Although she employed a cleaner, she cleaned up before they came.

Barbara, like Freddie, had exquisite taste. She adored luxury. She loved couture and designer shoes, the finest food and wines, the best hotels. She preferred to turn left on a plane, and she'd always had a thing for smart cars. She was so proud of her first, a Renault Floride roadster (also known as the Caravelle), bought with money she had earned herself. Her second was an E-Type Jaguar, a wedding present from her first husband Rolf. It impressed her less than it might have: he had sold her sports car from under her nose, and gambled away the proceeds at the casino.

Lars discovered a short handwritten manuscript, the rudiments of Barbara's own memoir, in a drawer after her death. She had managed no more than a single chapter, which focused on her 1960s experiences in Munich. He marvelled at her fluency, and was taken aback by the frankness and sensitivity with which she wrote about her men. He was moved by her painstaking attention to detail that brought the pages to life. If only she had got around to finishing it.

CHAPTER THIRTEEN

REDEMPTION

Barbara's son found himself wondering again after her death whether she had had an affair with Elvis Presley. He could remember her driving them to stay with friends in Saint Tropez on 16 August 1977. The singer's death was newsflashed on the radio. Barbara collapsed in floods of tears, later explaining that she had once got to know Elvis, and how fond she had been of him. The thirteen-year-old boy could well imagine that his mother was alluding to an affair. It's not so far-fetched. We know that Elvis visited Munich in 1959, on a fourteen-day army furlough from Frankfurt. America's greatest young entertainer and his cohorts made the most of Munich's Moulin Rouge, its bars and the clubs, cosied up to the strippers and the chorus girls and smuggled a chosen few into the Edelweiss Hotel for after-hours larks before relocating to wreak further havoc in Paris. Who's to say that Barbara, who would have been nineteen at the time, wasn't one of them? Not that the King of Rock'n'Roll would have been her most eminent suitor. That honour fell to a genuine king, Hussein the First of Jordan, who courted Miss Valentin before he fell for and married Antoinette 'Toni' Avril Gardiner from Suffolk. You lose some. 'I didn't love him,' was all that Barbara would share about the Hashemite monarch.[1]

Her lovers beyond her third marriage included an Israeli concert agent called Sascha, Helmut the gay doorman at Munich's 'New York' nightclub, who later died of AIDS, and a homosexual Russian exile by the name of Alex who claimed to be a CIA agent and who would fetch Barbara Beluga caviar from his jaunts. She ate it with a mother of pearl spoon.

'The people my mother knew were often celebrities,' said Lars. 'I managed to speak hardly a word with Freddie Mercury, even though he sometimes lived at my mother's place in the early 1980s, and I sometimes took them somewhere with me after a visit, in my Fiat 500.' On such excursions, Freddie was obliged to bend himself onto the narrow back shelf while Barbara crammed ample bosoms and buttocks into the front passenger seat.

'As a youngster,' he confessed, 'I found Queen's music silly. The same as many of Barbara's friends, not to mention her lovers. I very much regret my ignorance now.'

☿

Although her film career had peaked and was in decline, the theatre industry had come looking for her. Barbara was about to embark on a promising second career on the stage when she and Freddie got together. She gave it up for him, because he asked her to. At his behest and expense, she accompanied him to destinations around the world. From Barcelona to Ibiza, from Rio to Montreux, there was Barbara, glowing and proud on his arm. At Garden Lodge, she was given her own bedroom. She guessed that she must have stayed there forty or fifty times.

A key factor in their relationship was that she fell not for the rock legend but for the man.

'I vaguely knew who Freddie Mercury was, but to be a famous rock star was no great shakes in Munich,' she said. 'I was probably more famous here than him. He always had an entourage, he was an industry all by himself. He even had his own little corner in the "New York" club. He and his people referred to it as "the family corner".'

Barbara was aware that he was involved with Winnie Kirchberger. She remembered in great detail their break-ups and their make-ups, and how they couldn't give each other up.

Just as Spanish soprano Montserrat Caballé would become 'Freddie's personal opera singer', Barbara was his own personal film star. And she *was* the film star. She could be preposterously grand when she wanted to be: yet another characteristic that she and Freddie shared. She also relished the sleazier side of life, which again they had in common. They brought out and encouraged each other's wicked side.

In some ways, their affair was the most straightforward that Freddie ever had. They enjoyed the same simple pleasures: nights out in bars, a few lines of cocaine, a skinful of booze and 'a good fuck': preferably with someone new every night. They didn't need a cast of regulars to massage their egos or make them feel import- ant. Most of their nights on the tiles were spent simply talking to each other, oblivious of everyone else. Barbara was known and welcomed all over Munich. Freddie was content to take the back seat there, and let her be the diva du jour. He wasn't obliged to live up to his persona, because Barbara Valentin the movie star was doing all that for him. He could let his guard down in her company, confident that she would not exploit his vulnerability. There was vulnerability in Barbara's make-up too. This gave Freddie the unusual opportunity to play the caring role, which he was not often called upon to do.

Friends teased the 'the old married couple', calling them 'Fredl and Barbl'. When Freddie was in town, they'd be together every day. They would have coffee at Café NiL, named after the River Nile, on Hans-Sachs-Strasse. They might also eat a simple snack there: meatballs, schnitzel, toasted sandwiches or goulash. They would shop together in Beck's department store; and take tea at Dallmayers, buying cheeses, ham and treats there to take home for later. When they ate out, it was often at the Restaurant Kafer-Schänke on Prinzregentenstrasse, an elegantly rustic establishment famed for delicious international and regional specialities. There, they would eat some crispy Käfer duck or a little caviar, which Freddie liked to have with mashed potato, or some oysters. It was

Barbara who took charge in restaurants, ordering for them both as Freddie couldn't speak German. They would then begin the rounds. Their bar and club crawls – from the Frisco pub on Blumenstrasse, and the Teddy Bear with real furry teddies dangling from the ceiling on Pestalozzistrasse; the Ochsengarten (Ox Garden) and the bars around Müllerstrasse, the Pimpernel, the Peppermint, the Violine, the BAU; Le Clou pub, an old rockers' joint; Old Mrs Henderson on Rumfordstrasse (which later became Paradiso Tanzbar), and of course New York, on Sonnenstrasse – would last into the early hours. Freddie always drank vodka with tonic, preferring Stolichnaya when it was available. Barbara's poison was any good brandy with Coke. She could match him drink for drink and chaperoned him around town. They made an odd couple. Freddie seemed tiny beside Barbara. They sported matching leather jackets. Freddie gave her one of his, but she looked ridiculous in it. It was never going to dam the swell of her bosom. Friends of Barbara's remembered the pair discussing marriage soon into their relationship, but in such a light-hearted way that no one took them seriously.

Barbara knew where and how to lay her hands on just about anything. She had friends in high places as well as low. She shrugged off Freddie's frequent visits to Fisherman's, a gay sauna and pickup joint; and Die Deutsche Eiche on Reichenbachstrasse, a hotel and restaurant with facilities of a similar kind. She would reason with police officers she knew personally whenever the squad pitched up to bother gay men in the bars and clubs. Homosexual activity, under the German Civil Code, was still a punishable offence.

There was something else about Barbara that was key. Freddie's friendship and love for her did not drastically alter her circumstances the way that it had affected the lives of others: his parents, his sister Kashmira and her family, Mary Austin, Jim Hutton, Winnie Kirchberger, Peter Freestone, Joe Fanelli and the rest. Barbara came to the table as an equal. She could walk away whenever she chose and would still be his equal. That earned her his respect. There was nothing mousy nor apologetic about her. She was radiant and gracious; the kind of strong, glamorous, determined female he relished. Like Freddie, she was a mass of contradictions. Her imposing image concealed an intense sensitivity and fragility. Perhaps for the first and last time, he connected with another human being with whom he felt able to be completely himself.

☿

On their first night out together at the New York nightclub, Freddie and Barbara sat talking for hours on the floor of the ladies' toilets. The music in the club was so loud that they couldn't hear themselves, and anyway the ladies' room was rarely used. They became so engrossed in their conversation that nobody knew they were in there. When the evening ended and the bar closed up, they discovered that they were locked in. It was an auspicious beginning. Before the cleaners arrived the next morning and freed them, they had shared their life stories. Freddie opened up to Barbara about his childhood in Zanzibar and India to a degree that he had never done with anybody else. Crucially, only with Barbara did he revisit his refugee past and confess his survivor's guilt. He poured it all out, she said, and wept to her about the atrocities committed during Zanzibar's revolution. Barbara's own recollections of bombs falling on Bruchsal were fragmented, though she could remember feeling terrified. 'He was damaged by all that, just as I was damaged,' she said. 'He had never left it behind, the way everyone thought. In a way, we were both refugees. He couldn't work out why our lives had been spared when so many others were lost, through no fault of their own. He said he couldn't believe in God for that reason.'

On the subject of religion, Freddie was doubtful.

'In his view, no god would have allowed so many millions to suffer. He felt that he had been raised in blind faith by parents who accepted rather than questioned. He'd taken the path he chose precisely for that reason. As an antidote. He assumed that he would wake up from all the madness one day. We both thought that. That we would somehow find the answers. But Freddie didn't expect to grow old, he said. Perhaps it wasn't a death wish so much as his disregard for the importance of living a long life. He couldn't see the point, he said, of growing old and just fading away.'

☿

From the moment that Queen began work on tracks for their album *The Game* at Musicland, all four band members started taking advantage of Munich's liberated lifestyle.[2] They would work on tracks during the day, beginning well into the afternoon, and step out on the town late at night. For Freddie, the city would be both his revelation and his ruin. He loved the Munich lifestyle primarily because he was able to flaunt his homosexual side without fear of being outed in the press. He was never hounded there the way he was in London. You have to laugh that he was cavorting about town with a woman.

Barbara travelled with Freddie to Montreux, and would accompany him to recording sessions at Mountain Studios. She appears in the video for 'It's a Hard Life', a single from Queen's 1984 album *The Works*. Freddie's November 1985 solo single 'Love Me Like There's No Tomorrow', the final release from *Mr. Bad Guy* was, confirms Peter Freestone, inspired by her. She was with Freddie at the first Rock in Rio festival in January 1985, and at Live Aid in London that July. She was a VIP guest at his extravagant thirty-ninth birthday party at Henderson's on 5 September that year, at which everyone appeared in black-and-white drag. Remembered Peter Freestone, 'It was a crazy party. The first time I had seen a real champagne fountain with all the glasses standing on top of each other . . . constantly flowing.'

The party was filmed, and some sequences were later used in the video for Freddie's September 1985 single from *Mr. Bad Guy* – 'Living on my Own'. Freddie went as himself, in a harlequin catsuit and trainers and a gorgeous Russian Imperial jacket designed by Princess Diana's wedding dress creators David and Elizabeth Emanuel. He would wear it again on 5 November for his appearance, with actress Jane Seymour, at the Fashion Aid extravaganza at London's Royal Albert Hall.

The love affair with Munich was on the skids. Long absences from home were taking their toll on the band and their families. The *Magic* tour of 1986 concluded at the Knebworth Park Festival that August, after which Freddie would never again perform with Queen. Party over.

☿

The many conversations that Barbara had with Freddie about Mary played on her mind long after his death. Because he had promised to marry her, she said, he felt guilty.

'He was dutiful and had a deep sense of obligation. It had been expected of him, and he'd gone back on his word. The guilt never went away ... although I wondered how much of that guilt she herself made him feel,' said Barbara. 'It wasn't Freddie's fault that he turned out to be mostly gay. That's life. But he couldn't get over the way he had let her down. He said that he hadn't been gay, not in the beginning, but then he just turned around, flipped out completely, and started to live a gay life. It was a choice, not a biological thing, with him.'

Homosexuality, Barbara believed, was a role that Freddie chose to play.

'He *was* the Great Pretender,' she said. 'It excited him, because it was forbidden fruit. While all this was going on, he and I were lovers in the truest sense. We did have sex together regularly. Yes. Yes. It took a while. When it happened, it was beautiful and innocent. I was completely in love with him by this time, and he had told me that he loved me. We even talked of getting married. Of course, he'd still pick up dozens of gay guys and bring them back night after night, but I didn't mind. Sounds insane, doesn't it, but that's the life we were living, and I couldn't stop him even if I wanted to. I continued to take lovers myself. To a certain point I was allowed. Then Freddie started to show off, and would kick them out.'

Eventually, she said, Freddie no longer cared about sex.

'He'd get together with people just for tenderness, affection. His longings had nothing to do with the body anymore. He was like a little child. He'd cry like a baby. He'd say to me, "Barbara, the only thing they can't take from me is you."'

It was she who first noticed changes in Freddie's health and habits. It started, she said, with the little things. His appetite began to fade, which didn't concern her much. He had never been a big eater. Then his moods became erratic. He would criticise other members of the band, for no apparent reason. He started picking fights, sometimes ending friendships of many years' standing. Looking back, Barbara blamed it on stress. She felt sure that Freddie knew what was coming. The most obvious sign of illness was a growth in his gullet, which they referred to as 'the mushroom'. It flared and subsided for months, until one day it became obvious that it was permanent. Freddie confessed to her his fear that he was rotting from the inside out. Then one night, Barbara said, she was lying in bed with him and one of his boyfriends when Freddie had a terrible coughing attack. She realised in that moment that it was only a matter of time. Subsequent fits, and Freddie's terrified reaction when he cut his finger and screamed in her face to stay away from him, confirmed her worst fears. During the summer of 1987, when Barbara was staying with Freddie at Garden Lodge, he developed dark blue bruises on his face which she would blot out with her own make-up when he had to do TV interviews or video shoots. The marks were Kaposi's sarcoma.

'When we first met, he was either denying it to himself or he simply didn't know,' she said. 'After he made his first test, it changed his life.'

Barbara sought her own AIDS test immediately. The result was negative. They never again had sex together. Nor did they ever have the AIDS conversation. The killer blow was Freddie's departure from Munich towards the end of 1985, without explanation or farewell. For the woman with whom he had shared everything, it was unbearable.

'He just disappeared out of my life,' Barbara wept. 'I couldn't understand it. I sent the birthday card, I wrote, I called. He was never there. It didn't make sense. What he was doing was a lie. But OK, I thought, if he wants it over, then it's over. It really was a break without a reason.'

He did go back to her. Again, unexpectedly and without warning. Months after he'd fled, Barbara was dressing to attend the launch of a friend's boutique when her doorbell rang. Thinking that it must be her cab, she hastened down to the lobby to find Freddie standing there clutching a posy of white flowers. Not wanting to believe that it was really him, she ran away. At the boutique launch, she did her film-star bit and lent her celebrity to the occasion, before wandering home to find what she couldn't bear to see.

'Freddie was still there, sitting quietly on the couch, playing with the TV remote control. It was then that it hit me. I fell into his arms and cried. He did too. We cried and cried, and cried and cried, and cried.'

It was weeks before he could explain himself and his sudden disappearance. What Barbara deduced was that it had all got too much for him. More than a hundred of their mutual friends in Munich had died of AIDS. It had dawned on Freddie that he would soon be joining them. Desperate to turn over a new leaf when it was already too late to do so, he forbade his London household to refer to Munich again. He wiped the place of photos and other mementoes of Barbara, because she reminded him of that city. Her name, Freddie commanded, must never be spoken.

'He'd wanted to break free from those crazy times,' she said. 'To live a calmer, different life, and to die, eventually, in beauty. But he couldn't stay away from me.'

'Jim had replaced Winnie, but it was complicated with Barbara,' said Peter Freestone. 'I think Freddie had simply had enough at the time. Stories about Freddie and Barbara were appearing in the German press with alarming regularity, and Freddie got it into his head that Barbara was the one leaking the information. I don't believe she would do that, but Freddie was convinced. Could it be that the idea was put into his head, and rumours fuelled by those who wanted rid of Barbara for good? Who knows?'

They renewed their relationship. She resumed travelling with Freddie. She was invited to his forty-fourth birthday dinner at Garden Lodge on 5 September 1990, seated at Freddie's left while Mary sat to his right. She continued to converse with him on the phone until a fortnight before his death.

Years passed before Barbara got her answers. Freddie's cocaine habit had soared during the Munich years. Barbara was held responsible. The gunpowder of sin, the rock star's ruin, had robbed him of reason and taken him to the brink. As it does, it distorted his mind, depriving him of free will and making him paranoid. The Queen machine had concluded that this was all Valentin's fault. She was denounced as the drug dealer who had corrupted him.

But Barbara was never a dealer. Local friends and journalists found laughable the notion that she could ever have been mistaken for one. As her Munich-based jeweller friend told me, 'She was too well-known here. Her comings and goings, all the people she was connected with, everything was observed. She would never have got away with dealing for money. It must be the case that the authorities knew she was using. But she was obviously useful to certain people in other ways.'

While she moved in such circles and could always obtain supplies, especially of the highly favoured pure South American cocaine smuggled in via Israel and Holland, she did not sell it. She bought for her own use through her own regular dealers, and would order on behalf of friends such as Fassbinder and Freddie. She alluded to an 'arrangement' with local police, who knew what she was up to but would leave her alone. Most of the time. When one of her dealers was apprehended, charged and imprisoned, Barbara's number was found in his contacts book, and she was fined. That reality check was not enough to make her relinquish her habit. She remained a defiant user until her stroke, her addiction its most likely cause. The discovery that chronic cocaine abuse could lead to strokes and long-term blood-flow deficits resulting in paralysis, loss of speech and dementia had only been made during the mid-1980s.

Whatever they say, Barbara did not initiate Freddie's cocaine habit. She did not lure him into drug abuse. He was hooked long before Munich. All that she was, in this regard, was a casual partner in crime. She doubled up as another mother to care for him, lending an empathetic ear when the excesses got too much. Their mutual cocaine use was about escape, she explained, from reality. It fuelled their hedonism. Freddie could be shy, retiring and undemonstrative without it. When the marching powder kicked in, the king of Queen was able to convince himself that he was king of the world.

☿

Barbara's most ignominious moment occurred just after Freddie's death in November 1991. On the verge of departing for the airport to fly to London for his funeral, she received a phone call instructing her not to come. She refused to divulge who had made the call. Peter Freestone said he couldn't remember. Most likely it was an employee in Jim Beach's office. Mary was the featured widow that day, and Barbara would not be welcome.

'After all we'd been through,' she said. 'The pain was terrible. I have never got over it. The love I shared with Freddie I never had before, and I've never had it since. He was the greatest love of my life. He still is.' She was not, however, the greatest love of his.

At least, she said, he got to do what he told her that a star should always do, and quit while he was ahead.

'He used to tell me that you can never afford to fall from the top, be not as great as you once were. Fame had made him the loneliest person in the world. To compensate for this, his life became wilder and wilder, until it controlled him. He was over-compensating for his loneliness: Freddie did everything to extremes. The price he paid was the most terrible. I know he wouldn't have planned it like that. But he got his way. Immortality was what he wanted, and immortality was what he got.'

For Barbara, there was worse to come. The executors of Freddie's will tried to deprive her of her apartment, claiming that she had no legal right to stay there. Barbara was forced to engage lawyers at vast expense. She won. She would.

No invitation for her, then, to the tribute concert for Freddie at Wembley Stadium on Easter Monday, 20 April 1992. Not that she had expected one. 'I heard that it was broadcast to about eighty countries and got an audience of more than a billion people,' she said. 'I was one of them. I was at Wembley in spirit.'

One of Barbara's greatest assets was her ability to weep for the camera. Where other actors required glycerine drops in their eyes to give the impression that they were crying for real, she could produce tears to order without any trouble at all.

'How do you cry in a film, Mama?' her son wanted to know. 'I just have to think about a specific thing and the tears come flooding,' Barbara told him. 'What on earth do you think about?' he pressed her. 'I'll tell you some other time,' she promised, over Christmas 2000, on the last evening they spent together. She had been fretting for a fortnight about turning sixty, which she really didn't fancy. A few days into January 2001, she was having a snack and a drink at their old favourite Café NiL just along the street from her building when she dropped from her chair, felled by a stroke from which she would never recover. She lingered for a year in a persistent vegetative state, and died on 22 February 2002, aged sixty-one. They laid her to rest, appropriately, in a place where celebrities lie: in Munich's Ostfriedhof Cemetery at Obergiesing.

☿

Visit Munich today and you'll find little of Freddie's and Barbara's eighties playground. The Glockenbachviertel quarter, which includes Hans-Sachs-Strasse where they bought the apartment in which Barbara lived, is now Munich's most upmarket neighbourhood. Chic bistros, bars, boutiques and smart residential buildings line the streets.

'Munich has changed a lot since the 1980s,' says German journalist and author Nicola Bardola. 'Two factors play an important role in this: gentrification and liberalisation. Districts such as the Glockenbachviertel were very popular in those days because rents were low and the nightlife was strong. Bohemians felt comfortable in Munich. Discotheques and special bars and clubs shaped the cityscape. Gay and transvestite bars flourished. These quarters were paradise for people who moved away from the mainstream. The party continued to grow – until AIDS came along. The Bermuda Triangle disappeared. Where the gay clubs were, there are now espresso bars or pastry shops. The few remaining places that survived from the 1980s have closed or are struggling to survive because of Covid-19.'

Having said that, says Bardola, the modern LGBTQ community in Munich today is thriving:

'The gay movement has continued to fight in Munich since the 1980s until today. And it has achieved a lot, locally and nationally. Gay marriage is now allowed. When a gay couple kisses in public, nobody looks anymore. It has almost become normal. So normal that some gays almost regret that they no longer have special status. This development is far from over. In any case, the recognition of gay rights has led to the disappearance of the corresponding subculture and the special atmosphere that Freddie so loved. Today, yuppies and bankers dominate the streets.'

The main problem, for those in search of Freddie Mercury and Barbara Valentin there, is that nearly forty years have passed. Much of the city as they knew it has been renovated, repaired or replaced. Most of the people they played with are long dead. Music fans and the rock community are aware that Queen and Freddie Mercury were often in Munich. But not everybody there today is comfortable with that.

'On a superficial level, some people have a queasy feeling about it,' the writer admits. 'Freddie as a symbol of the city of Munich as a gay paradise, and as a symbol of decadence, is not so popular. But if you take a closer look, you will discover the enormous importance of Freddie and Queen in Munich. For example, Freddie at last gets a street named after him. This should have happened much earlier.'

Better late than never. After five years of campaigning, local radio station Rock Antenne convinced Munich's city council to recognise Freddie's importance to the community. During 2021, the thirtieth anniversary year of his death, Freddie-Mercury-Strasse gets its unveiling south of the Olympic Park close to the Olympic Hall where Queen performed several times. Just as Hamburg honours the Beatles on the Grosse Freiheit and beyond, and as Berlin remembers David Bowie at Hansa Tonstudio and Frank Zappa on his own street there, Freddie will finally have an official connection to Munich.

'I have never understood that in Munich the heritage of Freddie and Queen was not cultivated,' Bardola remarks. 'I think that was a disgrace. The low point was the film *Bohemian Rhapsody*. In a few minutes, Munich is portrayed as a cesspool of sin. I write biographies about artists and rock stars (Yoko Ono, John Lennon, Ringo Starr). I think it is my duty as an author to effect justice. When I became aware of the book *Bowie in Berlin*, I decided to write my own *Mercury in Munich*. I aim to show that their times in Munich were not only bad.'

☿

Only now, all these years later, does the way they treated Barbara make sense to me. In order to facilitate Freddie's ascension to iconic status, it was necessary to distance him from matters unpalatable. His memory had to be purified. All traces of seediness, zipless sex, drug-taking and alcohol abuse had to be eliminated, disguised or at least set in context, so that someone else, not he, was always to blame. The slate had to be wiped. A variation on the theme of Freddie – that tragic figure, him again, the gay man who fell in love with a woman – had to be consolidated and fortified. Barbara Valentin, the symbol and figurehead of Freddie's most reckless years, had to be sacrificed. They had no choice. The woman was by her own admission a loose cannon. Who knew what kind of stunt she might pull at his funeral? What if, beside herself with grief, she went and threw herself on the coffin, gnashing and wailing and spewing it all out, destroying the dignity of the occasion by revealing all to the press, and telling a few home truths about what *really* went on in Munich? Because, come on, she could have gushed the lot: what caused Freddie to disintegrate, what was behind his apparent death wish, the part she had played, the devilry they had shared, and (we can ignore her detractors, who were not actually there and who do not know) all that she had meant to him. Which would have muddied the waters, ridiculing the idealised image of Mary the widow. It would also have humiliated 'boyfriend' Jim and would have reduced Saint Freddie to no more than the creature his critics refused to unsee: a king who was in the altogether.[7] A self-indulgent wretch who had lost his way and who had blighted the lives of too many with his selfishness, his addictions and his loss of self-control.

The stage-management of Freddie's death and funeral, the banishment of Barbara and other undesirables, was an act of sanitation and sanctification. It was about preservation of the legacy. Elevation of Freddie Mercury to untouchable idol would uphold the Queen oeuvre in perpetuity. Untainted and intact, it would guarantee income far into the future. Which is what happened.

A biopic can never be more than a distillation of a life. Its running time would be years not hours otherwise. GK Films, Queen Productions, the band's manager Jim Beach and, yes, Brian and Roger, who I believe were to some extent misled, invited the world to believe their fact-bending celluloid simplification of Freddie's gigantic, tangled, self-destructive half-life. The world fell for it. The film makers laughed all the way to the bank. Then the backlash.

CHAPTER FOURTEEN
MONTSERRAT

There would also be one last love, a meeting of minds, a blending of souls. A redemptive, non-romantic, asexual relationship that lifted Freddie not only out of his comfort zone but out of himself. Projecting him into a dream world of possibilities and new beginnings, it contradicted dismal reality and gave him fresh purpose towards the end of his life. It also generated a song that came closer than anything Freddie had ever composed to matching and even eclipsing 'Bohemian Rhapsody'. The artist he wrote it for and with whom he sang it was Spanish soprano Montserrat Caballé. The song was 'Barcelona'.

That first ever rock-opera collaboration would inspire other artists to work with non-classical stars. Galvanised by the global success of 'Barcelona', the world's best-loved tenor Luciano Pavarotti gathered the Spice Girls, Elton John, Gloria Estefan, Mariah Carey, Celine Dion and more to perform at his 'Pavarotti and Friends' concerts of the late 1990s and early 2000s. His Three Tenors co-star Placido Domingo broadened his remit to sing with Julio Iglesias, John Denver and various Latin American stars. There was then the meteoric rise of cross-overs Katherine Jenkins and Andrea Bocelli: both classically trained but up for anything, including musical theatre numbers and rock and pop.

There was also Alfie Boe. The Blackpool-born car mechanic who trained to be a tenor, before taking a leap of faith into musical theatre and becoming Jean Valjean in *Les Misérables*, had been captivated as a child by Freddie Mercury. But it was not until almost twenty-two years after the composer's death that Alfie tackled 'Barcelona' for a performance at London's One Mayfair (the former Grade I listed St Mark's Church) on 5 September 2013, in honour of what would have been Freddie's sixty-seventh birthday.

'The more I practise, the more I realise how complex the song is,' said Boe during rehearsals, clips of which were included in an episode of the ITV series *Perspectives* entitled 'Freddie Mercury Saved My Life'. 'I find it extraordinary that Freddie, who as far as I know was an untutored, untrained rock singer, could write and sing this incredible piece,' he said. The programme explored his desire to find out how much of Freddie's lack of formal training made him the creative genius that inspired Alfie himself to get up on stage. He revealed that after gaining a place at the Royal College of Music, he struggled to cope with life in London, and soon found himself broke, starving and sleeping rough in Hyde Park. It was only when an opportunity arose to demo a tape of Queen songs at Abbey Road Studios that he found the strength to pull himself together and give music another go. On leaving the studio that day, Alfie 'was filled with this energy and drive to go and pursue what I wanted to pursue, to do what I wanted to do, to sing the music I wanted to sing, and discover emotion. The spur, for me, was listening to the real thing. I heard a raw freedom in Freddie's voice, from the very last tracks like 'The Show Must Go On' all the way back to the earliest Queen records. I wanted to explore what gave rise to that extraordinary voice.'

Boe's performance of 'Barcelona', duetting with mezzo soprano and crossover star Laura Wright, was the culmination of everything he had learned about Freddie along the way. He visited the remains of Mountain Studios and Freddie's statue beside the lake in Montreux; Mike Moran's Buckinghamshire studio; and the Barcelona Ritz Hotel, where he conducted one of the last-ever interviews with Montserrat Caballé, in the room where she and

Freddie had first met. He also talked to Freddie's mother and sister, his friend David Evans, Brian May, former roadie Peter Hince and (of course) Peter Freestone. He emerged 'humbled' to have received the training that Freddie 'knew he lacked'. The whole experience taught him, Alfie said, that there were 'no limits' in music.

'From rock to opera, it didn't matter to Freddie. It was either good or bad.'

☿

In 1985, the year of Queen's Brazilian victory at Rock in Rio, of Live Aid, of their tour of New Zealand, Australia and Japan, of Freddie's wildest birthday party ever, in Munich, and of his show-stopping appearance at Fashion Aid, he was still, in his own cock-sure words, 'an old slag who gets up every morning, scratches his head and wonders what he wants to fuck.' Back on the road in 1986, Queen's *Magic* tour was attended by more than a million fans across Europe, each city chosen for personal reasons by all four members of the band. It also included historic shows performed behind the Iron Curtain, in Budapest. Freddie was still every inch the searing superstar . . . out on stage. Away from the spotlight, his touring persona had undergone a dramatic transformation. The orgiastic frenzy of coke, cruising, catamites and craziness that had consumed his previous decade had given way, can you believe, to civilised games of Scrabble and Trivial Pursuit with his crew and cohorts. The Bacchanalia was behind him and the key had been thrown away . . . the same key that locked the stable door after the horse had bolted.[1]

It was during the early 1980s that the AIDS epidemic began its inexorable march across the continents, going on to claim up to forty million lives. AIDS-related deaths peaked in 2004. By the end of 2019, there were still more than thirty-eight million people throughout the world living with HIV.[2] The virus, which had been identified some sixty years earlier, was transmitted by bodily fluids including blood and semen, and attacked the immune system.

Those most at risk were intravenous drug users and people who had unprotected sex with multiple partners. It flourished among the gay community in New York before spreading worldwide. A lack of information coupled with raging homophobia let to its denunciation as a 'gay plague', before its indiscriminate nature was understood. In 1982, it was even referred to as GRID: Gay-Related Immune Deficiency. Scientists were baffled by the deaths from rare illnesses of so many otherwise apparently healthy people.

For many years, French Canadian Gaëtan Dugas was deemed to be to blame. The Air Canada flight attendant became globally infamous as 'Patient Zero': the first HIV-infected male who, having contracted the virus in Haiti or Africa, landed in America in 1974 and started spreading it around New York's gay bars. Dugas, thirty-one, died a pariah back home in Quebec in 1984, not from AIDS but from kidney failure. But his name has now been cleared. New testing of blood samples in 2016 proved that the HIV strain which infiltrated the US had crossed from Zaire to Haiti in 1967, and to New York City in 1971, thereafter spreading to San Francisco over the next five years. It had reached America ahead of Dugas.

Interviewed by doctors as part of a 1984 investigation to track down the sexual contacts of some forty homosexuals with Kaposi's sarcoma or showing other signs of advanced AIDS, Dugas supplied the names of seventy-two males with whom he'd had sex. There were probably hundreds more. Twenty per cent of the aforementioned forty, four in Southern California and four in New York, admitted to sex with an anonymous flight attendant. Dugas was consequently branded 'Patient Zero' and castigated worldwide. But the label was erroneous. He had in fact been listed as 'Patient O', denoting 'Outside Southern California'. That 'O' was read mistakenly as 'zero'. American journalist Randy Shilts went after him in his bestselling 1987 study, *And the Band Played On*, pillorying Dugas for having started the spread of the disease deliberately by continuing to indulge in unprotected sex after doctors had cautioned him not to. Shilts himself died of AIDS in 1994.

The most frequently asked questions about Freddie and AIDS – when and where did he contract the virus, and who gave it to him – are impossible to answer. We know that he began frequenting the more notorious New York gay clubs such as the Mineshaft and the Anvil from 1975, during Queen's major US tour. Letting his hair down on a scale he could never have got away with in London, Freddie lived promiscuously and even talked about it to the press. British journalist Rick Sky, who was invited to New York to interview Freddie exclusively, remembers him saying, 'I live life to the full. My sex drive is enormous. I sleep with men, women, cats – you name it! I'll go to bed with anything. My bed is so huge, I can comfortably sleep six. I prefer my sex without any involvement.' He is known to have had encounters with airline steward John Murphy, who had also had sex with Gaëtan Dugas. Freddie met Dugas several times, in New York clubs as well as in London's Heaven. Did they have sex? Thought to have been infected for around ten years when he died – so from about 1981 – Freddie and his hundreds of lovers could have gone on to infect hundreds more. By the time he woke up to the folly of his 'Fuck it, I'm doing everything with everyone' stance, it was too late. His first test towards the end of 1985 was inconclusive. His second – in 1987, when testing had become more sophisticated and the results were more reliable – was a death sentence.

Not that he faced up to it. He avoided the verdict. His doctor, unable to get hold of him, was forced to impart the awful news to Mary. She in turn had to break it to him, no enviable task. Though in some ways it feels quite right that it had to be her. Having received the devastating but not entirely unexpected confirmation, Freddie dealt with it by ignoring it. He barely discussed it with members of his household, all of whose futures would change course.

Jim Hutton later said that Freddie was in deep denial about the diagnosis. After he came to him and confessed it, they never discussed it again. 'It was his cross and he wanted to carry it the way he chose – without burdening me,' said Jim. 'If something came up on TV to do with AIDS, we'd turn channels.'

The first thing he should have done was inform his band-mates Brian, Roger and John, who had suspected for some time that something was wrong. They feared the worst anyway, and they had a right to know. It would change their careers too. But Freddie avoided the confrontation until the beginning of 1989, when he invited them to his house for the meeting. At which, Jim recalled, Freddie didn't say much. What he wanted to get across was that he wished to continue recording with them until he dropped.

☿

In a taped interview conducted ahead of his forty-first birthday party in 1987, at Pike's Hotel in Ibiza, Freddie revealed to David Wigg that he had given up sex completely.[3]

'I've stopped going out, whatever, and to be honest I've almost become a nun,' he said. 'I learned the hard way. I thought sex was a very important thing to me, because I lived through sex, and now I've gone completely the other way. You see, I'm one of those people who can go from black to white; I don't like intermediary measures or anything. It's quite easy for me to completely give up. I can give up alcohol at the drop of a hat. And yes, *it* (HIV/AIDS) has frightened me to death, and I have stopped having sex.'

He warmed to his theme, as if trying to convince himself.

'I just like titillation now,' he teased. 'I'm into titillation. What I was doing before . . . I was very greedy. People always want something more, and sex for me was fun. I was extremely promiscuous, but I've stopped all of that. Practicality came into it. And I'm an old bird now, dear. The word "solace" came into it, and you can't say you have a life of solace and then go round fucking half the world. And I don't miss it, I really don't. It was like a high. Everything was open to me, so in terms of music, sex was a very integral ingredient to what I was doing. It was a very major factor in a lot of what I did, but I would never have thought of sex and nothing else. It was all of these things, and I was living them to the full. There was excess in every direction. I was living what one would call a very full life, in every direction. And why not?'

In all the years leading up to this volte face, had Freddie ever taken a deep breath before engaging with his latest primed specimen, or searched his conscience before diving in? Had the bigger picture ever occurred to him?

'Probably not,' muses rock manager Simon Napier-Bell. 'I'm sure Freddie wasn't thinking too deeply about it all, he was just doing what he enjoyed. There's this tendency to moralise and disapprove. Even today, when people are supposed to be more enlightened, the prevailing opinion is, "Well, what do they expect when they swan round the world having sex with hundreds of rent boys?" In this regard, by the way, "rent boys" have had a bad rap. They are not like women prostitutes, who often have no choice, having been coerced into it by family members or murderous pimps. These young men are not victims. They know what they're doing. They don't lose their purity to it, and they tend not to feel violated. Most of them are country boys who migrate to the city because they want a better life. They are up for fun. They put up with sex for all the other benefits, such as dinner and drinks and money. It's a common arrangement that suits the kind of men who enjoy having friendships with younger people but who don't want to have to show affection.

'Freddie was in it for sex, not romance,' Simon reasons. 'He went with rent boys everywhere. It came with the territory. The fact that he was gay makes him no different from any straight rock musician. Is a groupie not a rent boy by another name? You have sex with a rock star, you get a ticket to the gig, it's the same thing. If the rock star gives a male groupie a little something, that makes him a rent boy. You have to look at it from Freddie's point of view. His job involves travelling all over the world. He wants to have sex. He also wants to meet interesting people who are different from people he's met before. So he meets young men in bars, buys them a drink, they talk about their lives. He could be talking to the local prime minister's son or a boy from the sticks with no money to buy himself a meal. It's more often about company than about anything else. But it usually becomes about sex because everything does, if you are attracted to someone. The sex is almost incidental. You end up in bed, then it's, "Ooh gosh, I've got to give you a bit of money, haven't I, because you haven't got any and I've got loads." This is a very different person from the man who frequents hardened brothels, with cubicles – where the girl's got a baby at home, and probably even a husband. Are we saying that Freddie was any worse than them? Aren't they the same?'

Why have so few come forward to kiss and tell about their experiences with Freddie Mercury?

'Because they were not there to meet Freddie Mercury! They were there to have sex! Most of them wouldn't have known who he was anyway. Then there's the fact that someone who has to be a rent boy is not someone who knows how to talk to journalists or get a publisher. Plus, they don't want to expose themselves. I think about George Michael . . .' – whom Simon managed for years, both as half of the duo Wham! and as a solo artist – '. . . trawling Hampstead Heath late at night for men to have sex with. None of those guys talked about George after his death. Why would they? Most of them were married men with families. They were not going to come out and say they'd had sex with George Michael while he was still alive, either, so George knew he was perfectly safe. He went with the kind of people who, like him, had too much to lose. So much sexual activity is covert, even today, but believe you me it's going on. It doesn't make it right or wrong, it makes it a fact. You might be amazed by some of the people who are doing that kind of thing. Freddie was no worse than any of them.'

☿

I used to look at her and wonder. Would Mary Austin have wanted Freddie back, had she known about the stuff he got up to? I studied her across rooms, that summer of 1986, when we were all in

Budapest. She still had the same pure, untouched air she had exuded in photos during the early seventies; a stoical mien that gave her something of the look of an Italian Renaissance Madonna. I imagined her putting up with anything and turning a blind eye to the lot, provided there was a chance that her Freddie would one day come back to her. Maybe she did know everything. Compliant, apparently complicit rock women tend to. 'No flies on her,' as my mother would say. After the funeral of the Who's bassist John Entwistle in Stow-on-the-Wold in 2002, I had a conversation, back at John's home Quarwood, with the wife of another band member. He was notoriously as wild and as unfaithful as 'the Ox' had been. 'Why do you put up with it?' I asked her. 'I couldn't give a monkey's what he gets up to or who with when he's out there, to be honest with you,' she said. 'Sex and drugs and rock and roll, as they say. The rocker-him does whatever he needs to, to let off steam and be the star who's bought us the life we have. Whose earnings pay for a new Bulthaup kitchen or Christmas in Antigua or another Range Rover whenever I want one. I'd be an idiot to cut my nose off to spite my face. Ask any of the wives here today, I bet you they'd all say the same. Better to be his Mrs than his mistress or his one-night stand. In any case, the real him is the one who comes home and shares a bed with me.'

☿

Beyond the last Queen show with Freddie as frontman, at Knebworth in August 1986, Freddie's life was largely one of domestic bliss. He and Jim set off from Garden Lodge on a spend-spend-spend holiday of a lifetime in Japan, reckoned to have cost Freddie a million pounds, and returned with their shopping bags to the shock of their lives. A splash exclusive in the *News of the World* outed Freddie; revealed the names of airline steward John Murphy and courier Tony Bastin, former lovers of his who had died of AIDS; exposed details of wild cocaine nights with Rod Stewart and David Bowie; and identified Jim Hutton and Winnie Kirchberger as two of

'All the Queen's Men'. It also divulged details about Freddie's first AIDS test. Several days' worth of sordid revelations followed, in 'the Screws' sister paper the *Sun*.[4] Freddie's former personal manager Paul Prenter had done the dirty for the paltry sum of £32,000, which he later claimed was to pay for his own AIDS treatment. Although the content was largely accurate, Freddie denied everything, refused to comment, and kept his head down. He found the betrayal unbearable and never spoke to Prenter again, despite the traitor's efforts to get in touch with him.

'It was an awful betrayal,' said Jim. 'It crushed Freddie's ability to trust others, except for a select few. He made no new friends after that.'

Which was not quite true.

During promotional interviews for the *Magic* tour, Freddie was asked by a Spanish broadcaster who, in his opinion, had the best voice in the world. Taking care to emphasise that he wasn't just saying so because he was in Spain, Freddie named Montserrat Caballé.

Peter Freestone, who had worked at the Royal Opera House and who had a genuine, well-informed love of ballet and opera, had introduced Freddie to recordings of Montserrat's voice five years earlier. In 1983, the dickie-bowed pair had repaired to Covent Garden to experience Pavarotti performing in Giuseppe Verdi's *Un Ballo in Maschera* (A Masked Ball). The prima donna on that occasion was none other than Miss Caballé, still stupendous in her fiftieth year. From the moment she came on, Peter said, Freddie forgot about the Maestro and turned his astonished attention to Montserrat. She sang like an angel, piercing his heart. 'He went to a couple more of Montserrat's concerts in New York, but he never wanted to meet her,' Peter added. 'I don't think he wanted his image of this amazing diva destroyed. He imagined Montserrat would be a grand opera character, the same way everyone imagined Freddie was a rock and roll animal.'

Montserrat's brother Carlos Caballé had been made head of entertainment for the summer 1992 Olympic Games by the

International Olympic Committee. When Barcelona was declared the host city in 1986, an idea was floated that Montserrat should sing a specially commissioned official Olympics theme song as a duet with Freddie Mercury. Why? Because no such thing had been done before? Whoever first thought of it, Freddie and Montserrat were both up for it. So it was that in March 1987, at the Barcelona Ritz, Miss Caballé and Mr Mercury came face to face. Also present was a most affable musician and friend of Freddie's, the gifted pianist, composer and arranger Mike Moran. They went prepared with a demo: of 'Exercises in Free Love', a piece of music they had co-written for her. It was Freddie's voice on the tape, imitating Montserrat's falsetto. Never in all the years he had worked for him, said Peter Freestone, had he seen Freddie so nervous:

'They'd arranged to have lunch at 1 p.m.' (or at 2 p.m., as he has said elsewhere.) 'In his suite, Freddie was chain-smoking and pacing. For the first time ever, he actually turned up for an appointment five minutes early ... Freddie always made an appearance fifteen minutes late. In the lobby, by four minutes past, Freddie said, "She's not going to come, she's not interested." Then this crowded lobby parted like the Red Sea and Montserrat walked through. She said later she was so happy because, when she took his hand, it was colder than hers, which meant he was even more nervous than she was. She'd been shaking at the thought of meeting this amazing rock star.'

The divas ate together in a private garden dining room in which a piano had been installed, 'just in case'. Peter remembered them being 'completely in awe of each other', but also thrilled by the idea of working together. Despite their thirteen-year age gap, their musical and cultural differences and a moderate language barrier – Montserrat spoke adequate English, while Freddie's Spanish was virtually non-existent – they fell for each other. She was soon calling Freddie 'my Number One'. He was addressing her as 'my Super-Diva.' She loved the piece, too, and requested their permission to sing it at the Royal Opera House the following week.

Freddie had not expected Montserrat to be so earthy. 'She jokes and she swears and she doesn't take herself too seriously,' he enthused. 'That really thrilled and surprised me, because up until then I had been labouring under the illusion that all great opera singers were stern, aloof and quite intimidating. But Montserrat was wonderful. I told her I loved her singing and had her albums and asked if she'd heard of me. She told me she enjoyed listening to my music and had Queen albums in her collection, too.'

His understanding had been that they would record one song together, the one destined for the Olympics. It was Montserrat who suggested that they produce an entire album together. Freddie, who was already assembling ideas for another solo album, had never imagined that he would be recording one with her.

'When I was planning to do my second solo project,' he said, 'I really didn't want it to be just another bunch of songs. I wanted it to be something different, to have another stamp to it that spearheaded the damn thing.' It was no secret that it had long been his dream to create a whole album combining rock with opera, harking back to what he had started with the Baroque'n'roll glory of 'Bohemian Rhapsody'.

With a schedule as packed as Montserrat's – opera singers are routinely booked for five years or more in advance – finding the time to create an album proved challenging. Having established that her diary would allow them a little time together in September, a few days the following January and perhaps a couple more in April, it was decided that producer Mike and Freddie would lay down everything required except Montserrat's vocal. She would join them to add her parts at the last minute. They recorded at Queen's Mountain Studios in Montreux, and at London's Townhouse.

As that engagement at the Royal Opera House would be bringing her to London a few days after their first meeting, Montserrat accepted an invitation to dinner at Garden Lodge.

'When Montserrat stayed at Freddie's home, to try ideas for the album, the two of them and Mike Moran the producer were still up at four in the morning,' recalled Peter – while Montserrat long maintained that she left Freddie's home at 6 a.m. 'And she was a hoot. I couldn't help thinking that Freddie really had met his match this time. She downed about two bottles of champagne by herself. At one point, she reached for Freddie's cigarette packet, took one out and lit up. Freddie was horrified. He banged on and on to her, how can you *do* this, what about your *voice*?! Afterwards, we said, well, who knew? She was as rock'n'roll as he was! They were as drunk as skunks together. They adored each other.'

Part of the original plan was that Freddie and Montserrat would perform at the Olympics' opener. Then came his AIDS diagnosis, before they had even begun to record. Although he could not summon the courage to confess to his bandmates, Freddie wasted no time in sharing it with his new best friend. He could not bear the thought of her being misled into thinking that he would still be around to sing live with her in 1992. In the end, he would die only eight months before the Olympics began.

'Barcelona' the single, backed by 'Exercises in Free Love', was released in October 1987. It became one of Freddie's greatest hits, reaching number eight on the UK singles chart. It would do even better five years later, when, as the soundtrack used by the BBC for their coverage of the '92 Olympics, it rose to number two. The eponymous album was released in 1988, the title track its masterpiece. Its appeal transcended its name and subject matter: I know two brides who walked down the aisle to it. Commented Mike Moran, 'The power and the passion he put into it is the same as a tenor in an opera.' Its accompanying video, directed by Queen favourite David Mallet, out-diva'd them all.

Freddie and Montserrat performed 'Barcelona' together just twice. The first was for the May 1987 Ibiza Festival, at the Ku nightclub (later the Privilege Ibiza, the 'world's largest nightclub'). Then on 8 October 1988 came Freddie's last-ever live performance, with Montserrat – at Barcelona's La Nit festival held to receive the Olympic flag from Seoul, in the presence of King Juan Carlos,

Queen Sofia and Princess Cristina. They were to sing live on a stage constructed in front of Barcelona's Font màgica de Montjuïc (Magic Fountain) on the Plaça de Carles Buïgas, world-famous for its water, light and music shows. It didn't get grander. José Carreras, Dionne Warwick, Rudolf Nureyev, Jerry Lee Lewis and other major stars had performed ahead of them. The pièce de résistance would be Freddie and Montsy accompanied by the Barcelona Opera House orchestra and choir, rounded off with a spectacular fireworks display.

But disaster struck ahead of the performance. Freddie's voice deserted him. Although the problem was described at the time as 'throat nodules', 'the mushroom' of which Barbara spoke was to blame. All involved went into panic mode. The city was teeming with British journalists who had been flown in to talk to Freddie and Montserrat about the momentous occasion. In no mood to talk to the media, Freddie pulled out of both press conference and exclusive interviews, which led inevitably to conjecture about his condition. But the show must go on, he insisted. He prepared himself to sing. As the day wore on, it became increasingly obvious that he was not going to be able to. Only at the last minute did he give in and agree to mime. He and Montserrat would perform three tracks, 'How Can I Go On', 'The Golden Boy' and 'Barcelona', to their own recordings. Which would not have been a problem had the playback not run slow. It had to be stopped and rewound while they were standing there on stage, thus revealing to all present that it would not, after all, be a live performance. Freddie lost it. He went screaming for the sound technicians who had screwed up so badly and exposed him as a fraud, before retreating to his tented dressing room to fill himself with vodka. By the time he was taken to meet members of the Olympic Games committee, he had calmed down. So what, he mimed to a live audience. He was by no means the first to have done so. It's still him on the record.

Footage of the two performances of 'Barcelona', accessible online, are incredibly moving. The delight and pride on Freddie's face as he raises Montserrat's bejewelled hand to kiss it, and his sublime expression as he pecks her cheek at the song's conclusion, say everything about what he felt for the music and for Montserrat.

☿

During an interview with popular Swedish television and radio host Jacob Dahlin in 1988,[5] the year of their album's release, Montserrat was asked what she thought was the difference between singing rock with Freddie Mercury and a grand opera with the third of the Three Tenors, José Carreras. In hesitant English, she explained.

'Well, the difference is the way you feel something that is so different in instrumentation, inspiration, but in the same time – and don't be shocked with what I am saying, because this is the way I feel – to be part of a creation,' she said. 'To be part of something that is created . . . for freedom, freedom of expression, and in music, and in lyrics. In the opera you have to do it in a way that you are . . . you have to go inside a big painting that is already done. You go inside, and you make yourself part of that big – whatever it is. With Freddie, we have to create something which is different. He created it. It's for me, and for him. I enjoy it enormously. I feel free. I don't feel that I have to follow a conductor. I can in the moment express inspiration, not only in the music but in the words . . . '

That. She would also later acknowledge her 'greatest blessing': that 'Barcelona' had made her, beyond her genre, a worldwide household name. But the music aside, her feelings for Freddie were simple. 'Musicians, they understand each other, very very well,' she said. 'They are married in music. This is what was happening with Freddie and with me.'

'I lovèd him,' she smiled, pronouncing the final syllable. 'And he lovèd me.'[6]

Was Montserrat, then, the love of his life? Imagine.

☿

She would outlive Freddie by twenty-seven years. How much of her life story and early career had he been able to catch up on during the relatively short time they knew each other? Beyond his appreciation of the clarity of her voice and her regal stage presence, what else did he know about her? Montserrat was no blower of trumpets. Could someone like Freddie truly understand her significance in the pantheon of world-class prima donnas?

He could, and did. He adored her sobriquet 'La Superba'. It projected her into the highest possible echelon alongside Australian soprano Joan Sutherland, 'La Stupenda', and Greek-American Maria Callas, who was known as 'La Divina'. Montserrat had 'ravished', 'shimmered' and 'melted' her way around the world's great opera houses . . . opera critics invariably effused when writing about her. Her pianissimo – the ability to sing so softly that what emerges is little more than a whisper, reckoned to be one of the most demanding operatic techniques and for which the singer requires a cast-iron diaphragm and better breath control than that of an athlete – was magnificent. She was once described as possessing one of the most beautiful voices ever to issue from a human throat. It lent itself so brilliantly to the bel canto repertoire, comprising works by Donizetti, Rossini, and Bellini, that she was later acknowledged as having been the reason behind the whole bel canto revival. She was acclaimed for her renditions of the German Lieder: songs from the fourteenth and fifteenth centuries that were basically poems in dialect set to music; the dramatic Spanish zarzuelas, an early musical theatre genre; Verdi's operas; Richard Strauss's *Salome*, her favourite role; and Donizetti's *Lucrezia Borgia*, her single performance of which, in 1965, shot her to international stardom. No wonder Freddie sometimes seemed lost for words in her presence. No wonder he deferred to her so sweetly, coming on like a coy little boy.

In a Spanish interview filmed in Ibiza, he sits smoking nervously and drinking a glass of beer beside her as she beams him her lipstick-caked smile. When Freddie speaks, he sounds almost

Estuary compared to her – whereas normally his accent was quite silver-spoon. Dressed in a loose blue-grey suit over a green Hawaiian-style shirt, he appears to be carrying weight in this piece. His clean-shaven face looks puffed. These were probably effects of his AIDS medication. Montserrat, in a flowing red, purple and mustard gown and made up as if for the stage, beams beside him. He glances at her and back at the camera, and raises his eyebrows cartoonishly. He calls her 'Montsy'. 'It was like a dream come true,' he tells the interviewer, about working with her. 'I wondered if our voices would match ... but now she's a rock and roller ... I'm finally doing something that I really wanted, to sing with her. I have to keep touching her (he does so) [to make sure] that she's here. I just hope there are some better things to come.'[7]

Montserrat, like Freddie, had stunned audiences all over the world by the time they met. One of the leading opera singers of the second half of the twentieth century, she had performed with the Basel and Bremen Operas before making her Carnegie Hall debut in Manhattan in 1965, at the age of thirty-two and not long married to Spanish tenor Bernabé Martí. Freddie, only nineteen at the time, was still finding his feet in London. She would return to 'the Hall' to perform annual concerts for years afterwards. She thrilled audiences at the San Francisco Opera and the Vienna State, and sang ninety-eight times with New York's Metropolitan Opera. Covent Garden and Milan's La Scala were among her favourite venues. Unusually for a soprano, she sang well into her sixties, more than ten years beyond the usual retirement age. It gave her a career spanning almost half a century. Her audiences routinely screamed, stamped and generally erupted into the kind of fervour usually reserved for rock'n'roll gigs. She was more than accustomed to public hysteria by the time she met Freddie. It was just another thing for them to giggle about together.

Her voice, Montserrat often said, was a gift from God. It's not hard to see why she felt such gratitude for the talent that transported her from poverty to wealth and stardom.

Born Maria de Montserrat Viviana Concepción Caballé i Folch in Barcelona on 12 April 1933, she was named after the Blessed Virgin Mary of Montserrat, the patron saint of Catalonia, whose image is one of the Black Madonnas of Europe. She lived through both the Depression and the Spanish Civil War. In years to come, she would deftly sidestep questions in interviews about whether her family had been Nationalist supporters of dictator Franco or Republicans, on the side of the democratic Spanish government. Music is not political, was her view. Her love of it had been encouraged by her middle-class parents, Carles Caballé i Borrás and Anna Folch, who cherished their collection of operatic recordings. By the time she was eight years old, she had committed to memory the aria *Un Bel Dì* from Puccini's *Madama Butterfly*, and was performing it for her parents, aunts and uncles. Her lofty imaginings afforded escape from the family's penury. At one point during her childhood, she had only one dress, which she wore to school every day for a year. It explained her adult passion for lavish couture, fur coats and jewellery. Her precocious talent prompted her mother and father to scrape together the wherewithal to send her to Barcelona's Conservatori Superior de Música del Liceu, where she studied piano and voice. But before she turned sixteen, her father fell ill and could no longer meet the fees. She left the conservatory to work in a handkerchief factory. Salvation arrived a year on, in the form of wealthy Barcelona patrons who sponsored her return to the Liceu and supported her family. She graduated at twenty with her college's highest honour to her name, a gold medal for voice. Lacking confidence, she failed auditions with all the Italian opera companies she tried for; but found a home in Switzerland in 1956, with the Basel Opera. Her break came when the company's soprano fell sick and Montserrat replaced her, performing as Mimì in Puccini's *La Bohème*. It was her performance as Lucrezia Borgia in that American Opera Society concert production at Carnegie Hall that established her international career.

There were obstacles. She was diagnosed with a benign brain tumour in 1989, and treated for a heart problem in 1993. Her son and daughter were born surgically, by Caesarean section, which took her out of circulation for months. She suffered a stroke in 2012. Two years later, in a Spanish tax fraud case, she was forced to accept a six-month suspended sentence and a hefty fine, having falsely claimed residence in the tax haven of Andorra. She actually lived between homes in Vienna and in the countryside beyond her beloved Barcelona.

She gave her last performance in 2014, in the Catalan coastal town of Cambrils. She had been ill for several years, and was admitted to Barcelona's Sant Paul hospital on 22 September 2018 with a suspected gall bladder problem. She died on 6 October, at the age of eighty-five. Her funeral, held two days later, was attended by former Queen Sofia of Spain, leading politicians, and cultural figures including José Carreras. 'She was an irreplaceable artist, the soprano of the twentieth century along with Maria Callas,' her friend the Catalan tenor said. They buried her beside her parents, in the Sant Andreu cemetery.

☿

I have long been fascinated by the fact that the two people with whom Freddie identified most keenly were both women: Barbara and Montserrat. They, like him, had survived war, and had lived through adversity. Each had been displaced from childhood homes and had their lives turned upside-down. Each had overcome challenges against the odds to make something outstanding of themselves, achieving wealth, fame and acclaim. Like Freddie, they lived life on their own terms, cowering to no one.

☿

The obvious theme of Queen's fourteenth studio album, *Innuendo*, their last to be released during Freddie's lifetime, is mortality. The band tackled their subject matter full-on, with dignity and defiance.

Brian came up with the banger, 'The Show Must Go On'. Roger's haunting offering was 'These Are the Days of Our Lives', released as a single on Freddie's forty-fifth birthday. The mournful 'Don't Try So Hard' was bassist John Deacon's oblation. These special, quintessentially Queen songs heave with all the conversations their writers were unable to have with the friend who was slipping away. All the agony and despair they couldn't express in spoken words found their way into these wonderful tributes. The title track, however, is the sensation. Written by Freddie and Roger and six and a half minutes long, it exceeds 'Bohemian Rhapsody' by thirty-five seconds. In terms of scope and scale, it outclasses their signature song, to the point that it was dubbed 'Bohemian Rhapsody II'. Its epic tapestry of changing tempos, metal, choral interludes, Flamenco and other Spanish influences, the clenching guitars, the 'Bolero' beat, Freddie's soaring, liberated vocal, as well as its operatic sequence and echoes of early Queen, seem to magic-carpet the band back through their entire career, delivering them deftly to the doorstep of their original dream. Complex and deep, its lyrics throb with home truths: war and greed and false gods are futile . . . destruction is pointless . . . human existence must be worth more than this . . . Freddie is leaving us . . . and then the lifeline: 'You can be anything you want to be.'

'The music, at the end, was what kept Freddie alive,' said Jim. 'If he hadn't have had that, I'm sure that he would have died sooner.'

CHAPTER FIFTEEN
LOVE OF MY LIFE

How marvellous Freddie was and how brave, they said. Keeping himself so busy during those final years, improving his home, snapping up and doing up houses in the mews behind Garden Lodge, buying a Montreux apartment with a balcony looking out over Lake Geneva all the way to the snow-capped mountains – a view he loved more than anywhere else, though he had once pronounced the place 'boring'; and continuing to record with Queen, as fast as the others could write and hurl him songs. It must have occurred to those close to him that he was in denial; that he was occupying his mind with to-do lists and work for a reason. Which was that there could be no room left in it to ponder, fret or consider his brewing fate. It was what it was. Nothing could be done about it. There was, and is, no cure. He knew better than anyone what was coming. Even so, there must have been concomitant hope that if he cut all excess living, hunkered down and toed the line, he could beat this thing.

Did he ever stop to think, at that stage, about the many co-stars and walk-ons who had passed through his blockbuster life? Of sweet Mary, as she was when they first met? Of those innocent early days when they set up home together so quaintly, and had seemed so perfectly matched? Of their final two years together, when inner conflict set in, when guilt and duty kept him heading home at night while desire of another kind was dragging him away?

Of his monumental infidelity towards both Mary and David Minns, his first real boyfriend? Of all those other good old-fashioned lover boys? Of the many nameless, faceless turns who peopled the turning-point New York years? Of Barbara, Winnie and Jim and the upset and confusion he caused them during the derangement that was Munich? Of his mother and father, his sister and her own family, of their innocent pride in him? Of what they might think if they knew what he didn't want them to ... which, it turns out, they knew anyway. Of Brian, Roger and John (who knew some of it), and what would become of Queen when the ride stopped and they had to get off? For how could the show go on without him? Queen minus Freddie would be like the Beatles without Lennon. To soldier on minus their frontman or to try to replace him could never work. Could it? Wouldn't that make them figures of fun, little more than their own tribute act? Just as well, then, that they would probably clean up in the aftermath of his passing, without having to lift a finger. As rock manager Simon Napier-Bell famously said, the best thing a rock star can do for his back catalogue is die young. Once the possibility of further product by that artist has been extinguished because he is no longer here to record any, his fans will value him even more highly and his – their – stock will soar. No, Freddie didn't worry on their behalf.

Closer to home, he had taken care of his household. Neither Phoebe, Jim, Joe nor others would leave empty-handed. All would depart with enough cash in their back pocket to buy a home outright elsewhere. But money aside, how would they fare psychologically? Would they cope without him? Having put their own lives on hold to devote themselves unconditionally to his, what would be the emotional impact of his loss?

The fall-out, for those who have served celebrities, can be cataclysmic. Take Jane Andrews, who never adjusted back down to normal life after losing her job as Sarah, Duchess of York's dresser and companion. Fergie's aide was arrested in 2000 after killing her boyfriend because he declined to marry her. Found guilty of murder and sentenced to life, she escaped nine years in but was caught and re-incarcerated. Her 2015 parole was short-lived. After harassing a lover she went back to jail, walking free in 2019.

Paul Burrell made a more successful transition after the crash that killed the Princess of Wales. Diana's 'rock' had swapped a Derbyshire mining village for the royal household. Her Majesty's personal footman became the princess's butler and right-hand man. It was he who laid out her body in Paris; he who collected and incinerated her blood-soaked clothes. As a representative of Diana's Memorial Trust, he went fundraising to America and found fame … which led to him reclining on Elizabeth Taylor's bed, watching the Oscars on her television. After the Palace paid him off, he gave talks, wrote an etiquette column for the *Daily Mail* and a bestselling book, *Entertaining with Style*, which shifted a hundred thousand copies. Accused of selling royal belongings, he wound up in court, but his trial collapsed. He became a florist in Cheshire, came out as gay and left his wife, graced Channel 5's *Big Brother* house and came second in *I'm a Celebrity … Get Me Out of Here* in 2004. Each time I flick through the channels, there he is on some doc or other, chatting, reminiscing and pontificating about the royals.

I had my own experience of the phenomenon, if not in any professional capacity. I was friendly with a Hollywood actress for a while. Raquel Welch and I met in a beach bar in Mustique. She was, as I later wrote, 'a fabled and faded drama queen who was old enough to be my mother. I was an upstart nobody, young enough to be totally in awe.' Celebrity friendships are always symbiotic but rarely equal. Never devoid of ulterior motive, they are inevitably short-lived. We seemed inseparable for a while: hanging by the pool at the Beverly Hills Hotel, getting our nails done, having lunch in the Polo Lounge, going for dinner at the Rainbow Bar and Grill. I couldn't fathom at the time why the most legendary sex symbol since Marilyn Monroe wanted to hang with me. The reason, I worked out later, was that she was deeply insecure. My gig was to compliment her constantly; to reassure her that she still looked pretty, sexy and *young*. Because, come *on*, Baby, a girl's gotta know. After I left Los Angeles and returned to live in London, I never heard from her again.

To be a Have-Not living through Have-Everythings can be akin to dicing with death. Ask Peter Freestone. He knows to his cost how the lines become blurred. One minute you're the hired help, the next an official best friend. But you're still on the payroll, so how equal can the friendship be? As Freddie's PA for the final twelve years of his life, Phoebe found himself on call around the clock, in charge of everything. Keeper of the boss's purse and passport. Mopper-up of his sick.

'For twelve years I was in close contact with Freddie on an almost daily basis,' is the authorised line on Peter. 'I was the handyman, waiter, butler, secretary, cleaner, babysitter and responsible for his personal correspondence. I was with him when he was at the top, just as I was present during the empty periods. I saw the inspiration and I saw his frustration when things were at their worst. I was his bodyguard when necessary. And, in the end, of course, I was one of his "nurses".'

Peter was born in Carshalton, Surrey, but was educated for some years at a hill station boarding school in India, just like Freddie. His parents Leslie and Olga ran a hotel in Calcutta. He left school at sixteen and worked at Selfridges on London's Oxford Street. A part-time job in the wardrobe department at the Royal Opera House led to a full-time position. It also facilitated his first meeting with Freddie. The rising Queen star was due to take part in a charity gala performance organised by Royal Ballet principal Wayne Eagling. Accompanied by Paul Prenter, who was managing the band at the time, Freddie rocked up at the ROH to organise his stagewear. The gala was a success, and Prenter was soon back looking for a new assistant to manage Queen's wardrobe on the road during their forthcoming UK tour. Peter was hired. His life became a whirlwind of all-expenses-paid jaunts to exotic locations. He travelled the world, Access All Areas. His working relationship with Freddie evolved into friendship. He was privy to the innermost workings of one of the planet's most creative minds. A kind and loyal man, he has made a living since Freddie died in a jumble of ways. He worked at London's Guy's Hospital. He opened and ran a small hotel, the Kintyre in Torquay, Devon, where the walls were lined with framed photographs, gold discs and other Freddie memorabilia. I visited him there and saw for myself that it wasn't really him. He didn't settle. He moved on to become the director of an opera company. In 1995, having searched his soul as to whether he should but deciding on balance that it was his duty to set the record straight, he committed six months to co-writing his first book about Freddie with their mutual friend David Evans. *Freddie Mercury: An Intimate Memoir by the Man Who Knew Him Best* was published in 1998. His follow-up, launched eighteen years later in 2016, was *Freddie Mercury's Royal Recipes*. It brims with memories of cooking for Freddie and shares details of his favourite meals. Also that year, Peter co-authored the libretto of a ballet entitled *Queen – The Show Must Go On*, staged by the Moravian Theatre in the ancient city of Olomouc.

Peter was granted official Czech citizenship in August 2020 after nineteen years' residence. He lives in Třebechovice pod Orebem, a village in the region of Hradec Králové city, two hours or so east of the capital, Prague . . . itself the capital of Bohemia. See what he did there? No small coincidence, either, that his home lies only five hours north-east of Munich. He teaches locally, and works for the Titanic Freddie AIDS Project, an awareness and prevention initiative for school-age children. He appears at the annual conventions held in Montreux each September, to mark Freddie's birthday. He has been involved in a number of musical and charitable enterprises; has hosted tours of Queen- and Freddie-related locations in and around London and other cities; has appeared in many a Mercury documentary, including *The Untold Story*; presents YouTube videos addressing Freddie's fans throughout the world in his softly spoken and gentle style, reminiscing and reassuring fans who miss Freddie; and he was employed as a fact and continuity consultant by the producers of the *Bohemian Rhapsody* film. Engaged for a year, he was remunerated inadequately. For a fee that I would call insulting, he was required to get himself to the set at the crack of dawn each day and sit there for ten or twelve hours, advising the director and pointing out things they'd got wrong. One of which was the colour of Rami Malek's eyes.

'I told them, right at the beginning,' Peter despaired to me. 'It didn't make sense to me that Rami Malek was allowed to perform with his own light blue eyes. Freddie's eyes were so dark they were almost black. They were such a vital component of his face and personality. There were times when he only had to glance at you and they drilled right through you. How could this guy be Freddie with pale eyes? But of course the script kept changing, as did the director. No one could keep up, least of all me. Things that I'd flagged up to them right at the beginning didn't get handed down to the eventual team. They got lost in translation, so to speak. Apparently, dark contact lenses were fitted and made for Rami, but he couldn't get on with them. Some people just can't get used to wearing lenses no matter how hard they try, and he was one of them. This was all wasting time, and they soon gave up on the idea. That and other slip-ups were so disappointing. He couldn't be Freddie, for me, because those eyes that were staring down from the screen simply weren't his. On reflection, perhaps, it was a good thing.'

Rami took piano lessons and singing lessons. Choreographers and body movement specialists were brought in to coach him. He was required to fill his mouth with prosthetic teeth. So much work went into making him over in Freddie's image, yet he was allowed to get away with pale blue eyes. To anyone on the lookout for the production's biggest mistake, it might be that one.

☿

Could Peter Freestone, then, have been the love of Freddie's life? It's not as far-fetched as it sounds. Who but Phoebe fulfilled the traditional wifely role, seeing to all things domestic and personal and leaving Freddie undistracted by minutiae and therefore free to focus on his work? They were made in heaven, these two. Always more than a mere servant, Peter understood the artist's psyche, got to know Freddie's modus operandi, and perceived instinctively how to work around him. He knew him so well that towards the end he could almost read his mind. Freddie depended on Peter. Peter cared for Freddie selflessly, enduring the bad and enjoying the good. He was never less than there for him.

'We were very close as a group,' said Roger Taylor, soon after his bandmate's death in1991. 'But even we didn't know a lot of things about Freddie.'

But Phoebe knew. He knew everything there was to know. Almost. Most importantly, as we know, it was he who introduced Freddie to opera, inspiring a new passion, escorting him to the Royal Opera House and plonking him down in front of Montserrat Caballé . . . thus giving rise to the most important breakthrough of his creative life.

Peter's tone to this day when speaking about his lost friend, especially when he recalls a sweet or funny anecdote, is wistful and touching. So many of his utterances are prefaced with 'It seems like only yesterday . . .' Thirty years on, he is still living Freddie Mercury's life. Should I say, re-living it. Going through the motions and the moods, over and over, he has never been allowed to leave it all behind. Although the place he calls home is far from London, and while he has certainly made an effort to distance himself, he continues to exist through the achievements of a dead rock star. By his own admission, it took him several years to adjust to life after Freddie. But he has never come to terms with life *without* Freddie. His pivotal role in the Great Pretender's reality still defines him. The connection and the relationship continue. His name is, and perhaps will always be, synonymous with Freddie's. He may be loath to admit it, but it's all that really matters to him.

☿

While he was promoting his 2019 official autobiography *Me,* Sir Elton John was interviewed on the Hammersmith Apollo stage one night before a celebrity-studded audience.[1] Talk turned eventually to Freddie Mercury, at which point pink-suited Elton went misty-eyed behind his rose-tinted specs. The seventy-two-year-old was soon choking back tears as he recalled the final days and demise of his close friend. Freddie's drag name for Elton had been 'Sharon'. Elton called Freddie 'Melina', after the late Greek actress turned politician Melina Mercouri. Freddie cared so much about his friends, said Elton, that even during his dying days he was still flicking through the catalogues of his favourite auction houses, ordering presents for them.

'I have a house in London which wasn't too far from the house where he spent the last few years of his life,' Elton said. 'I didn't go and see him often because I found it really, really painful. AIDS was terrifying. He was physically terrifying to look at. Freddie loved collecting Japanese art . . . at auction. So while he was dying, he was still buying . . . He would be surrounded on a bed . . . by medicine cabinets and pills and auction catalogues.'

Freddie revealed neither fear nor sadness about dying, Elton told his audience. All he wanted to do was buy things. The Rocketman's interpretation of this was that Freddie was still thinking about art, and therefore that he 'still had such a love of life.'

'I collect a painter called Henry Scott Tuke,' he said. ' . . . a Cornish painter who painted boats and naked boys at the end of the nineteenth century and early twentieth century. He was ostracised for his paintings of boys. But I like to collect them. Not just the boys, the boats as well. On Christmas morning (after Freddie died, our mutual friend) Tony King came round and gave me this pillowcase . . . (containing) this watercolour by Henry Scott Tuke.

The note that went with it said, "Dear Sharon, I saw this at auction and thought you would love it. I love you, Melina."

'It was really moving,' Elton wept. 'He was dying and he still thought of his friends, and he bought me this. I still have it on its easel and I still have the pillowcase next to my bed. That is the kind of person he was. He was so, so full of love and life. I don't think I've ever met anyone quite like that.'

It wasn't the first time Elton had told the story. In his 2012 book *Love is the Cure: On Life, Loss and the End of AIDS*, he pre-echoed his later account with the following:

'I was overcome, forty-four years old at the time, crying like a child. Here was this beautiful man, dying from AIDS, and in his final days he had somehow managed to find me a lovely Christmas present. As sad as that moment was, it's often the one I think about when I remember Freddie, because it captures the character of the man. In death, he reminded me of what made him so special in life.'

Pause . . . to consider the life and work of Tuke, a Yorkshire-born impressionist painter and photographer who worked in Italy, France and the West Indies before making his life in Cornwall. He is best known for his homoerotic paintings of boys and young men, including *Nude Boy on Rocks*, *A Cadet on Newporth Beach, near Falmouth with Another Boy in the Sea*, and *The Bathers*. His intimate paintings of nude males resulted in rejection during the years preceding his death in Falmouth in 1929. He came back into fashion during the 1970s, and was exalted by the LGBTQ+ community, particularly young, openly gay artists. Elton started collecting his works during the 1980s. During the summer of 2008, he lent eleven works from his private collection to the *Catching the Light* exhibition at the Royal Cornwall Museum in Truro and the Falmouth Art Gallery, mounted to mark the one hundred and fiftieth anniversary of the artist's birth.

'Tuke's fascination with youth – including unclothed male adolescents – has raised difficult yet intriguing questions about how to judge his work morally and sensitively in today's context,' commented Flora Doble, Operations Officer at Art UK.

He was acquainted with Oscar Wilde and other distinguished writers and poets who classed themselves as 'Uranian': a nineteenth-century term describing a person who was believed to have 'a female psyche in a male body', but who would later be understood as homosexual. Their work was heavily influenced by a romanticised take on ancient Greece. Their poetry celebrated pederasty: sexual activity between adult males and pubescent or adolescent boys. They thus revived the lost Hellenic tradition of 'man-manly love'. Uranians enjoyed and promoted homosexual desire and liberation as though thumbing their noses at the risk: sexual activity between men at that time was still a criminal offence. In one of his celebrated pieces, Tuke depicts a naked male adolescent leaning against shoreline rocks, wearing the winged helmet and holding the caduceus (serpent-entwined wand) of the Greek deity and messenger of the gods, Hermes . . . whose equivalent in Roman mythology is Mercury. We don't know which particular Tuke painting Freddie gave Elton, to be delivered to him for Christmas from beyond the grave. I hope it was that one.

Did Freddie ever submit to analysis? Peter thought not when we discussed it over dinner at Shezan in June 2019. How could he be sure? 'I would have known about it,' Peter insisted. In which case, maybe Freddie should have. It might have helped him to understand his issues, come to terms with his problems and prepare for his premature death. I guess his response to such a suggestion would have been, 'Get stuffed!' 'What's the point?' or 'I already know what I need to. The rest, I don't *want* to know!' Given his self-obsession, I am surprised he didn't try it. Then again, ask any rock star and it's a predictable retort: that they consider what they do on stage to be the best therapy. Dodging the issue? Well. They know about self-obsession.

There are exceptions to every rule. Not every rocker has been a prisoner of his or her own narcissism since childhood, but it's uncanny how many have. Because they are and always will be their personal focal point and their own Number One, they are often incapable of sustaining normal long-term relationships. Falling in love with yourself at an early age, which is what it amounts to, leaves little room for anyone else. Dysfunction and abandonment in infancy are rarely overcome. The realm inside an artist's head is not only his creative crucible but his original safe space, to which he will always return when he feels threatened or overwhelmed.

What evidence exists that Freddie was like this? See footage of his intoxicating live performances. Utterly self-absorbed, there is something self-sacrificial about the way he flirts with and sells himself to his audience. But what he is really doing is inviting his fans to pay homage to *him*. What he is really saying is, 'You, you and all of *you*, throw yourselves at *me*.' As his friend David Evans remarked in Alfie Boe's episode of ITV's *Perspectives*, 'I sometimes got the feeling when he approached the audience, it was almost like he was cruising in a gay bar. He was, like, *challenging* people. There was a huge libido there in the performance that he could draw on, to almost say, "Come and get me ... you want a bit of this, *come and get it*."

'He was always an outsider, all his life. That was a huge key to Freddie. He was very conscious of always being ... maybe *inferior*, even. He always was very awkward in social situations to start with.'

☿

No rock star in it for the duration is going to own up to the life-negating reality of being in love with himself. Confessing that he had fallen for himself at an early age and that he is hooked for life is no way to win friends or influence people. What is he saying, that no one else counts? I'm outta here. No, he soon twigs that he has to play it down and cool if he wants his subjects to stick around and take care of his shit for him. So he turns down the volume on his superiority complex. He develops a streak of false humility, believing that the devaluation of self and the rejection of praise will make him more tolerable. He practises the art of self-deprecation, unaware that what this amounts to is fishing for compliments. In the case of someone like Freddie, his very domestic set-up is the furnace of his narcissism. It is reminiscent of the young-family home in which life revolves around a treasured new child. All eyes are on him. Every little thing he does is magic. Everyone claps hands and squeals with delight when he staggers across the room for the first time like a keeling drunk. Every arm stretches to catch him when he falls. Every last choo-choo-train mouthful of carrot and potato sludge wins him applause. Each performance on the potty provokes a standing ovation. What was the set-up at Garden Lodge if not like this?

Freddie would have laughed you all the way to Earl's Court tube had you dared to put this to him. But you would have made his teeth itch and got his gut bubbling. He wasn't stupid, he knew the truth. Freddie was the only one who truly mattered to him. He was the only person to whom he would ever be completely faithful. Not just emotionally but also physically. His delight in his own body was blatant, even when he wasn't throwing it around for the entertainment of the paying masses. It manifested itself in all those highly charged onanistic performances that had them peeing in the aisles. His soul mate, his inspiration and his raison d'être was Freddie.

'Artists *are* self-obsessed,' says artist manager Simon Napier-Bell. 'The reason they become artists in the first place is to try and find themselves, and to make sense of why they feel the way they do about themselves. I've never met a single artist who did not know that this was the case. Knowing Freddie, he wouldn't have denied it. I remember (the art critic) Andrew Graham-Dixon saying that George Michael reminded him of Rembrandt and his self-portraits. Because George would sit around listening to his own music all day long, the way Rembrandt used to sit staring at his paintings for hours on end. It was the same with Elton, who'd lie around stuffing coke up his nose while playing his own records over and over, trying to come to terms with who he was. You look at Francis Bacon's paintings to try and find out who he was. But that's exactly what Bacon himself was doing, by painting them. And that's exactly what Freddie was doing by writing songs.'

The artist's tragedy, then, is that he is enslaved for life to the art that drives him, to the point that it becomes the thing he resists?

'Exactly. He can never stop worrying about what it's all about, because the meaning of the universe is the meaning of ourselves. Most of us don't need the outlet. We just get on with life and make the best of it, because that's what people do. Most of us can root ourselves a little more in normal society. But artists can't. They create the outlets because they can't live without pouring it all out. They are exceptionally unstable. They regurgitate their own art in order to get to the heart of who they are. Meanwhile, we the punters are also looking for our *own* selves in their output. We think artists have all the answers, and we consume their art in order to get at those answers. But they are more in the dark than we are.'

Which could explain Freddie's fatalism; why he continued to do 'everything with everybody', even after HIV and AIDS had been identified, fully aware that such rash behaviour was going to kill him.

☿

Rock stars are also driven by self-loathing. This is explained by the psychological theory they call the 'Narcissistic Wound'. At some point in his past, the individual was demeaned or humiliated to such a degree that he can never regain confidence or restore his sense of self-worth. A parent or a teacher can casually put a child down in some way, and that child will carry his hurt to the grave. A classmate or companion can be carelessly disapproving or censorious, and the effect will stay with him for life. However magnificent he later becomes, the wounded infant will always be inside, churning and aching and reliving the crushing blow of yore. To conquer this, he needs constant reassurance, approval and adulation. On these things he comes to depend. Addicted to the fix, he sets himself higher and higher goals, thus justifying his need for ever-increasing approval and fan worship. Whenever he fails – to meet his own standards or those imposed by others – he relives the original anguish, again and again. The vicious circle increases. It becomes the rhythm of his life. He is the hamster in the wheel, longing to jump but terrified to so. Each successive achievement brings fresh opportunity to heal the 'Narcissistic Wound'.

'The two traumas in Freddie's developmental life are very clear,' says psychotherapist Richard Hughes. 'That is, his childhood and his relationship with his parents, and being sent away to boarding school at such a young age. A child sees himself reflected in his mother's eyes. If she is physically not there, if he is removed from her in some way, he spends the rest of his life both searching for himself and seeking to have his needs met. Which is what we mean by the Narcissistic Wound. It is the seeing of oneself reflected in one's mother's eyes that creates a sense of self. And this very much defines Freddie. I get a strong sense that he was striving to get his emotional, sexual and physical needs met all the time, frantically and desperately, which led him into some very deep water. All those who featured prominently in his life and who were mistaken for normal healthy relationships were in fact mother substitutes. It certainly explains his relationship with Mary Austin.'

It also explains Freddie the alpha narcissist:

'Which is an outcome of a developmental stage, a character style and not a diagnosis,' cautions the psychotherapist. 'Narcissism is a good, healthy thing, by the way. It's a fundamental part of child-hood development. It's about primary validation, and what we learn we can get away with. If our needs don't get met and bound-aries aren't set, they spin off into character outcomes that might not always serve us well. Because Freddie had long felt alienated from himself, he created a "false self". He started behaving outrageously, in order to get attention and control his environment. Rock stars are not the only ones who do this. We see it in CEOs, heads of companies, heads of state ... and we witness people in their lives offering them narcissistic tribute. Almost on bended knee, deferring to them and fawning all over them as if to a king or a god. Alpha narcissists create homes filled with gorgeous antiques, art and nick-nacks. They surround themselves with beautiful things. Only the best will do. They create an opulent environment around themselves which they then have to find a way of feeling worthy of.

'So it reaches the point at which Freddie *is* the king. His god-needs are constantly met, and he comes to expect that. This explains why someone like him gets upset when he is not given presents. Not because he needs things. He can afford to send someone out to buy whatever he wants anyway. It's because he wants and needs to be honoured with material indications of his worth to others. So he immerses himself in people who *are* the tribute. They can't supply the material goods because they are not in his league and don't have his fortune to spend. He therefore tributes himself with all the spending and the buying, cocooning himself in luxury in his palace.'

Had Freddie been interested in self-exploration, he might have undergone the relational psychoanalysis that was emerging during the eighties. But it was a huge commitment. We don't think that Freddie submitted to it. Peter Freestone believes that he didn't. He was probably, thinks Richard Hughes, too 'adapted', and committed to the 'false self' and his alpha narcissism, to want to do that work on himself. But he didn't need to have done therapy to be knowledgeable about it, which he appears to have been. There are many therapy references in his lyrics. Take 'Somebody to Love', which could be described as the very anthem of the narcissistically wounded. Here he is, looking in the mirror, trying to find somebody to love: it's all there, in that very song. And it is the key to Freddie Mercury. The fact that it was his mother's favourite of all his songs makes it even more fascinating. Freddie lacked the very mirroring in his childhood of which he writes in the song. At that most crucial developmental stage, his mother wasn't there to show him how to be. Because he was at school in India, thousands of miles away, while she was at home in Zanzibar.

Then there's 'The Great Pretender'. No Mercury original, it was the work of American songwriter Buck Ram, who penned it for the Platters. The group's recording earned them a number one on the US Top 100 Billboard chart in February 1956. Freddie had probably heard the original while he was still at school in Panchgani. His cover of it thirty-one years later was metaphorical. Freddie himself declared that the song summed up both his career and his stage persona. There is an air of send-up, however, in both his cover of the song and its promotional video. The latter features tongue-in-cheek takes on scenes from earlier Queen videos, including 'I Want to Break Free', 'Bohemian Rhapsody', 'Radio Ga Ga' and 'I Was Born to Love You'. Drummer Roger Taylor, Freddie's Jamaican-born actor friend Peter Straker and Freddie himself all appear in vulgar drag, as exaggerated backing vocalists. The record's B-side is 'Exercises in Free Love': the first piece written by Freddie and Mike Moran for Montserrat Caballé. The suggestion here is that the A-side was a kiss goodbye to the histrionic cartoon rock of Queen's heyday, because he was done with all that. Flip it over and you find Freddie the new rock opera king, vocalising: singing melody without words. His voice is the dirge of the opera diva, basically la-la-la-ing. He swoops, he reels and he coos. The sound is sorrowful, and bleeds with lament. What was he telling us? That he had at last located the groove in which he felt most comfortable? That he had found the way forward in terms of expressing himself as he truly was? It's the size of it. He's also telling us that he knows his days are numbered. He has reached the slippery slope of no return.

Flip it back again and the A-side now makes more sense. Oh yes, this is infinitely more than a cover version. The lyrics express him exactly. It's all about playing games, being left to dream alone, admitting that no one else can tell how lonely he is because he has been pretending too much, and the killer, about wearing his heart like a crown ... which could have been written specifically with him in mind.

'It's that line, "My need is such, I pretend too much",' says Richard Hughes. 'He couldn't create anything that packed the punch of that song better than the one that had been written already. It conveys the sentiment perfectly. It can't be improved on. So he covers this one.'

Looking at Freddie in terms of the more poetic Jungian approach – a branch of analytical psychology in which analyst and patient work together to balance unconscious elements of the psyche with conscious awareness and experience, and which uses characters to explain personality types, Freddie clearly conforms to the 'Hero' archetype.

'He is also an "Outlaw" and a "Magician",' says Hughes. 'His homosexuality defines him as that. It was still against the law while Freddie was at school, and when he first came to London and enrolled at college. Which we tend to forget. So to a certain extent he was literally an outlaw. The impact of going through your adolescence as illegal is huge.

'The "Outlaw" archetype creates conflict, causes problems and breaks things down. All of which leaves others feeling shot to pieces. People in the life of someone who routinely behaves that way end up disrupted and destroyed by it. But it feeds his sense of self, and enables him to go out and be the "Magician" character on stage, working his magic and thrilling the life out of an audience until they can barely stand. Being the "Freddie Mercury" character loved and adored by the whole world.'

Throw in his sexuality and the dilemma becomes denser. Leaving Freud aside (we'd be here all night) and turning to 'Attachment Theory', Hughes concludes that people like Freddie with inconsistent childhoods are 'constantly in fight or flight mode' when it comes to the feelings brought up by relationships. Pleasure made up for a lack of deeper connection.

We know what Freddie would have preferred, don't we? Part of him would have been happier with a male partner more cultured and refined than those he coupled with. Public-school, perhaps, with a background not dissimilar to his own; although that wouldn't necessarily have been a deal-breaker. A man of the world with an appreciation of music, ballet and art. Someone familiar with fine wine and cuisine, who was well-read and attuned to the ways of romance. The fact was, however, that he was not attracted to the opera-loving 'dickie-bow' brigade. The men he fancied were the Winnies and Jims: rough-edged, plain-talking, basic blokes who wouldn't know how to behave in an opera house if you gave them lessons. The fact is, he had distilled right down what he needed in life, which was a simple man who could satisfy him physically. All the rest, he could deliver himself! This made Freddie's male relationships a bit gentleman versus 'rough'. Which was what got the Beatles' urbane manager Brian Epstein into so much trouble back in the sixties. And do you remember when Liz Taylor married Larry Fortensky at Michael Jackson's Neverland ranch in 1991? The construction worker was like Richard Burton but without the Shakespeare or the talent. But she no longer needed Burton's brilliance or profile, as in the end it was *she* who was the star! Observers took it to mean that this 'lesser' kind of guy was her true preference, her basic need. They said the same thing about Freddie. Wouldn't he have adored the idea of being with somebody more like himself?

But darling, that's what he had already. He had Freddie.

CHAPTER SIXTEEN

FINALE

He lives because he died.

We hear him loudly and clearly because he no longer sings.

We might have forgotten him by now. There would have been no Freddie Mercury tribute concert beamed to billions, no juke-box musical to re-seduce them in dozens of countries, no lavish 'same product, new wrapper' archive sets, no navel-gazing documentaries, no box-office movie sensation. There may not have been the many commercials soundtracked by Freddie compositions, because he found that kind of thing 'common'. At least, he did back then. We have no way of knowing how his views might have changed over time. But it's interesting to note that only since his death has Queen's presence boomed in the relentless arena of advertising. Would he have wanted his songs to become synonymous with sofas and nappies? I'm guessing not. Despite which, Queen music has been used on commercials around the world over the thirty years since his passing to flog everything from chewing gum, chocolate and cars – 'Don't Stop Me Now' for Toyota, 'I'm in Love with my Car' for Jaguar – to hair dye, erectile dysfunction medication and hotels. 'I Want to Break Free' was used to sell vacuum cleaners (obviously), and 'Somebody to Love' to market Amazon Music, with the tag 'a voice is all you need'. How has this happened? One explanation is that the Queen organisation make it easier than most artist management companies to license their material. Any advertising agency will tell you that negotiating rights and fees amounts to more than half the battle, and that the guys down at the Queen office are all ears. Which has led to livid criticism of Taylor and May down the years for having sold their old friend down the river. The counter argument has to be that eighties music emerges as the most popular and effective among advertisers; and that Queen as a heritage act have more than paid their dues. They are in the global public consciousness, if not embedded in our DNA. It's their right to use their back catalogue to generate income. I suspect that they have done it less to stoke the coffers, overflowing as they are, and more to keep the music alive and maintain its relevance for younger generations – who are not as bothered as their squeamish parents by having it played to them in order to try and sell them something. Because like it or not, music has moved on. Arduous months in extortionate studios have long given way to recording on laptops, calling in the expertise of session musicians remotely. Hip-hop rules, and the kids all want to be rappers. Traditional record companies have all but disappeared. Stadium rock tours have for some years been losing out to the summer festival experience. The power of radio exposure has ceded to TV and internet advertising, which ram the message home. Still, do I want to see a bunch of men jigging down a street like spritzed-up Morris dancers to the tune of 'We Are the Champions', bowled over by the effects of Viagra? To be fair, Freddie might have seen the funny side of that one. But, bad mistakes . . . I've made a few . . . talk to your doctor.[1]

Post Live Aid, post-*Magic* tour, what were Queen's scope and prospects? Wasn't the writing on the wall? Freddie was done with the road by 1986. He had put down roots. He had his dream home, his affluent lifestyle, his devoted entourage, his Mary, his Phoebe. He had a new lease of musical life thanks to Montserrat Caballé, which would have continued to lure him away from the band and into more elite dimensions. He would have exchanged exhausting juggernaut rampages across the globe for a handful of exclusive, civilised concerts and recitals every other year in the world's most exquisite venues: the Romanian Athenaeum, say; the Palacio de Bellas Artes in Mexico City, the Amsterdam Concert-Gebouw, Milan's La Scala, Barcelona's spectacular Palau de la Música. All of which are unique, and so up his *Strasse*. He would have risen to the occasion and have recorded further albums along the lines of *Barcelona*. It's likely that he and Mike Moran, who is still going strong, bless him, and whom I still see at this birthday celebration or that Unsung Singers show – in which he accompanies Tessa Niles, Gina Foster and other renowned session and tour singers on keys – would have consolidated their collaborations and have become a truly dynamic force. Freddie would have divorced the rock world that he wasn't much part of anyway. He would have proceeded elegantly into his fifties and sixties as a crossover artist. In which case, the rest of Queen would most likely have called it a day too. The astrophysicist had his PhD thesis to finish, which he at last handed in to Imperial College thirty-six years after having started it. He was also awarded an honorary doctorate by the University of Exeter in 2007. The drummer had his solo projects. Deacon had long had other things on his mind, and would succumb to retirement. But Freddie died, and they were struck by a meteorite of obligation to keep the dream alive. The commercial advantages being obvious; the flagrant cashing-in being offset by a vast no-brainer of a charitable opportunity, to relaunch Freddie as the greatest gay icon in history and reap the riches for the fight against AIDS via the Mercury Phoenix Trust. The title of one of rock's most iconic singles and Freddie's all-time signature is then purloined to promote the fantasy film of his life. His magic is re-worked for a new generation, many of whom weren't even born before he died.

Exhilarating artistry aside, what do they see in him?

The music, first and foremost. The best-selling album in the UK charts is *Queen's Greatest Hits*, ahead of ABBA's *Greatest Hits*, the

Beatles' *Sgt. Pepper's Lonely Hearts Club Band* and Adele's *21*. Which seems uncanny. As far back as July 1985, Freddie Mercury on the Wembley stage was already a dinosaur. Those whose parents followed Queen, who came to the band via family vinyl LP collections and old cassettes collecting dust in the jalopy's glove compartment; who might have been taken to see the stage musical as teenagers, and who watched the film as twenty-somethings; who worship Freddie and won't have a 'bad' word said against him, tend to be flummoxed when asked what exactly it is that they 'love' about him. It's not as if Queen's music, which evolved and changed dramatically over the years, is evocative of any specific era – the way the Beatles define the Swinging Sixties, Bowie, Fleetwood Mac, Pink Floyd, the Eagles and Elton the seventies, or Cool Britannia's BritPoppers Blur and Oasis the nineties. The simple answer appears to be nostalgia. Queen serve up an apparently more innocent time when life seemed less complicated, rock was pre-corporate, and their particular brand of rebellion could be taken home to mum.

Perhaps part of his appeal is the fact that Freddie apparently anticipated a new sexual revolution decades ahead of its dawn. He pre-lived today's precarious young adult hook-up culture and inhabited its casual sex environment as though he himself had invented them. It looks to them as though he did so brazenly at a time when prejudice was still rife; they are perhaps unaware of what it cost him, in terms of living a double life. Because gay stars couldn't just come out during the seventies and eighties the way they can today, no matter how experimental they were in their private life. Which must be so surprising for young people who are used to seeing it all paraded on Instagram and OnlyFans. They worship Freddie for having risen above the rampant racism and homophobia of his age. He risked his life for the sake of a good time and it killed him, for which they applaud him. Nay, they revere him. Why? He wasn't as brave as all that. He stayed in the closet. He quit the cruising, cottaging and carousing and hunkered down with a live-in lover, but humiliated the poor man by never admitting him to the world. You could say that this does actually make Freddie a wonderful role model for those still struggling with sexuality and gender identity issues, having to skulk about pretending to be who they are not; who, for family, religious, racial, legal or cultural reasons, cannot face or are prevented from emerging as their true selves. But thrusting his groin and camping it up for an audience in front of a line-up of heterosexual musicians was never an adequate declaration of his true identity. Had he gone the whole hog, hurled caution into the ether and invited the consequences come what may, we could have admired him for that. Instead, we felt sorry for him. Those who champion him today for having 'lived life on his own terms' are missing the point. Then again, that, too, is part of the Freddie mystique, and another reason why he is cherished.

Nostalgia depends on things coming to an end. We can't look back on them otherwise. Freddie had no time for it. He was all about the here and now, about the living of life while it's happening. He never wanted to look back, as his whole life proved. He moved on from Zanzibar and India. He couldn't be bothered with being African or Asian. The artist he turned himself into was to all intents and purposes British and white. He let good friends go, making no effort to keep in touch, and resisting the attempts of others to maintain contact with him. They belonged to his former lives. They were the larvae of his past. He had pushed through the pupa and was out the other side, a magnificent Painted Lady. Those people served only to remind him of the grub he had been, and had grown out of. What would he make of his fame today, there being nothing current about it? It's not that he wanted to be remembered differently. As he said himself on more than one occasion, perhaps not really meaning it, he didn't want to be remembered at all.

☿

It always comes back to the big one. No matter how many times, however fervently they deny interpretations, insisting that he never explained what the obscure song was about and that he carried its secrets to the grave, most people accept it as Freddie's 'coming-out song'.

'Bohemian Rhapsody' was a rudimentary opera condensed into a pop song with all the elements: conflict, light, shade, the glorious climax. It was as if his whole life until that point had been a pressure cooker of pent-up emotion, duplicity and concealed torment waiting to blow . . . then at last, the eruption, the gush, the release. This 'miniature operatic-rhapsodic-symphonic-tone-poem', as one lofty critic described it, became one of the most requested tracks at the height of the karaoke boom in the mid-2000s. Which must have been influenced by the 1992 *Wayne's World* take, in which Mike Myers, Dana Cavey and chums head-bang along to it in a flame-accented powder blue AMC Pacer in Aurora, Illinois. Freddie was shown the sequence just before he died. He adored it, and approved its use in the film. The box office smash helped to re-establish Queen's reputation in the US after Freddie's demise. Eagle-eyed fans spotted the favour's return in Queen's own film, when Mike Myers as record company executive Ray Foster dismisses a demo of the song with, 'No one is going to be head-banging in a car to "Bohemian Rhapsody".' According to Brian May, Freddie once lamented, 'I suppose I'll have to die before we get America back.'

'And in a sense, that's what happened,' said Brian. 'And it was *Wayne's World* – which came completely out of nowhere – that made it happen.'

The 1975 hit, which topped the charts a second time after Freddie's death in 1991, was described as being 'about relationships'. Oscar-winning lyricist Sir Tim Rice, who knew Freddie well, socialised with him often and co-wrote songs for the album *Barcelona*, remains convinced that the song's hidden drift was Freddie's confession of homosexuality. 'It's fairly obvious to me this was Freddie's coming-out song,' Tim told me. 'I've spoken to (drummer) Roger Taylor about it. There is a very clear message in it. This is Freddie admitting that he is gay. In the line "Mama, I just killed a man," he's killed the old Freddie, his former image. With "Put a gun against his head, pulled my trigger, now he's dead," *he's* dead, the straight person he was originally. He's destroyed the man he was trying to be, and now this is him, trying to live with the new Freddie. "I see a little silhouetto of a man" – that's him, still being haunted by what he's done, and what he is.

'Every time I hear the song, I think of him trying to shake off one Freddie and embrace another – even after all these years. Do I think he managed it? I think he was in the process of managing it rather well. Freddie was an exceptional lyricist, and 'Bohemian Rhapsody' is one of the great pieces of music of the twentieth century.'

I leapt at my chance to put the theory to Freddie in 1986, during a reception in his hotel suite in Budapest. At which he laughed, muttered 'Bad timing!' and swanned off with his two bottles of champagne. But according to Jim Hutton, the theory was correct. 'You were right,' he told me. 'Freddie was never going to admit it publicly, because he had to carry on the charade about being straight, for his family. But we discussed it many times. It was Freddie's confessional. It was about how different his life could have been. How much happier he would have felt, had he been able to be himself. The world heard a masterpiece of imagination. It was so intricate, and had so many layers, but its message was simple. 'Bohemian Rhapsody' was Freddie as he truly was.' My heart bleeds as I remember Jim telling me that Freddie had given him as a present the original handwritten lyrics to the song. He had taken them out of storage about a year before he died. They were Jim's most prized possession. He placed them carefully in his trunk of precious belongings he had collected throughout his life, which he kept in his workshop at Garden Lodge. He forgot to retrieve it when he was asked to leave. The trunk was never returned to him.

But was 'Bohemian Rhapsody' really the song that best defined Freddie? What about 'Don't Stop Me Now' from 1978's *Jazz* album, cited by some as 'Queen's greatest-ever song'? An unvarnished ode to debauchery and indulgence, it features on several film and television soundtracks including *Shaun of the Dead*, *Hardcore Henry*, *American Dad*, *Skins*, *Glee* and *Doctor Who*. Its message is unequivocal. Here's Freddie floating in ecstasy, making a 'supersonic man' and a 'supersonic woman' out of this one or that one, being a sex machine ready to reload, and having a ball. After he died, Brian told of his struggle with the lyrics because the song related to a 'difficult' time in Freddie's life when he was 'taking lots of drugs and having sex with lots of men.'[2]

'I thought it was a lot of fun,' he later commented. 'But I did have an undercurrent feeling of, "Aren't we talking about danger here?" Because we were worried about Freddie at this point. That feeling lingers, but it's become almost the most successful Queen track as regards to what people play in their car or at their weddings. It's become a massive, massive track and an anthem to people who want to be hedonistic. It was kind of a stroke of genius from Freddie.' If any single song could be said to have summed up Queen's frontman, showcasing his devil-may-care attitude and what really mattered to him in life, it was this one.

☿

During the spring of 2018, I visited Freddie's last resting place. I was taken there by a lawyer I was working with at the time, whose late father had owned the land. Although the grave is not marked with his name or his life dates, a certified entry in a legal register and the coordinates of the grave confirm that he is there. The information, which arose in conversation by chance, was strangely comforting. All these years, people have wondered. It was Jim's belief that Freddie's ashes were buried by Mary under a cherry tree at Garden Lodge. Peter Freestone's assumption was that they had been divided, and shared between Mary and Freddie's parents. Rumours swirled that they had been scattered over the waters of Lake Geneva, close to the spot where Freddie had purchased his final home. Others believed that they must have been carried back to the place of his birth, thence to be entrusted to the sea. We know that Freddie asked Mary to take responsibility for his remains, because she talked about it in an interview. As to their whereabouts, she would never say. All she has ever divulged is that she had kept his urn in Freddie's bedroom for about two years. She then drove the ashes unaccompanied to the secret location in which they now lie. I have seen it, and have photographed it for posterity.

In February 2013, the London *Evening Standard* ran a speculative piece suggesting that Freddie's ashes had been interred in the place where he was cremated, West London Crematorium in Kensal Green. A plaque bearing his name and dates had been added to a tall plinth there, leading fans to believe that their idol may have been strewn in the Scattering Garden.

'In loving memory of Farrokh Bulsara, 5 Sept 1946 – 24 Nov 1991,' stated the plaque. '*POUR ETRE TOUJOURS PRES DE TOI. AVEC TOUT MON AMOUR. M.*' – which translated from the French, reads, 'To be close to you always, with all my love, M.' But the plaque disappeared soon afterwards. He was not there anyway, insisted Mary. 'Nobody will ever know where he is buried, because that was his wish.' What she meant was that she didn't want to invite desecration. Did she really believe that Freddie's fans would do such a thing?

What I have found, over all the years spent writing about music, getting to know and trying to make sense of bands and musicians and fans and what the magic's about, and how it affects people, is that most fans are simply genuine music-lovers. They're not nutters. They don't expect much. They don't want Disneyfied. They don't need tip-of-the-iceberg, gauzed-lensed, here's-one-I-made-earlier versions of their idols. They identify with humans, not gods. They want truth. They want to understand why that person became that legend. When did it first occur to them, how did they do it, what did they have to overcome to reach the top? Most of them rejoice in the fallibility of a rock star. It makes him sympathetic. It makes him more like them. They comprehend and forgive his shortcomings. They love him all the more for them. They accept him as he is. Freddie knew that.

CHAPTER NOTES

CHAPTER 1 – SOUVENIRS

1 Irena Sedlecká (7 September 1928 – 4 August 2020) was a Czech-born sculptor who trained at Prague's Academy of Fine Arts. Escaping communist rule in 1967, she fled to the UK with her family. Notable creations include portrait heads of Sir Laurence Olivier, Bobby Charlton and Charlie Chaplin. Her statue of Freddie, which she created from photographs and videos, was a gift to Montreux from the remaining members of Queen. Freddie's figure faces outwards across the lake and is a popular tourist destination, particularly among Queen fans, who congregate there at sundown and leave floral tributes.

2 The Château de Chillon, dating back to the twelfth century, stands at the eastern end of Lac Léman (Lake Geneva) between Montreux and Villeneuve. One of Europe's most visited castles, it has a tragic history. It features in Lord Byron's 1816 poem 'The Prisoner of Chillon' and in Henry James's novella *Daisy Miller* (1878).

3 Queen played Stockholm's Rasunda Fotbollstadion on 7 June 1986, supported by Gary Moore and Treat. Widely considered to be the finest rock concert ever performed in Sweden. Attendance was 37,500. On 5 July 1986, they performed at Slane Castle, Slane, Ireland, before 95,000 fans, Supported by the Hits, Chris Rea, the Fountainhead and the Bangles. The last

date of the *Magic* tour and their last-ever gig with Freddie as their frontman, not that they knew this at the time, took place on 9 August 1986 at Knebworth Park, Stevenage. The support acts were Belouis Some, Status Quo and Big Country. 120,000 fans attended. The occasion is remembered for the customised helicopter that dropped Queen in for their performance, and for the fatal stabbing of twenty-one-year-old Scottish fan Thomas McGuigan.

4 Daphne's: a posh South Kensington, London, Italian restaurant favoured by aristocrats and celebrities. Opened in 1964 by Daphne Rye, the theatrical agent who discovered Richard Burton.

5 Some spell it 'Parsi', others 'Parsee'. Both are correct.

6 Black Lives Matter: the international social movement founded in the USA in 2013, to campaign against racism, violence and particularly police brutality. Inspired by earlier organisations such as Black Feminist, Black Power, the Civil Rights Movement and the LGBTQ movement.

7 Interview with author, UAE, 2019.

CHAPTER 2 – REFLECTIONS

1 Ritch C. Savin-Williams is the author of *Mostly Straight: Sexual Fluidity Among Men,* Harvard University Press, 2017.

2 *Coronation Street,* launched in December 1960 and on air ever since, is Britain's longest-running television soap opera.

3 Dick Emery (1915–83), English actor and comedian whose long-running BBC series *The Dick Emery Show* featured a clique of grotesque characters played by the host – including buxom peroxide blonde 'Mandy' and her catchphrase 'Oooh, you are awful . . . but I like you.'

Stanley Baxter (1926–) Scottish comedian, impersonator and actor. Star of several popular TV comedy series including *The Stanley Baxter Show*. His impersonations included the Queen ('the Duchess of Brendagh'). His only wife died in

1997 after forty-six years of marriage. He came out as gay in 2020. His wife had always known and accepted his homosexuality, and had even allowed him to bring men to the marital home for sex. In his biography he describes his anguish over his sexuality: 'Anybody would be insane to choose to live such a very difficult life. There are many gay people these days who are fairly comfortable with their sexuality, fairly happy with who they are. I'm not. I never wanted to be gay. I still don't.'

Danny la Rue (Daniel Patrick Carroll, 1927–2009), the 'Grande Dame of Drag', was an Irish Catholic female impersonator and singer.

4 'The Pink Pound' refers to the spending power of gay men and lesbians, an increasingly lucrative market targeted by advertisers from the 1980s onwards.

5 Singer/songwriter-actor Adam Lambert (1982–) was a runner-up on TV talent show *American Idol* in 2009. He has worked with Queen on recordings and tours since 2011, while maintain his hugely successful solo career.

CHAPTER 3 – ROOTS

1 The Republic of Djibouti is the obscure Horn of Africa territory believed to have been part of ancient kingdom the Land of Punt, from which the Egyptian Pharaohs plundered gold.

2 America's National Aeronautics and Space Administration. Further information: https://history.nasa.gov/SP-45/ch8.htm

3 Coir is the fibre from the outer husk of coconuts, used to make matting, ropes and brushes, and potting compost.

4 Senegal's capital Dakar, Tanzania's Dar Es Salaam, Lomé, the capital of the Togolese Republic, Angola's Luanda and Cape Town have all been bestowed with the epithet 'the Paris of Africa' at one time or another.

CHAPTER 4 – RITUAL

1 Betel nuts are the seeds of the fruit of the areca palm. They are
chewed with betel leaf as a stimulant. Now known to be both
carcinogenic (causing cancers of the mouth and oesophagus)
and psychoactive, they are these days controlled or banned in
several countries but are (curiously) freely available in the UK.
The 'nuts', consumed by hundreds of millions of people worldwide, are referred to as 'Asia's deadly secret'. They provide a
buzz akin to that achieved by drinking six cups of coffee.
Regarded as a symbol of love and marriage, and used as a cure
for indigestion and impotence, they are used freely by women
and children but especially by working men who chew them to
keep themselves awake and alert during long gruelling shifts.
India, Thailand and Taiwan have all launched campaigns to
discourage betel-nut chewing. But they are fighting an uphill
battle, as the cancers can take up to twenty years to appear.

2 Freddie's classmates Subhash Gudku and Ajay Goyal interviewed for the *Hindustan Times* in November 2018.

3 **Poona** is known today as Pune. The second largest city in
Maharashtra state after Mumbai, it is the eighth most densely
populated in India, the country's second most important IT
hub, and its primary car and manufacturing centre. It is also
known as 'the Oxford of the East', on account of its numerous
schools and colleges. **The Gateway of India** in South Mumbai,
the city's top tourist attraction, was built to commemorate the
arrival in 1911 of the first British monarch to visit India, King-
Emperor George V, and Queen-Empress Mary. Contrary to
popular belief, Queen Victoria never visited India. The furthest
east she ever travelled was Tuscany. The Gateway of India and
the Taj Mahal Palace afford spectacular views over the Arabian
sea and famous beaches such as Chowpatty, Juhu and Versova.
But the sea there is contaminated with untreated sewage, and
the beaches are among the most polluted in the world. Nobody
swims. **The magnificent Gothic railway station** in Mumbai

formerly known as Victoria was completed during the Queen and Empress of India's Golden Jubilee year, 1887. It is today a UNESCO World Heritage Site. The name was changed to Chhatrapati Shivaji Terminus in March 1996. Shivaji was a seventeenth-century warrior chieftain. 'Chhatrapati' in Sanskrit means 'great king', and is a compound made up of chhatri ('parasol or umbrella') and pati ('lord, master ruler'), to denote a protector of people. In 2017, the station's name was revised again, to 'Chhatrapati Shivaji Maharaj Terminus', 'Maharaj' meaning 'great king' or 'emperor'. The station is the most important transport hub in the world's busiest commuter rail network, serving both long-distance and suburban destinations. It features in all splendour in Danny Boyle's 2008 film *Slumdog Millionaire*. The photograph here of the terminus to and from which Freddie journeyed as a schoolboy was taken by the author during a visit to Mumbai in 2012, before its most recent renaming.

4 S. Moutrie and Co., founded by Londoner Sydenham Moutrie who moved to Shanghai and started a business importing pianos, were the first company in China to begin manufacturing the instruments during the 1870s. He eventually expanded to Yokohama, Japan, but died unexpectedly in 1907, leaving his company to the board and shareholders. Messrs S. Moutrie & Co. kept pace with technological developments in music and continued as important purveyors of musical instruments throughout the 1930s. They suffered a downturn in the late 1930s, due to impending war and to a trend for people moving away from playing instruments and more towards listening to recordings on the radio or gramophone. But during the World War II era, Moutrie's extended their influence and operations into several Asian countries. Made of solid, superior teak from Bangkok, and specially varnished to counteract the effect of insects and damp in the Tropics, Moutrie pianos were renowned for being reliably built, with a beautiful tone. Freddie played a

wide variety of pianos during his professional career, including models by Steinway, Bechstein, Bösendorfer, Yamaha and Kawai.

5 Nonagenarian Lata Mangeshkar, known as 'the Queen of Melody' and 'the Nightingale of India', is a fabulously celebrated Bollywood playback singer whose voice has graced a thousand Hindi films and who has sung in more than thirty-six languages both regional and international. Playback singing is an industry itself in India, in which the singers make recordings of songs to which the movie actors mime on screen. Although playback singers never appear in the films, the best become as famous as the actors who lip-sync their voices. Although Freddie was claimed in later years to have been a passionate fan of her music, his school friends refuted this, and Freddie himself gave no indication that he admired her vocal style and technique.

6 Interviews with Derrick Branche, Victory Rana and Bruce Murray courtesy of the late advertising guru and writer Anvar Alikhan, who conducted them in 2016 for Scroll.in just before his sad death from pulmonary disease the following year.

7 Zanzibar's last Sultan was bankrolled by the British Government to the tune of £100,000. Banned from ever returning to Zanzibar, he relocated from his London hotel to a small semi-detached house on a back street in Southsea, Hampshire, where he lived for the next fifty-six years. In September 2020, at the age of ninety-one, he was at last granted permission to live in Oman and see out his days among the last-remaining members of his family.

8 Rare clips of the Zanzibar Revolution can be found on YouTube. N.B., content is graphic.

CHAPTER 5 – STONE FREE

'Stone Free' was the second song recorded by the Jimi Hendrix Experience. Written by Jimi, it was released in December 1966 as the B-side of 'Hey Joe', their first UK single.

1 'No Blacks, No Irish, No Dogs' was the wording of signs all too often displayed in the windows of properties advertising for tenants.

2 Jim Hutton author interview, County Carlow, 1997.

3 In 1993, Isleworth Polytechnic and Hounslow Borough College became West Thames College.

4 The term 'Blighty' was coined in India during the nineteenth century, to denote a British or English visitor. Its source may have been the Urdu word 'vilāyatī' meaning 'foreign'. It was commonly used in the trenches during the Great War, in reference to Britain.

5 'This royal throne of kings, this sceptred isle, this earth of majesty, this seat of Mars, this other Eden, demi-paradise . . .' From John of Gaunt's Act 2 death-bed speech prophesying the downfall of an idealized England under the rule of this monarch. *Richard II*, William Shakespeare.

6 Pete Townshend would later reveal that he wrecked his first six-string in the front room of the family abode when he was thirteen, after his grandmother complained once too often about 'that bloody racket'.

7 Adrian Morrish and Patrick Connolly in an article for *Mojo* magazine. In 2018, Morrish published *Freddie Mercury: The Fantasy Recording Sessions 1965*. A factional novel about a fictitious band called Bulsariana, it is based on the author's friendship with and recollections of Freddie.

8 Writing on his website https://brianmay.com/ after Freddie's mother died in November 2016.

9 Tim Teeman for *The Times*, 2 September 2006.

10 'I'm Not in Love' by 10cc, the second single from their third album, *The Original Soundtrack*, released May 1975, number one in the UK for a fortnight and the band's breakthrough international hit. It has become an all-time radio classic and film-soundtrack fixture. Queen were doing OK themselves at the time: on 1 May that year, they performed the last concert of

their hugely successful *Sheer Heart Attack* tour at the Nippon Budokan Hall in Tokyo. Freddie returned home to receive an Ivor Novello Award for 'Killer Queen', which made it to two in the UK and twelve on the *Billboard* Hot 100.

CHAPTER 6 – JIMI HENDRIX

1 Millions have wished ever since that they had been there. I actually might have been, had it happened a dozen years later, as I attended the same establishment to study Modern Languages. By then, the college was known as the Polytechnic of Central London. It has since reverted to varsity status, and is these days the University of Westminster. Three members of the future Pink Floyd read architecture there: Nick Mason, Roger Waters and Richard Wright. The college also educated fashion designer Vivienne Westwood, DJ Annie Nightingale, actor Timothy West, Quentin Crisp (the original Englishman in New York) and Rolling Stone drummer Charlie Watts.

2 The Chitlin' Circuit was a string of performance venues across America's East, South and upper Midwest that welcomed African American musicians, comedians and other performers to entertain black audiences during racial segregation. It was dubbed 'chitlin' because chitlins or chitterlings – the small intestine of pigs, boiled or fried and sometimes filled with mincemeat, along the lines of the traditional Scottish dish haggis – were sold along with other soul food dishes on the premises.

3 The French-owned Cheetah Club on Broadway and 53rd St occupied the site of the old Arcadia Ballroom, near the Theater District. Launched in spring 1966, it was the first real disco club in New York. Its clientele looked like 'a kook in a Kubla Khanteen' (according to *LIFE* magazine). It boasted a dance floor and its own dance style, a library, a small cinema, colour television and a boutique selling fashion direct from London's Carnaby Street for clubbers to change into and dance in – hotpants, mini minis and fishnets and long, swishing hair were

the order of the day – and a hotdog stand. Every surface was black velvet-clad except for the bar, which was covered in fake fur.

4 Linda Keith interviewed for the documentary commissioned by the Hendrix estate, *Jimi Hendrix: Hear my Train a Comin'*. Her part in Hendrix's pre-fame story was told in the 2013 film *All Is by My Side*, starring Outkast's André Benjamin as Jimi and Imogen Poots as Linda.

5 Café Wha?, 115 MacDougal Street between Bleecker and West 3rd Streets, New York City, was and is a live music, comedy and other performance venue in the basement of the Players Theatre. Many musicians and comedians began their careers there, including Bob Dylan, Peter, Paul and Mary, the Velvet Underground and Bruce Springsteen, and Lenny Bruce, Woody Allen, Richard Pryor, Bill Cosby and Joan Rivers.

6 Ringo had to evict Hendrix for hurling whitewash at the walls during an acid trip. He eventually sold the lease on 34 Montagu Square in 1969. The property now bears an English Heritage blue plaque, recognising it as the former home of Starr's former bandmate John Lennon. Which Ringo might think is a bit rich.

7 Robert A. Heinlein's *Stranger in a Strange Land* was published in 1961. When Walter Tevis's novel *The Man Who Fell to Earth* was published in 1963, comparisons were drawn; even more so when Nicolas Roeg's film adaptation starring David Bowie appeared in 1976.

8 The infamous Chelsea Hotel, 222 W23rd Street in the Chelsea district of New York City, has featured on America's National Register of Historic Places since 1977. Formerly the residence of musicians such as Jim Morrison, Iggy Pop, Bob Dylan, Jimi Hendrix, Pink Floyd; of poets Allen Ginsberg and Dylan Thomas; where Arthur C. Clarke penned *2001: a Space Odyssey*; where Madonna shot nude portraits for her book *Sex*; where Mark Twain, Arthur Miller, Tennessee Williams, Jack Kerouac, William S. Burroughs and Quentin Crisp all wrote; where

Nancy Spungen, the girlfriend of Sex Pistol Sid Vicious, was murdered; where Leonard Cohen and Janis Joplin had a steamy affair, which he wrote songs about. Stay there. I did. It's wall-to-wall ghosts.

CHAPTER 7 – LEADER

1 As Bowie told society portrait photographer Fergus Greer during a *Sunday Times Review* photo session during the nineties, which Greer related to the author in 2016 during an interview for *Hero: David Bowie* (Hodder & Stoughton, 2016).

2 The boots were by Alan Mair, a Glaswegian musician who'd been in and out of bands including the Beatstalkers, Scotland's answer to the Beatles, before getting involved in fashion. He established stores in Kensington and Chelsea, where his handmade designs were favoured by the rock and pop crowd. 'Daisy roots' is Cockney rhyming slang for 'boots'.

3 'Auntie', a nickname for Britain's national broadcaster the BBC, dates back to the 1950s and echoes an era when the BBC was prim, proper and puritanical. It was short for 'Auntie knows best'. The BBC had chosen David's 'Space Oddity' ('Ground control to Major Tom . . .') as the soundtrack for their extensive television coverage of the Apollo 11 moon mission. The exposure earned David a hit. The single, produced by Gus Dudgeon (Tony Visconti had rejected it) was recorded in June and released on 11 July 1969. It featured Rick Wakeman on Mellotron. 'I really wouldn't like to make singing a full-time occupation,' David told my friend the former *Melody Maker* writer Chris Welch. 'The record is based a lot on the film *2001: a Space Odyssey*. It's a mixture of Salvador Dalí, *2001* and the Bee Gees. Really, it's just a record which amuses people.'

4 'Under Pressure' was the single co-written, composed and produced by David Bowie and Queen, released in single format in October 1981 and a track on the Queen album *Hot Space* the following year. The single became Queen's second

UK Number One hit (Bowie's third) and flew high around the world. Freddie and Bowie fell out over the mixing of the track. Queen bassist John Deacon is usually credited as having created the track's famous bass riff (Bowie said so too), although Deacon has always credited David Bowie. While Queen did perform 'Under Pressure' live, David did not ... until the 1992 Freddie Mercury Tribute Concert after Freddie's death, when he duetted it with Eurythmics' Annie Lennox. Thereafter, David performed it regularly, duetting with his bassist Gail Ann Dorsey.

5 David was parodying the lyrics of 'The Hokey Cokey', a mass-participatory song and dance routine possibly dating back to the late 1800s. Claimed by various countries and cultures, it became popular in Britain during the music hall era.

6 Brian May recalling his Jimi Hendrix experience to loudersound.com in October 2015.

CHAPTER 8 – QUEEN

1 Dhansak, one of Freddie's favourite dishes, is a traditional Zoroastrian Parsi dish that combines elements of Persian and Gujarati (Indian) cuisine. Mutton or goat is cooked with lentils and vegetables to create the curry. Vegetarian versions are favoured too. In Parsi families, the dish is made on Sundays, because it takes a long time to prepare and cook. It is also served on the fourth day after the death of a loved one, prior to which no meat may be eaten for three days beyond the death.

CHAPTER 9 – SECRETS

1 The largest-ever search for genes linked to sexual orientation, the 2019 genome-wide association study involved 493,001 participants from the US, UK and Sweden.

2 Speaking to Penny Wark for *The Times* newspaper; also on the Channel 5 TV documentary *Freddie Mercury: A Christmas Story* (19 December 2019), produced and directed by Mark Turnbull.

3 Dr Patrick Willis Woodcock (1920–2002) was described in one obituary as having been 'the most celebrated and cherished general practitioner in the capital.' He numbered among his close friends Christopher Isherwood, David Hockney, Tony Richardson, John Gielgud and Nöel Coward.

4 As recorded in the 2006 Omnibus Press book *Freddie Mercury: A Life in His Own Words*, a definitive collection of Freddie's interviews and statements

CHAPTER 10 – MARY

1 Nottinghamshire miner's son David Herbert Lawrence (1885–1930) was one of the earliest and most significant writers to tackle the subjects of sexuality and emotions. At least bi-curious himself, he was said to have had an intense romantic relationship with a young coal miner when he was about sixteen, and other sexual encounters with men throughout adulthood. Although his reputation was in tatters at the time of his death, he has come to be regarded as one of England's most important novelists. *Women in Love* was banned temporarily for what was considered to be obscene content – as was its predecessor *The Rainbow*. Lawrence would also become embroiled in an obscenity trial over his 1928 novel *Lady Chatterley's Lover*.

Larry Kramer (1935–2020), who wrote the screenplay for the film adaptation and also produced the picture, was still in the closet when he wrote it. The American playwright, author and producer would go on to become the world's most famous AIDS activist.

2 Rosemary Pearson revealed her *Women in Love* experience with Freddie to one of the directors of acclaimed BBC TV series *A Life In 10 Pictures*, in which the author also took part.

3 Anita Dobson's character Angie Watts was the blousy, boozy landlady of the 'Queen Vic' public house in long-running TV soap *EastEnders* from 1985 to 1988. Anita's clandestine affair

with Brian May, which began in 1986, ended his first marriage. She and Brian tied the knot in November 2000.

4 Launched in December 1960, *Coronation Street* is Britain's longest-running 'soap'.

5 The Salvador Dalí Society www.dali.com

6 Music publicist Bernard Doherty, who masterminded the publicity for Live Aid, talking to the author in 2011.

7 Jo Burt spoke to *Somerset Live* in November 2018.

8 Mary Austin speaking to *OK!* magazine.

CHAPTER 11 – JIM

1 Peter Freestone talking to *Express* online, 28 October 2019.

CHAPTER 12 – BARBARA

1 **Greta Garbo** (1905–90), Swedish-American actress born Greta Louisa Gustafsson, who began her screen career at sixteen. She migrated to Hollywood and made her name in her silent debut *The Torrent* in 1926. She perfected the role of enigmatic heroine in films such as *Anna Karenina* (1935) and *Camille* (1936) After twenty-eight films she retired at thirty-five, never to return. In later life, she famously said, 'I never said, "I want to be alone". I only said, "I want to be let alone".'
Marilyn Monroe (1926–62), American screen legend born Norma Jeane Mortenson, major sex symbol of the 1950s and a cultural icon to this day. Her films included *Gentlemen Prefer Blondes, How to Marry a Millionaire, Niagara* and *The Seven Year Itch*. Her death at thirty-six from barbiturate overdose prompted conspiracy theories still unresolved. **Jean Harlow** (1911–37), American actress born Harlean Harlow Carpenter, known as 'the Baby', 'the Platinum Blonde', 'the Blonde Bombshell' and 'the Laughing Vamp'. Major Hollywood icon and the star of nine films including *Dinner at Eight, Reckless* and *Suzy*, she was dead at the age of twenty-six, from kidney failure. The 'Jean Harlow' cocktail named after her is a blend of equal

parts light rum and sweet vermouth. **Carole Lombard** (1908–42) was an American comic actress who made her debut at sixteen and appeared in a number of films including *Twentieth Century* and *Hands Across the Table* before marrying screen idol Clark Gable and becoming part of one of Hollywood's most legendary super-couples. Their bliss was short-lived: she died in a plane crash at thirty-three. **Brigitte Bardot** (1934–) is a French-born former actress whose exquisite beauty made her one of the most famous sex symbols in the world during the 1950s and '60s. She married film director Roger Vadim when she was eighteen. Her debut, *And God Created Woman* (1956) established her worldwide. Forty-seven films, sixty songs and several musicals later, she retired in 1973 to concentrate on her animal rights activism. **Faye Dunaway** (1941–), American actress, is best known for the pictures *Bonnie and Clyde, The Thomas Crown Affair, Network* and *Eyes of Laura Mars*. She played Joan Crawford in *Mommie Dearest*, and opera diva Maria Callas in *Master Class*. Her second husband was a British celebrity photographer, the late Terry O'Neill. **Meryl Streep** (1949–), twenty-one-times Academy Award-nominated and three times winner, best known for *The Deer Hunter, Sophie's Choice, Out of Africa, Kramer vs Kramer, The Iron Lady* and *Mamma Mia!* **Jayne Mansfield** (1933–67), American actress born Vera Jayne Palmer who became known as 'the working man's Marilyn Monroe'. An acclaimed Hollywood sex symbol famed for her hourglass figure, extraordinary bosom and 'accidental' wardrobe malfunctions, she spoke five languages, played the violin and could quote Shakespeare endlessly off the top of her head. The first high-profile American to perform a nude scene on film (in *Promises! Promises!* 1963), she also starred in *The Girl Can't Help It* (1956) and *Too Hot to Handle* (1960). Like Marilyn Monroe, she was rumoured to have had affairs with both John F. and Robert Kennedy. She was killed in a car crash in 1967, aged thirty-four.

2 Both the Arabella-Haus and the Musicland Studios in its basement have now vanished from Arabellastrasse. Today, the Sheraton Arabellapark Hotel and several shops stand in their place.

Freddie is said to have composed 'Crazy Little Thing Called Love' in the bath on an acoustic guitar at the historic Bayerischer Hof Hotel in Munich's city centre. Drummer Roger Taylor stated this in an interview, while others have said that the song was conceived at the Hilton München Park. In his *Queen in 3-D* published May 2017, Brian May included a photo of Freddie that he had taken on a balcony of the Hilton in July 1979. Perhaps Roger's reference to the more luxurious hotel was ironic.

3 *Daily Express*, October 2020.

4 As Peter Freestone recounted in his memoir *Freddie Mercury: An intimate memoir by the man who knew him best*, co-authored by David Evans and published by Omnibus Press in 1998.

CHAPTER 13 – REDEMPTION

1 King Hussein and Antoinette Gardiner met when his bride-to-be was only nineteen, while her father was working in Jordan as a military adviser on water conservation. They married in 1961.

2 Queen worked on four studio albums at Musicland, Munich: *The Game*, 1980; *Hot Space*, 1982, also partially recorded at Mountain Studios, Montreux; *The Works*, at Record Plant LA and Musicland; *A Kind of Magic*, 1986, at Musicland, Mountain and London's Townhouse, with the orchestra recorded at Abbey Road. Freddie also recorded his solo album *Mr. Bad Guy* there. It took nearly two years to finish, because of all the distractions. Queen's affection for Munich extended to live performances. Between 1978 and 1986, they played the Olympiahalle beside the Olympic Stadium seven times.

3 'The king is in the altogether' is the chorus of the song 'The King's New Clothes' from the 1952 musical *Hans Christian*

Andersen. It refers to the nineteenth-century Danish folk writer's story for children, *The Emperor's New Clothes*, about a vain ruler who was duped by rogue tailors into believing that he was dressed in regal finery, with which his loyal subjects agreed, until his obvious nakedness was pointed out by a little boy. The story's message flags up the willingness of people, for whatever reason – vanity or acceptance by their peers, perhaps – to disbelieve a thing or circumstance that they know full well to be true.

CHAPTER 14 – MONTSERRAT

1 To 'lock the stable door after the horse has bolted' is an old proverb which warns of the futility of taking precautions after the damage has been done.

2 Global HIV and AIDS statistics: www.unaids.org/en/resources/fact-sheet

3 The David Wigg Interviews, included with the 2000 ten-CD/two DVD *Freddie Mercury: Solo* boxed set, and also released as *Freddie Mercury talking to David Wigg*, audio download, 2006, in commemoration of what would have been Freddie's sixtieth birthday.

4 'The Screws', 'The News of the Screws' and 'The Screws of the World' were common nicknames, at the height of its popularity, of the world's biggest-selling English-language newspaper, the *News of the World*. Founded in 1843, the paper folded for good in 2011 following a sensational phone-hacking scandal during which editors and other staff members were arrested. Queen named their sixth studio album after the Sunday tabloid in 1977. It marked a change in style to a leaner, harder rock sound, and met with critical backlash on release, but went on to become one of the band's most popular albums. Its singles 'We Are the Champions' and 'We Will Rock You' have become classic rock anthems.

5 Montserrat appeared on Dahlin's TV show *Jacobs Stege* ('Jacob's Ladder', a biblical reference from the Book of Genesis about a

ladder leading to heaven). Multilingual, homosexual Dahlin regularly welcomed international stars onto his chat show. He died from HIV/AIDS-related illness on 10 October 1991, a few weeks ahead of Freddie. He was thirty-nine.

6 Montserrat Caballé speaking in *Freddie Mercury: the Untold Story By Those Who Knew Him Best*, released 8 December 2000. Produced by Queen manager Jim Beach, Rudi Dolezal and Hannes Rossacher. Featuring members of Freddie's family, friends, colleagues and partners, including Mary, Montserrat, Barbara and Jim.

7 Freddie and Montserrat interviewed for RTVE, Spain's state-owned broadcasting corporation, at the Ku Club Ibiza, 29 May 1987.

CHAPTER 15 – LOVE OF MY LIFE

1 Elton John's memoir was ghost-written by the *Guardian* newspaper's pop critic Alexis Petridis. This sold-out 'Evening with Elton John', during which Elton was interviewed by comedian and writer David Walliams, took place on 19 November 2019, at the former Hammersmith Odeon – the hallowed rock venue where both Elton and Queen had often performed.

CHAPTER 16 – FINALE

1 Brian, Roger and Adam Lambert recorded an updated version of 'We Are the Champions' in support of frontline healthcare workers during the 2020 coronavirus pandemic. Entitled 'You are the Champions', and released during April 2020, all proceeds were donated to the World Health Organisation's Covid-19 Solidarity Response Fund.

2 Brian May talking to *Mojo* magazine, 1991.

☿

TRIBUTES

He had an extraordinary capacity to energise people and make them feel excited. We knew he was something very special, he made people feel like they could do it too.
Brian May

He wasn't the kind of persona that he put over on stage, because he was an entertainer.
Roger Taylor

As far as we are concerned, this is it. There is no point in carrying on. It is impossible to replace Freddie.
John Deacon

It never really sank into me, up to the last two weeks, that he was dying. I think I really carried on my normal work just to keep myself occupied. I didn't want to go absolutely crazy thinking about it all the time. I wouldn't say he died in my arms, but I was there.
Jim Hutton

We were both trying far too hard to be happy. Because we were *not* happy. You get drunk, you take blow, you play the monkey, you lay as many people as you can, all as if you are daring your body to stay alive. It is a sort of death wish. In the end it just makes you

more lonely, more empty. Freddie and I were both as bad as each other. We identified with each other. In the end, we were the only one that each other could turn to. If he hadn't had me, and I hadn't had him, I think that we would both have been dead much sooner.
Barbara Valentin

I got Freddie Mercury straight away. From the minute I met him, I loved him . . . he was just magnificent. Incredibly smart and adventurous. Kind and generous and thoughtful, but outrageously funny. Oh God, if you went out clubbing with him and Tony King – they were great friends – you'd spend the whole night howling.
Elton John

When Freddie died, it affected me a lot more than I thought it would. It was almost like part of my childhood just disappeared.
George Michael

Of all the more theatrical performers, Freddie took it further than the rest. He took it over the edge. And of course I always admire a man who wears tights!
David Bowie

I adored Freddie Mercury and Queen had a hit with 'Radio Ga Ga'. That's why I love the name. Freddie was unique, one of the biggest personalities in pop music. He was not only a singer but also a fantastic performer, a man of theatre and someone who constantly transformed himself. In short, a genius. It's all about him and David Bowie.
Lady Gaga

If I hadn't had Freddie Mercury's lyrics to hold on to as a kid, I don't know where I would be. It taught me about all forms of

music . . . it would open my mind. I never really had a bigger teacher in my whole life.
Axl Rose

There's so few people behind the glamour who really make it as true performers. It's a very strange thoroughbred condition to be a successful musician and still be able to project it with confidence. Freddie had that, and there's not many people who have had it.
Robert Plant

Freddie Mercury was – and remains – my biggest influence. The combination of his sarcastic approach to writing lyrics and his 'I don't give a fuck' attitude really inspired my music.
Katy Perry

Freddie's voice has so much texture to it. It's super-sexy. He kind of grabs at everything, he squeezes it. He was completely over the top in the best possible way.
Adam Lambert

For me he represents an era when people were less afraid of living life to the full. This was in the seventies when rock's extravagances went berserk. Perhaps we're not living in that time any more. There's a glorious rebelliousness about it, of freedom attached to it, that represents that whole spirit of rock 'n' roll.
Annie Lennox

We are here to tell the whole world that (Freddie), like others we have lost to AIDS, died before his time. It needn't have happened. It shouldn't have happened. Please, let's not let it happen again.
Elizabeth Taylor

I first saw the band as a teenager and later became great friends with them. For me, Freddie Mercury was the best front man in the

world. He was also the sweetest, kindest, most generous bloke, and one of the best drinking partners I've ever had in my life.
Tony Hadley

Musicians, they understand each other very very well. They are married in music, you know? This is what was happening with Freddie and me. He lovèd me a lot, and I lovèd him too. (And re performing together): For him was normal, but for me no. And I told him, Freddie, listen: do you think really I have to perform with you? I don't feel like. I am old, I am big, I am . . . I don't know. And he says, listen: music has not age.
Montserrat Caballé

Freddie on Monserrat: I love music, and she *is* the music.

He never stopped being creative. He could have easily given up and disappeared somewhere and lived the rest of his life in isolation, but he did not do that. It's another example of how brave the man was. He was out working until he could actually work no more.
Mike Moran

I believe (opera) was one way of Freddie having love for women which he could really express and indulge in. Because Freddie adored women. He revelled in their femininity, the way they looked and dressed, and smelled, even. In their differences from men. He quite obviously loved Mary. When I used to go out to dinner with him and Elaine (Paige), he really enjoyed her company. There was no question of him cutting women out. He very much wanted them in his life. I never went to any of his wild parties, but I did go to some dinner parties of Freddie's. There might be twenty, thirty people there, and at least half of them were always ladies.
Sir Tim Rice

He had a greater influence on me than any other artist. I remember as a kid being captivated by Freddie the first time I saw him on TV. I watched and admired as he wrote one of the biggest-selling singles ever. With Queen, he practically invented the pop video. He even embraced ballet, and finally he took my world, the opera world, by storm ... in many ways, my musical journey is the reverse of Freddie's. he went from rock to opera. I'm a classically trained opera singer escaping the constraints of my formal education, and embracing all kinds of music. After years of training, performing Freddie's signature pop opera classic ('Barcelona') shouldn't be a problem. But the more I practise, the more I realise how complex the song is. I find it extraordinary that Freddie, who as far as I know was an untutored, untrained rock singer, could write and sing this incredible piece.
Alfie Boe

The moments that always stood out for me were when he was at home laughing. I know this sounds quite ordinary, but whenever you see Freddie smiling or laughing during an interview, he always uses his top lip to cover his teeth, or else he brings up his hand to cover his mouth. The reason for this was that he hated his teeth and always tried to cover them up. When he was at home, he wasn't self-conscious surrounded by friends, and he would just throw his head back and laugh out loud with his mouth wide open. Those were the times when the warm, funny and relaxed man was able to appear, without having to be wary of strangers seeing him without the 'Freddie Mercury the Rock Star' persona.
Peter 'Phoebe' Freestone

He was just my piano player ...
Bruce Murray

I saw a man become incredibly brave. I saw a man become incredibly emotional at times. I saw depths of this person that was an exaggeration of what was . . . and I respected and admired him even more.

Mary Austin

He was very generous and kind, and he always used to spoil me.

Kashmira Cooke

None of them love him as much as his mother.

Jer Bulsara

☿

SELECT BIBLIOGRAPHY

Adams, Marcus K., *The Racialization of Jimi Hendrix*, Eastern Michigan University Senior Honors Thesis, Department of African American Studies, 2007

Brooks, Greg and Lupton, Simon, *Freddie Mercury: His Life in His Own Words*, Omnibus Press, 2008

Courtauld, Pari, *A Persian Childhood*, Rubicon Press, 1990

Freestone, Peter with Evans, David, *Freddie Mercury*, Omnibus Press, 2001

Hogan, Peter K., *The Complete Guide to the Music of Queen*, Omnibus Press, 1994

Hutton, Jim, with Wapshott, Tim, *Mercury and Me*, Bloomsbury, 1994

Laing, Olivia, *The Lonely City*, Picador, 2017

Paglia, Camille, *Sexual Personae: Art and Decadence from Nefertiti to Emily Dickinson*, Yale University Press, 1990

Paglia, Camille, *Free Women Free Men: Sex, Gender, Feminism*, Pantheon Books/Penguin Random House, 2017

Reichardt, Lars, *Barbara*, btb Verlag Random House GmbH, 2018

Sheriff, Abdul and Ferguson, Ed, *Zanzibar Under Colonial Rule*, James Currey Ltd, 1991

Shilts, Randy, *And the Band Played On: Politics, People and the AIDS Epidemic*, Penguin Books, 1987

NOTE FROM THE AUTHOR

My personal connection to Freddie and Queen, forged when I was a Fleet Street journalist during the 1980s and neither more nor less than that, has somehow never waned. In September 2011, I was a guest of Universal Music at the 'Freddie for a Day' celebration at London's Savoy Hotel, in honour of what would have been Freddie's sixty-fifth birthday and an AIDS fundraising dinner for the Mercury Phoenix Trust. In October 2012, I was invited to speak about Freddie at the Tata Literature Live! book festival in Mumbai, alongside bestselling Indian authors Jeet Thayil, Amish Tripathi and Anil Dharker. On 4 March 2013, I accompanied Brian May and Sir Tim Rice to a celebration of the life of veteran *The Sky at Night* BBC television presenter Sir Patrick Moore in Selsey near Chichester, Sussex, on what would have been the astronomer's ninetieth birthday. The following day, I was a guest of the Performing Rights Society (PRS) at Imperial College, London to witness Brian and Roger unveil a plaque commemorating their first-ever official gig as Queen, which they had performed in the college's Union Hall on 18 July 1970, forty-three years earlier. On 11 June 2015, I took part in '32 Londoners', a series of talks on the London Eye attraction hosted by Antique Beat and A Curious Invitation. The great wheel was slowed to a special rotation speed, and each of its thirty-two capsules was dedicated to a presentation by an authority on a featured personality. Biographer Claire Tomalin spoke about

Charles Dickens, Charles Moore about Margaret Thatcher, Robert Elms on footballer Stan Bowles and royal correspondent Jennie Bond on Diana, Princess of Wales. Our diverse subjects – mine was Freddie – were a cross-section of people from elsewhere whose talents and stories helped shape the capital. That October, I took part in Chicago's Ideas Festival, addressing a large Cadillac Palace Theatre audience on the subject of Freddie Mercury during their presentation 'Cultural Icons: You Know the Headlines, Now Learn the Truth'. And in January 2019, I was invited to appear on a series-best edition of BBC Radio 4's *Great Lives* with comedian, actor, writer and fervent Queen fan Matt Lucas and former Conservative MP turned author, journalist and broadcaster Matthew Parris. We discussed at length the band described by the *New Statesman* in their laudatory review as '99.8% Freddie Mercury and 0.2% good-humoured backing guys (to suggest otherwise is akin to the insane idea that Liam Gallagher would be nothing without his brother. Without Liam, Noel would be a Beatles copyist in a pub.)' Not that Matt, Matthew or I agreed with them, but the point was fairly made … says the reviewer reviewing the reviewer who reviewed the show.

'I do relate to the idea that Freddie wasn't an Everyman,' said Matt Lucas, recalling the moment he first fell for Freddie, and his own experiences as a stand-up unable to simply saunter out onto a stage with a pint. Freddie, we concurred, may well have been all things to all people: 'the world's greatest children's performer'; 'the Persian elf with an overbite gargling coloratura to truck drivers'; 'the prancer in a unitard serenading headbangers': Who else could have come up with that?

During the Covid-19 lockdown, I contributed to five documentaries about Freddie Mercury and/or Queen. In October 2020, I became involved in Chicago's Legacy Project: a mile-long outdoor public installation celebrating LGBT contributions to history and culture. This, the world's only outdoor museum of its kind, attracts more than a million and a half visitors each year. The organisation raises awareness of the loss of self-esteem in young LGBT people caused by bullying and abuse at school or at home. Freddie was an inductee. I wrote the inscription for his bronze plaque, appeared at the event on 11 October alongside the project's co-founder Victor Salvo, and answered questions during the live global Q&A. Thirty years after Freddie's death, barely a week passes that I am not asked about him: on radio and podcasts, by students, researchers and editors, by journalists from Japan, Croatia, Estonia and Russia to Finland, Brazil and Taiwan. How ironic, given that Freddie lived a mostly closeted life, that he has become the world's most celebrated homosexual.

ACKNOWLEDGEMENTS

It's hard to believe that almost a quarter of a century has passed since I began working with Hodder & Stoughton on books about Freddie Mercury. My first, brokered by the late Giles Gordon and edited by Simon Prosser, was published in 1997. The second, with agent Ivan Mulcahy and issued in 2011, marked the beginning of a long collaboration with Hannah Black. It was she who republished my second biography of Freddie as *Bohemian Rhapsody* in 2018, seeing it to the top five of the *Sunday Times* Bestseller List. Hannah also conceived and commissioned this new study. She is a wonderful publisher and editor – compassionate, committed, likes writers – and she is also my friend. I owe her, Erika Koljonen and all of her support team for having worked so hard to make this book.

I am indebted to Clare Hulton, my literary agent; Leila French, my translator in Florence; Bridie Shine BA (Hons), sexual politics consultant; and in so many ways to psychotherapist Richard Hughes, not least for his remarkable insight, expertise and unconditional friendship.

With heartfelt thanks to the following:

Marcus K. Adams, R.I.P.
Anvar Alikhan, R.I.P.
Keith Altham
Larry André, US Ambassador to the Republic of Djibouti

Dan Arthure
Martin Barden
Nicola Bardola
John Blunt
Montserrat Caballé R.I.P.
Gita Barucha Choksi
Federica Dini
Sandy Evans
Nicholas Gordon R.I.P.
Valerie Finn
Peter Freestone
Karen French
Monica French
Jim Hutton R.I.P.
Julie Ives-Routleff
Berni Kilmartin
Leo McLoughlin
Mike Moran
Simon Napier-Bell
Justin Parker
Edward Phillips
Professor Steven Pinker
Remy Quinones
Sir Tim Rice
Torrence Royer
Fiz Shapur
Rick Sky
Phil Swern
Barbara Valentin R.I.P.
David Wigg
Jane Wroe Wright
Richard Young
Susan Young

African Voice Global: https://africanvoiceglobal.com
The Mercury Phoenix Trust: www.mercuryphoenixtrust.com
The Elton John AIDS Foundation: www.ejaf.org

To Mia, Bridie and Henry, as always.
L-AJ, London, September 2021

RECOMMENDED

Never Boring box set of Freddie's non-Queen recordings, including 1985's *Mr. Bad Guy,* his only solo album, and 1988's *Barcelona,* his collaboration with Monserrat Caballé.

INDEX

Adams, Marcus K. 87, 88
al-Said, Jamshid bin Abdullah 55
Alberti, Irmgard 179
Altham, Keith 77–9, 82, 83, 84,
    89–90
And the Band Played On (Shilts)
    204
André, Larry 30
Andrews, Jane 222–3
Atkinson, Gordon 155
Austin, Mary
  and Freddie Mercury's sexuality
    16–17, 124, 126–7, 128,
    129–30, 135–6, 208–9
  and Barbara Valentin 21–2, 191
  at Freddie Mercury's thirty–
    ninth birthday party 24
  at Garden Lodge 36, 38–40,
    144, 145–6, 147–8, 168
  memories of Val Finn 102,
    104–5
  first meets Freddie Mercury
    137–8

  similarities with Freddie
    Mercury 138–9
  as mother-figure 142
  moves in with Freddie Mercury
    142–3
  end of relationship 143–4, 147
  on Queen tours 144–5
  and Freddie Mercury's ashes
    247
  tribute to Freddie Mercury
    271–2

Bacon, Francis 233
Baker, Roy Thomas 82
Band of Gypsys 81
Barbara (Lüder) 182
'Barcelona' 201–2, 212–15
Bardola, Nicola 197, 198
Barker, Steve 75
Baron Cohen, Sacha 4
Bastin, Tony 131–2, 209
Beach, Jim 16, 83
Beatles, The 61–2, 94

Beck, Jeff 74
Berry, Chuck 78
Beyrand, Dominique 115
Bilimoria of Chelsea, Baron 35–6, 60
Blauel, Renate 126
Boe, Alfie 201–3, 231, 271
Bohemian Rhapsody (film) 3–8, 21, 25–6, 52, 72, 105, 152, 198, 226
'Bohemian Rhapsody' (song) 111, 113, 244–6
Bolan, Marc 95, 96
Bon Jovi 24
Bono 27
Borrás, Carles Caballé i 218
Bowie, Angie 21, 97
Bowie, David 21, 95–9, 268
Boy George 24
Branche, Derrick 51, 52–3
Brown, Les 100
Bulsara, Bomi
  portrayal in *Bohemian Rhapsody* 5, 6
  relationship with Freddie Mercury 41–2, 61, 64–6
  life in England 60–1
Bulsara, Jer
  at memorial to Freddie Mercury 35
  gives birth to Freddie Mercury 41
  and Freddie Mercury's assumed name 42

life in England 60–1
  relationship with Freddie Mercury 64
  and Freddie Mercury's sexuality 67–8
  tribute to Freddie Mercury 272
Burdon, Eric 78
Burrell, Paul 223
Burt, Jo 146–7

Caballé, Carlos 210–11
Caballé, Montserrat 2, 24–5, 139, 187, 201, 202–3, 210–20, 236, 240, 270
Cameron, Piers 147
Carreras, José 219
Chandler, Chas 74, 76, 79, 80–1, 102
Chimera, Paul 141
Choksi, Gita 46–9, 51–2, 60
Clapton, Eric 73–5, 78–9
Clark, Dave 155–6
Connolly, Patrick 63
Cooke, Kashmira 35–6, 272
Cooper, Dominic 4
Cosmos Rocks, The 113
'Crazy Little Thing Called Love' 24, 111, 174
Crown, The 6–7

Dahlin, Jacob 215
Dalí, Salvador 141
Dannemann, Monika 83–4
Darunkhanawala, Perviz 41

Deacon, John
  writes 'I Want to Break Free' 18,
    139
  joins Queen 110
  retirement 111, 241
  relationships of 115
  and *Innuendo* 220
  tribute to Freddie Mercury
    267
'Death on Two Legs' 83
Dietl, Helmut 181
Deixler, Susan 125–6
Diana, Princess of Wales 223
Dini, Federica 15
'Do They Know it's Christmas?'
  112
Dobson, Anita 34, 114–15, 139
Doherty, Bernard 142
'Dolly Dagger' 84
'Don't Stop Me Now' 246
Douglas, Lord Alfred 125
Dugas, Gaëtan 204, 205
Duncan, Lesley 96
Dylan, Bob 39

Ealing Art College 63–4, 69–70,
  72, 96–7
Earth/Step on Me 107
Evans, David 203, 225, 231
Everett, Kenny 126, 176
'Exercises in Free Love' 213, 236

Fanelli, Joe 131, 145, 160, 178
Farthingale, Hermione 96

Fassbinder, Rainer Werner 175,
  180
Ferguson, Sarah 222–3
Finn, Val 101–5
Fisher, Ronnie 130
Fletcher, Dexter 4
Folch, Anna 218
Foster, Ray 244
Frampton, Owen 95
Freddie Mercury: An Intimate
  Memoir by the Man Who Knew
  Him Best (Freestone & Evans)
  225
Freddie Mercury Tribute Concert
  for AIDS Awareness 27
Freddie Mercury's Royal Recipes
  (Freestone) 225
Freestone, Peter 2, 203
  on Freddie Mercury's early life
    10
  on Freddie Mercury's sexuality
    15–16, 130, 131, 133–4
  and memorials to Freddie
    Mercury 36, 38–9
  celebrations of Freddie Mercury
    37
  on Freddie Mercury's musical
    talent 45
  on Freddie Mercury's need for
    conflict 137
  at Garden Lodge 145, 148
  and death of Freddie Mercury
    155–6, 157–8, 220
  on Jim Hutton 164

on Barbara Valentin 176, 194

and Freddie Mercury's HIV
diagnosis 177–8

at Freddie Mercury's thirty–
ninth birthday party 190

and Montserrat Caballé 210,
211

relationship with Freddie
Mercury 224–8

on narcissism of Freddie
Mercury 230

tribute to Freddie Mercury 271

Furnish, Dave 126

Gambaccini, Paul 22

Game, The 190

Gillespie, Dana 96

Glover, Julie 115

'Golden Boy, The' 214

'Good Old Fashioned Lover Boy'
131

Graham-Dixon, Andrew 232

'Great Pretender, The' 236–7

Green Book 26

Green Day 94–5

Gudka, Subhash 45

Hadley, Tony 270

Harrison, George 94

Harvin, Ernestine 125

Haythe, Justin 4

Hendrix, Jimi 12, 73–82, 83–90

Heretics, The 49–51

Hey Joe 75

Hillman, Joe 80

Hince, Peter 203

Holford, Nicholas 147

'How Can I Go On' 214

Hughes, Richard 17, 18, 176–7,
234–5, 237

Humpy Bong 108

Hussein of Jordan, King 185

Hutchinson, John 96, 97

Hutton, Jim 134, 209
on Freddie Mercury's
personality 15
and Freddie Mercury's HIV
diagnosis 16, 205
and Freddie Mercury's
childhood 41–2, 56–7
and Freddie Mercury's
relationship with father 64–5,
66
and Freddie Mercury's sexuality
66–7, 245
at Garden Lodge 145–6, 148,
165, 167, 168
early life of 152–4
and Freddie Mercury's death
154–7, 166
on relationship with Freddie
Mercury 157–9
start of relationship with
Freddie Mercury 159–62
unbalanced relationship with
Freddie Mercury 162–6
after Freddie Mercury's death
167–9

in *News of the World* 209–10
tribute to Freddie Mercury 267

'I Want to Break Free' 18–19, 111,
    139–40
Ibex 108–9
Innuendo (album) 112, 219–20
'Innuendo' (song) 220
Irani, Farang 50, 51
Iron Lady, The 8
Isleworth Polytechnic 61–3
'It's a Hard Life' 20, 190

Jackson, Michael 24
Jafferji, Javed 34
Jagger, Mick 27, 78, 84, 94
Jazz 23, 246
Jeffrey, Mike 76, 79–82, 83, 85
Jenkins, Jim 110, 111
Jimi Hendrix Experience 77, 78,
    79–81, 88, 89
John, Elton 126, 155, 228–9,
    232–3, 2268
Jones, Brian 76, 94
Jones, Eddie 'Guitar Slim' 74
Joplin, Janis 78

'Keep Yourself Alive' 111
Keith, Linda 75–6
Kemp, Lindsay 96
Kief, Garry 126
'Killer Queen' 111
Kirchberger, Winnie 134, 161,
    174, 186, 209–10

Knight, Curtis 75
Korniloff, Natasha 96

Lady Gaga 268
Lambert, Adam 8, 28, 113, 269
'Laughing Gnome, The' 95
Ledersteger, Hans 179–80
Lee, Sujin 136–7
Leng, Debbie 115
Lennon, Freddie 77
Lennon, John 76, 94
Lennox, Annie 269
Lewis, Jerry Lee 78
*Life on Two Legs: Set the Record
    Straight* (Sheffield) 83
Live Aid concert 3, 11, 57, 112
'Living on My Own' 24
Lloyd, Constance 125
*Love is the Cure: On Life, Loss and
    the End of AIDS* (John) 229
'Love Me Like There's No
    Tomorrow' 190
'Love of My Life' 131
'Love You till Tuesday' 96
Lüder, Lars 181, 182–3, 185, 186
Lüder, Rolf 181

Mack, Reinhold 174
Made in Heaven 26, 113
Mail on Sunday 36
Malden, Mark 69–71, 88
Malek, Rami 4, 25, 26, 226
Malhotra, Seema 35
Mallet, David 140

Manilow, Barry 125–6
Martell, Marc 4
Martí, Bernabé 217
Martin, Paul 63
May, Brian
  and *Bohemian Rhapsody* 6
  and Freddie Mercury's assumed
    surname 29
  in Zanzibar 34
  memorials to Freddie Mercury
    35, 36
  and Freddie Mercury's
    relationship with father 66
  in Smile 71, 99–101, 107–8
  first Queen concert 110
  and Freddie Mercury's death
    112, 113
  relationships of 114–15, 139
  and Freddie Mercury's HIV
    diagnosis 117
  on Jim Hutton 169
  and *Innuendo* 219–20
  tribute to Freddie Mercury 267
McCarten, Anthony 4
McCartney, Sir Paul 39, 78, 94
Mercury, Freddie
  statue in Montreux 1–2
  meeting with author 2–3
  and *Bohemian Rhapsody* 5–6, 7,
    25–6
  early life in Zanzibar 9–10, 11,
    31, 41–4
  early life in England 11–12,
    59–60

  sexuality 12–14, 15–19, 49,
    66–8, 114, 121–4, 126–7,
    129, 130–4, 135–6, 139–41,
    191–2, 206–8, 244–6
  relationship with Mary Austin
    16–17, 104–5, 124, 126–7,
    128, 129–30, 135–49, 208–9
  HIV diagnosis 16, 116–17,
    192–3, 205–6, 210, 213
  relationship with Barbara
    Valentin 20–2, 139, 164,
    171–200
  stories of excessive lifestyle 22–5
  popularity of 27
  and assumed name 29–32, 42
  memorials to 34–40
  relationship with father 41–2,
    61, 64–6
  at school in India 44–51, 53,
    56–7
  musical influences 50, 61–2, 63,
    77, 79
  snubs childhood friend 52–3
  at Isleworth Polytechnic 61–3
  at Ealing Art College 63–4,
    69–70, 72
  musical ambitions 70–2
  stall at Kensington Market 71–2,
    101–2
  identifies with Jimi Hendrix
    85–7
  rejects solo career 91–5
  meets David Bowie 95–9
  memories of Val Finn 101–5

in Liverpool 108–9
gigs with Wreckage 109–10
last days with Queen 112–13
relationship with Rosemary
  Pearson 122–3, 135–7
relationships with men 130–4
relationship with Jim Hutton
  134, 145–6, 148, 151–69,
  209
at thirty–ninth birthday party
  190–1
and 'Barcelona' 201–3
calmer lifestyle of 203, 209
outed in *News of the World* 209–10
and Montserrat Caballé
  210–20
relationship with Peter
  Freestone 224–8
narcissism of 230–8
reasons for appeal of 241–3
speculation about ashes of
  246–7
tributes to 267–72
Mercury and Me (Hutton) 15
Mercury Phoenix Trust, The 27,
  241
Michael, George 208, 232, 268
Middleton, Audrey 126
Minns, David 130–1
Minogue, Kylie 24
'Miracle, The' 89
Mr Bad Guy 24, 146, 161, 190
Mitchell, Mitch 77, 79, 80
Monterey Music Festival 78

Mooney, Bel 6–7
Moran, Mike 25, 211, 212, 213,
  236, 270
Morgan, Peter 4, 5, 133
Morrish, Adrian 62–3
Mortensen, Viggo 26
Moseley, Diana 139
'Mother Love' 113
Mott the Hoople 111
Mountain Studios 23, 35, 113,
  190, 202, 212
Mullen, Christine 114
Murphy, John 205, 209
Murray, Bruce 50–1, 271
'My Fairy King' 29
Myers, Mike 4, 244

Napier-Bell, Simon 92–3, 207,
  222, 232

Ono, Yoko 76

Paige, Elaine 139
Pearson, Rosemary 122–3, 135–7
Penniman, 'Little' Richard 125
Perry, Kate 269
Pitt, Ken 96
Plant, Robert 27, 269
Porter, Cole 125
Potgieter Taylor, Sarina 38, 115
Prenter, Paul 161, 174, 210, 224
Presley, Elvis 39, 185
Presley, Lisa Marie 39

Queen
  Live Aid appearance 3
  and video for "I Want to Break
    Free" 18–19
  and Sheffield brothers 82–3
  first gig 110
  rise of 111
  and last days of Freddie
    Mercury 112–13
  after Freddie Mercury's death
    113–14, 241
  music used in commercials
    239–40
Queen 111
Queen II 111
*Queen + Adam Lambert Live
  Around the World* 26
Queen's Greatest Hits 241–2

Radiohead 94
Rana, Victory 50, 51
Raw Silk 70–1
Rawat, Prem 103
Red Hot Chili Peppers 94
Redding, Noel 77, 79, 80, 81
Redgrave, Vanessa 125
Reichardt, Ernst 181
Reichardt, Nicola-Babette 'Minki'
  175, 181
Reid, Bill 133–4
Reid, John 24, 126, 131
Rice, Sir Tim 244–5, 270
Richards, Keith 75–6, 94
Richardson, Tony 125

Rock Roadie (Wright) 83
Rocos, Cleo 126, 176
Rodgers, Paul 113
Rolling Stone magazine 27
Rolling Stones 94
Rose, Axl 268–9
Rose, Tim 75
Roskowski, Greg 50
Ross, Robert 125
Ruby Tuesday 76

St Peter's Church of England
    School 44–51
Savin-Williams, Ritch C. 17
Schofield, Philip 128–9
Sedlecká, Irena 2
*See Me Linda, Hear Me, I'm
    Playing the Blues* 76
Send My Love to Linda 76
Serelis, Vytas 96
Sheer Heart Attack 111
Sheffield, Barry 82–3
Sheffield, Norman 82–3
Shelley, Emma 115
Shilts, Randy 204
'Show Must Go On, The' 220
Simon, Paul 39
Singer, Bryan 4
Smile 71, 99–101, 107–8, 110
Smith, Blossom 49
Smith, Janice 49
'Somebody to Love' 235–6
Sour Milk Sea 110
Squires 75

Staffell, Tim 71, 99–100, 101, 108, 110
Starr, Ringo 76, 94
'Stormtroopers in Stilettos' (exhibition) 35
Straker, Peter 160, 236
Strange, Steve 24
Streep, Meryl 7

'Take My Breath Away' 131
Tavener, Roger 2
Taylor, Elizabeth 269
Taylor, Roger
   memorial to Freddie Mercury 38
   in Smile 71, 100, 101, 107–8
   and death of Jimi Hendrix 87
   stall on Kensington Market 101
   first Queen concert 110
   and Freddie Mercury's death 112, 227
   relationships of 115
   and Innuendo 220
   on 'The Great Pretender' 236
   tribute to Freddie Mercury 267
Tetzlaff, Veronica 115
Thatcher, Margaret 7
'These Are the Days of Our Lives' 112–13, 220
Thomas, Linda Lee 125
Top of the Pops 62
Townshend, Pete 64, 78
Tuke, Henry Scott 228–30

U2 94
'Under Pressure' 99
Underwood, George 95

Valentin, Barbara
   on Freddie Mercury's personality 15
   relationship with Freddie Mercury 20–2, 139, 161, 164, 171–200
   and Mary Austin 21–2, 191
   on Jim Hutton 162
   first meets Freddie Mercury 174–5
   and Freddie Mercury's HIV diagnosis 177–8, 192–3
   early life and career 179–83, 185–6
   at Garden Lodge 186
   and Freddie Mercury's sexuality 191–2
   drug use 194–5
   and Freddie Mercury's death 195–6
   death of 196–7
   tribute to Freddie Mercury 267–8
Valentin, Erwin 180
Varadkar, Leo 154
Vince the barman 132–3
Visconti, Tony 96
Volkmann, Elisabeth 175–6

Walker, Scott 89, 90

Walker, 'T-Bone' 74
Wayne's World 244
'We Are the Champions' 240
'We Will Rock You' (musical) 3,
    35, 38
Wedow, Robbee 121
Welch, Raquel 223–4
Whishaw, Ben 4
Wigg, David 57, 132, 138, 143,
    145, 148, 176, 206
Wilde, Oscar 125
Wilkinson, Christopher 5
Wilson, Devon 84
Wood, Ronnie 64
Wood, Roy 103
Woodcock, Patrick 123
Woodrow, Linda 126

Woodstock 81
Works, The 111, 190
Wreckage 71, 109–10
Wright, James 'Tappy' 83
Wright, Laura 202

Zanzibar
    and Freddie's Mercury's early
        life 9–10, 11, 31, 41–4
    gay oppression in 13, 33–4
    and Freddie's Mercury assumed
        surname 29–32
    as tourist destination 32–3
    museum to Freddie Mercury in
        34–5
    colonial past of 53–7